KAPLAN pmbr

FINALS
Civil Procedure

CORE CONCEPTS AND KEY QUESTIONS

ROBERT FEINBERG, ESQ.
Editorial Consultant

JAMES PALMER, ESQ.

Reviewed by: EVAN SLAVITT, ESQ.

KAPLAN
PUBLISHING
New York

Series Editor: Lisa T. McElroy, Associate Professor, Drexel University College of Law
Editorial Director: Jennifer Farthing
Editor: Michael Sprague
Production Editor: Fred Urfer
Cover Designer: Carly Schnur

Published by Kaplan Publishing, a division of Kaplan, Inc.
1 Liberty Plaza, 24th floor
New York, NY 10006

Printed in the United States of America

August 2007
10 9 8 7 6 5 4 3 2 1

ISBN13: 978-1-4277-9637-0

Kaplan Publishing books are available at special quantity discounts to use for sales promotions, employee premiums, or educational purposes. Please email our Special Sales Department to order or for more information at kaplanpublishing@kaplan.com, or write to Kaplan Publishing, 1 Liberty Plaza, 24th floor, New York, NY 10006.

INTRODUCTION

Kaplan PMBR Finals: Core Concepts and Key Questions is a law school preparatory series from one of the leading companies for preparing for the Bar exam. It is designed to provide students with focused study to succeed on their law school exams. Remember that *Kaplan PMBR* is not simply another commercial outline series. Rather each edition consists of several integrated sections. This edition contains a substantive outline, capsule summary outlines, objective law school exam questions, essay exam questions, and fully detailed explanatory answers.

Finals is designed to be used as a pre-exam study aid. You should be aware that most law schools are now implementing objective *and* essay questions on their final examinations. In the past virtually all law school exams were written solely in an essay format. Now the trend is to test students with objective and subjective questions.

Objective questions on exams eliminate the subjectivity of essay grading. They provide uniformity and a basis for reliable grading. Law schools are also recognizing the necessity to prepare students for the Multistate Bar Examination (commonly referred to as the "MBE"). The MBE is a uniform, national, 200-question multiple choice exam covering the six subject areas of Torts, Contracts, Real Property/Future Interests, Evidence, Constitutional Law, and Criminal Law/Procedure.

Finals is designed as a national law school study aid. Many of the questions and answers follow the majority rule of law in effect in most jurisdictions. Many of the rationales and explanations refer to the national norm. This is to make the series as applicable as possible for students across the country.

This edition includes 100 multiple choice questions to review Civil Procedure. The questions require knowledge of the black letter law and some legal reasoning skills. Reviewing the questions will help you prepare for your exams and assist you in your comfort with the black letter law.

Kaplan and PMBR wish you the best of luck on your exams and in your legal career.

I. PERSONAL JURISDICTION

A. THE EVOLUTION OF PERSONAL JURISDICTION

INTRODUCTION. The plaintiff's objective is to sue the defendant in the court most convenient and favorable to plaintiff. The forum chosen is generally a court in plaintiff's home state. How does the 14th Amendment Due Process Clause of the United States Constitution serve to protect the nonresident defendant and limit the forum shopping available to plaintiff? It is a story told in three phases of ***personal jurisdiction law*** by decisions of the United States Supreme Court from 1877-1987.

1. **PHASE ONE (1877-1945)**

   (a) *Pennoyer v. Neff*, 95 U.S. (5 Otto) 714 (1877). (Personal jurisdiction is acquired by personal service ***inside*** the ***territorial limits*** of the forum state or by the voluntary appearance of the defendant there to contest the suit on its merits.)

   (b) *Hess v. Pawloski*, 274 U.S. 352 (1927). (Personal jurisdiction may be acquired by enactment of a nonresident motorist statute. The decision rests upon state ***police power***.)

   (c) *Blackmer v. United States*, 284 U.S. 421 (1932). (Personal jurisdiction authority can be based upon U.S. ***citizenship***.)

   (d) *Milliken v. Meyer*, 311 U.S. 457 (1940). (Personal jurisdiction may be based upon the defendant's ***domicile*** within the forum.)

2. **PHASE TWO (1945-1980)**

   (a) *International Shoe Co. v. Washington*, 326 U.S. 310 (1945). ("Due process requires only that in order to subject a defendant to a judgment in personam, if he be not present within the territory of the forum, he have certain minimum contacts with it such that the maintenance of the suit does not offend traditional notions of fair play and substantial justice." *I-Shoe* is the foundation for analyzing ***modern personal jurisdiction*** issues. It is commonly referred to as ***minimum contact*** jurisdiction.)

   (b) *Perkins v. Benguet Consol. Mining Co.*, 342 U.S. 437 (1952). (If the defendant's activity in the forum state is ***continuous and systematic***, there is personal jurisdiction even on ***a cause of action*** unrelated to that forum activity. *Perkins* is commonly referred to as a ***general jurisdiction*** case.)

   (c) *McGee v. International Life Ins. Co.*, 355 U.S. 220 (1957). (Although the defendant has only ***single or isolated*** contact with the forum state, there is personal jurisdiction on a cause of action related to that forum activity. *McGee* is commonly referred to as a ***specific jurisdiction case***.)

   (d) *Hanson v. Denckla*, 357 U.S. 235 (1958). ("[I]t is essential in each case that there be some act by which the defendant purposefully avails itself of the privilege of conducting activities within the forum state, thus involving the benefits and protections of its laws." *Hanson* is the beginning of the ***purposeful availment*** requirement.)

(e) *Kulko v. Superior Court*, 436 U.S. 84 (1978). (In order for the defendant to be subject to personal jurisdiction based on an act done outside the forum state that has effects there, the act must be "wrongful activity" or "commercial activity affecting state residents." *Kulko* is the leading case about the meaning of so-called ***effects*** jurisdiction.)

During this **PHASE TWO** period (1945-80), the states began to enact long-arm statutes. Illinois led with its version in 1956. The long-arm statutes vary from lengthy pronouncements that describe events, transactions or occurrences (e.g., commits a tortious act within the state) that provide the statutory basis for personal jurisdiction, to the brief statement of the California Code of Civil Procedure §410.10 ("A court of this state may exercise jurisdiction on any basis not inconsistent with the Constitution of this state or of the United States."). If the statute is of the "event oriented" type, the first step in the personal jurisdiction analysis is to apply the facts to the statute. If the facts fit the statutory language, then the analysis proceeds to the question of the constitutional limitations of the Due Process Clause. With a statute of the California type, the analysis is focused only on the 14th Amendment Due Process Clause.

Another feature of the **PHASE TWO** period is the beginning of the modern law regarding the enforceability of a forum-selection clause. In *The Bremen v. Zapata Off-Shore Co.*, 407 U.S. 1 (1972), the Supreme Court indicates that a forum clause should be honored unless "enforcement would be unreasonable and unjust, or . . . the clause was invalid for such reasons as fraud or overreaching." To determine whether a forum-selection clause is enforceable, the following factors are considered relevant: "[T]he identity of the law that governs the construction of the contract, the place of execution of the contract, the place where the transactions have been or are to be performed, the location of the parties, the convenience of the prospective witnesses, and the accessibility of evidence; and the presence or absence of fraud, undue influence, or other extenuating (or exacerbating) circumstances." *Heyco, Inc. v. Heyman*, 636 F. Supp. 1545, 1550 n. 7 (S.D.N.Y. 1986).

3. **PHASE THREE (1980-Present)**

(a) *World-Wide Volkswagen Corp. v. Woodson*, 444 U.S. 286 (1980). ("[I]f the sale of a product of a manufacturer or distributor . . . is not simply an isolated occurrence, but arises from the efforts of the manufacturer or distributor to serve, directly or indirectly, the market for its product in other States, it is not unreasonable to subject it to suit in one of those States if its allegedly defective merchandise has been the source of injury to its owner or to others. The forum state does not exceed its powers under the Due Process Clause if it asserts personal jurisdiction over a corporation that delivers its products into the stream of commerce with the expectation that they will be purchased by consumers in the forum state." *W-W Volks* is the beginning of the stream of commerce analysis in defective product litigation; it is also landmark on the definition of where the defendant can ***anticipate*** or ***foresee*** being haled into court.)

(b) *Keeton v. Hustler Magazine, Inc.*, 465 U.S. 770 (1984). (The ***plaintiff's lack of contacts*** with the forum state will not defeat otherwise proper personal jurisdiction.)

(c) *Calder v. Jones*, 465 U.S. 783 (1984). (Defamation actions do not have special constitutional limitations on the exercise of personal jurisdiction over nonresident media defendants. ***First Amendment concerns do not enter*** the 14th Amendment Due Process Clause equation of ***personal*** jurisdiction analysis.)

(d) *Helicopteros Nacionales de Colombia, S.A. v. Hall*, 466 U.S. 408 (1984). (If the cause of action does not arise out of or relate to the nonresident defendant's activity in the forum state, the defendant cannot be sued there unless there is ***significant*** continuous and systematic forum activity. *Helicopteros* is the leading case on the principle that the activity required for general jurisdiction must be more ***substantial*** than that required for ***specific*** jurisdiction.)

(e) *Burger King Corp. v. Rudzewicz*, 471 U.S. 462 (1985). ("If the question is whether an individual's contract with an out-of-state party alone can automatically establish sufficient minimum contacts in the other party's home forum, we believe the answer clearly is that it cannot . . . . It is these factors—prior negotiations and contemplated future consequences, along with the terms of the contract and the parties' actual course of dealing—that must be evaluated in determining whether the defendant purposefully established minimum contacts within the forum." *Burger King* is a landmark decision about the personal jurisdiction analysis in contract cases. *Note* that the decision makes forum-selection clauses relevant to the *personal jurisdiction analysis*.)

(f) *Asahi Metal Indus. Co. v. Superior Court*, 480 U.S. 102 (1987). (Justice O'Connor, joined by three other Justices, says: "The placement of a product into the stream of commerce, without more, is not an act of the defendant purposefully directed toward the forum State. Additional conduct of the defendant may indicate an intent or purpose to serve the market in the forum State, for example, designing the product for the market in the forum State, advertising in the forum State, establishing channels for providing regular advice to customers in the forum State, or marketing the product through a distributor who has agreed to serve as the sales agent in the forum State. But a defendant's awareness that the stream of commerce may or will sweep the product into the forum State does not convert the mere act of placing the product into the stream into an act purposefully directed toward the forum State."

Justice Brennan, joined by three other Justices, says: "As long as a participant in this process is aware that the final product is being marketed in the forum State, the possibility of a lawsuit there cannot come as a surprise . . . . A defendant who has placed goods in the stream of commerce benefits economically from the retail sale of the final product in the forum State, and indirectly benefits from the State's laws that regulate and facilitate commercial activity."

Justice Stevens wrote separately to say: "Whether or not . . . [the] conduct rises to the level of purposeful availment requires a constitutional determination that is affected by the volume, the value, and the hazardous character of the components.")

Asahi is a ***plurality*** opinion (4-4-1) on the meaning of ***stream of commerce***. Justice Stevens seems by his language to lean toward the Brennan view.

Asahi, however, does give a picture of the meaning of "traditional notions of fair play and substantial justice." Eight Justices agree, that in the context of litigation involving ***international parties***, "a court must consider the burden on the defendant, the interests of the forum state, and the plaintiff's interest in obtaining relief. . . . The unique burdens placed upon one who must defend oneself in a foreign legal system should have significant weight in assessing the reasonableness . . . of personal jurisdiction over national borders."

(g) The courts are divided on how to apply these principles of law to the Internet. Although the law is still very unsettled, initial indications are that a website that simply presents information is insufficient for jurisdiction; a website that permits full ordering and payment will probably be enough, and there is no consensus concerning a website that allows some interaction (such as making a request for more information), but does not permit the completion of a full sale.

B. PERSONAL JURISDICTION IN FEDERAL COURT

INTRODUCTION. From *Pennoyer* (1877) through *Asahi* (1987), the Supreme Court has defined the limitations of the 14th Amendment Due Process Clause on the exercise of personal jurisdiction over nonresident defendants. What are the sources of personal jurisdiction in federal court? Does the Fifth Amendment Due Process Clause require a ***minimum contact*** analysis to determine the personal jurisdiction grasp over defendants sued in federal court?

1. FEDERAL RULES OF CIVIL PROCEDURE

(a) Rule 4(f) (Personal jurisdiction over persons served inside territorial limits of state where federal court sits and 100 miles distant as to parties added pursuant to Rules 14 or 19).

(b) Rule 4(e) (Personal jurisdiction may be acquired by borrowing the forum state's long-arm statute).

2. FEDERAL STATUTES

(E.g., 28 U.S.C. § 2361) (Nationwide service of process authorized in *interpleader* actions)

3. CASE LAW

Omni Capital Int'l v. Rudolf Wolff & Co., Ltd., 484 U.S. 97 (1987). (Even in federal question cases, unless a federal statute permits nationwide service of process, the service authority of a federal court is limited to that granted by Federal Rules 4(e) and (f). *Omni* means that unless the defendant is amenable to service of process there is no personal jurisdiction; and *Omni* implies that, even if a federal statute expressly grants service of process authority, the Fifth Amendment Due Process Clause could still apply to prevent an unreasonable exercise of personal jurisdiction over a nonresident defendant.)

C. CHECKLIST OF PERSONAL JURISDICTION FACTORS

INTRODUCTION. Each Supreme Court case from *Pennoyer* (1877) through *Asahi* (1987) provides some part of the collection of rules of law applicable to personal jurisdiction issues. There is no substitute for familiarity with those case principles. To assist in remembering the case law, it may be helpful to focus on the following factors from the *Restatement Second of Conflict of Laws* §§ 27, 41 and the *Restatement Second of Judgments* § 5 (the lists are also relevant to topic **"II. JURISDICTION OVER PROPERTY"**, *infra*).

1. **JURISDICTION OVER AN INDIVIDUAL:** (a) presence (b) domicile (c) residence (d) nationality or citizenship (e) consent (f) appearance (g) doing business in state (h) doing an act in state (i) causing effect in state by act or omission done elsewhere (j) ownership, use or possession of thing in state (k) other relationships.

2. **JURISDICTION OVER A BUSINESS ENTITY:** (a) incorporation in state (b) consent (c) appointment of agent (d) appearance (e) doing business in state (f) doing an act in state (g) causing effect in state by act or omission done elsewhere (h) ownership, use or possession of thing in state (i) other relationships.

II. JURISDICTION OVER PROPERTY

A. THE EVOLUTION OF JURISDICTION OVER PROPERTY

INTRODUCTION. The plaintiff's objective is to gain either a ***personal judgment*** or a ***quasi in rem*** or an ***in rem judgment***. A ***personal judgment*** for damages is enforceable in its amount if there is ***personal jurisdiction*** over the defendant. A ***quasi in rem judgment*** that affects interests in designated property is enforceable to the extent of the property's value if there is ***quasi in rem jurisdiction***. An ***in rem judgment*** that affects the interests of all persons in the world in particular property is effective to dispose of that property, if there is ***in rem jurisdiction***, although the court clearly cannot have jurisdiction over the entire world. From *Pennoyer* (1877) through *Asahi* (1987), the law of personal jurisdiction has changed. How has the jurisdiction-over-property law changed from *Pennoyer* through *Shaffer v. Heitner* (1977)? How does the 14th Amendment Due Process Clause of the United States Constitution serve to protect the nonresident defendant's property? The story unfolds in two stages by decisions of the United States Supreme Court from 1877-1977.

1. **STAGE ONE (1877-1977)**

   (a) *Pennoyer v. Neff*, 96 U.S. (6 Otto) 714 (1877). (Quasi in rem and in rem jurisdiction are acquired by the ***presence of*** the nonresident defendant's property within the forum state and the attachment of the property at the commencement of the action.)

   (b) *Harris v. Balk*, 198 U.S. 215 (1905). (The ***presence-of-property rule*** of *Pennoyer* applies to an intangible, i.e., the ***situs*** of a debt is not the place where the creditor is located, but wherever the debtor may be: In *Harris*, the debt seized was not related to the plaintiff's cause of action.)

2. **STAGE TWO (1977 - PRESENT)**

Shaffer v. Heitner, 433 U.S. 186 (1977). ("[A]ll assertions of state-court jurisdiction must be evaluated according to the standards set forth in *International Shoe* and its progeny.")

Shaffer means that the ***minimum contact*** analysis of personal jurisdiction is ***now applicable to quasi in rem*** and ***in rem jurisdiction***. What is left of *Pennoyer*? The Supreme Court has never expressly overruled the holding in *Pennoyer* that permits personal jurisdiction to be acquired by personal service to the defendant inside the territorial limits of the forum state. In fact, at least one state supreme court decision after *Shaffer, Humphrey v. Langford*, 246 Ga. 732, 273 S.E. 2d 22 (1980), holds that personal jurisdiction may still be attained by personal service to a nonresident within the forum. Ultimately, the U.S. Supreme Court will determine the vitality of that part of the *Pennoyer* decision relating to personal jurisdiction. It is very clear, however, that *Shaffer* does overrule that part of *Pennoyer* that permits the ***presence*** of the nonresident's ***property alone*** to provide the basis for quasi in rem and in rem jurisdiction. What is the impact of *Shaffer*? In the type of quasi in rem case where the cause of action is closely related to the property seized (e.g., a seller's suit to foreclose on a buyer in default), the factual nature of the controversy is likely to provide the necessary ***minimum contacts among the forum state, the defendant, and the litigation***. The analysis will probably produce the same result in an in rem action (e.g., proceedings to determine title to real property), because the presence of the property within the forum state suggests that there would be ***other ties among the defendant, the forum state, and the litigation***. But what about the case where the property seized (e.g., a bank account) and the cause of action (negligence-personal injury) are unrelated? Applying *Shaffer* to that situation surely means that, unless there are other forum contacts with the nonresident, there is no jurisdiction.

III. SUBJECT MATTER JURISDICTION

A. NATURE OF THE LIMITED JURISDICTION

INTRODUCTION. A federal court can hear only cases described in Article III of the United States Constitution; ***only*** to the extent Congress has by statute executed the ***limited*** power contained in Article III; and to the extent of the construction given by the United States Supreme Court to the jurisdictional grant of power to the inferior federal courts created by Congress. There are, therefore, three sources of limitation: (1) the Constitution; (2) Acts of Congress; and (3) Supreme Court cases that construe the meaning of Article III and the Acts of Congress. How do those three areas define the ***limited*** subject matter jurisdiction of the federal courts?

1. **ARTICLE III**

"Section 1. The judicial Power of the United States, shall be vested in one Supreme Court, and in such inferior Courts as the Congress may from time-to-time ordain and establish . . .

Section 2. The judicial Power shall extend to all Cases, in Law and Equity, arising under this Constitution, the Laws of the United States, and Treaties made, or which shall be made, under their Authority;—to all Cases affecting Ambassadors, other public Ministers and Consuls;—to Cases of admiralty and maritime Jurisdiction;—to Controversies to which the United States shall be a Party;—to Controversies between two or more States;—between a State and Citizens of another State;—between Citizens of different States;—between Citizens of the same State claiming Lands under Grants of different States, and between a State, or the Citizens thereof, and foreign States, Citizens or Subjects."

2. **FEDERAL QUESTION JURISDICTION**

(a) Title 28 U.S.C. § 1331: "The district courts shall have original jurisdiction of all civil actions arising under the Constitution, laws, or treaties of the United States." This statute is commonly referred to as the source of "general" federal question jurisdiction.

(b) Cases defining the meaning of arising under: *Louisville & Nashville R. Co. v Mottley*, 211 U.S. 149 (1908) (The federal claim must arise on the face of a well-pleaded complaint. The plaintiff does not create a federal question by anticipating, in the complaint, a federal defense.); *Franchise Tax Board v. Construction Laborers Vacation Trust*, 463 U.S. 1 (1983) (Even though state law creates the cause of action, the claim may still "arise under" if the state-created cause of action requires resolution "of a substantial question of federal law in dispute between the parties."); *Merrell Dow Pharmaceuticals Inc. v. Thompson*, 478 U.S. 804 (1986) ("[A] complaint alleging a violation of a federal statute as an element of a state cause of action, when Congress has determined that there should be no private, federal cause of action for the violation, does not state a claim 'arising under . . . .' ").

(c) **Cases "Arising Under" Federal Law:** It is problematical to formulate a summary of the case holdings as to when an action "arises under" federal law. The following shall, however, provide some assistance: A case arises under federal law if the plaintiff is alleging a right or interest that is substantially founded on federal law, which consists of federal common law, federal constitutional law, federal statutory law, treaty law, and federal administrative regulations. The following list, although not exhaustive, provides many examples of cases ***"arising under"*** Federal Law:

1. Bankruptcy Proceedings [28 U.S.C. 1334]
2. Patent and Copyright Cases [28 U.S.C. 1338]
3. Cases where the United States is Involved

Note, however, that under the doctrine of sovereign immunity, there is no jurisdiction in the courts to hear cases against the United States unless the United States has consented to be sued.

4. Cases in which Consults, Vice-Consuls or Ambassadors are Sued as Defendants [28 U.S.C. 1351]
5. Antitrust Cases [*Freeman v. Bee Machine Co.*, 319 U.S. 448 (1943)]
6. Admiralty Cases
7. Foreign State
8. Postal Matters [28 U.S.C. 1339]

9. Internal Revenue [28 U.S.C. 1340]
10. Securities Exchange Act [15 U.S.C. 78(a)]

Exception: Cases brought against defendants other than the United States, its agencies, or employees under section 23(a) of the Consumer Product Safety Act. That section authorizes action by any person who sustains injury by reason of a knowing violation of a consumer product safety rule, or any other rule issued by the Commission. In such cases, at least $10,000 must be in controversy [15 U.S.C. Section 2072].

a. ***No Minimum Amount in Controversy Required in a Federal Claim Case:*** There is ordinarily no minimum amount in controversy required in federal claim cases.

3. **DIVERSITY JURISDICTION**

(a) ***Statutory Provision:*** District courts have original jurisdiction of civil actions, where the matter in controversy exceeds the sum or value of $75,000, exclusive of interest and costs, and which are between:

(1) ***Citizens of different states;***
(2) ***Citizens of a state and citizens or subjects of a foreign nation;***
(3) citizens of different States and in which citizens or subjects of a foreign state are additional parties; and
(4) a foreign state . . . as plaintiff and citizens of a State or of different States.

[A]n alien admitted to the United States for permanent residence shall be deemed a citizen of the State in which such alien is domiciled."

(b) "Citizenship" of an individual: Except as to a "permanent resident alien," a person must be both a citizen of the United States and a state domiciliary. ***Domicile*** means actual ***residence*** in a state ***with the intent to make that place home***, *Mas v. Perry*, 489 F.2d 1396 (5th Cir. 1974).

(c) "Citizenship" of a corporation: Title 28 U.S.C. § 1332(c)(1) provides that "a corporation shall be deemed to be a citizen of any State by which it has been incorporated and of the State where it has its principal place of business . . . ."

(d) A legal representative of an infant, incompetent or of the estate of a decedent shall be deemed to be a citizen of the same State as the infant, incompetent or the decedent.

4. **EXCLUSIVE JURISDICTION**

Congress has by statute granted to the federal courts exclusive jurisdiction over specific actions, e.g., Title 28 U.S.C. § 1338(a) (patent and copyright); 28 U.S.C. § 1346(b) (Federal Tort Claims Act). But most federal statutory claims fall into the area of ***concurrent jurisdiction*** and may be brought ***in either federal or state*** court, e.g., Title 45 U.S.C. § 56 (As to Federal Employers' Liability Act claims, "the jurisdiction of the courts of the United States . . . shall be concurrent with that of the courts of the several States."). Moreover, there is a ***presumption of concurrent jurisdiction*** that is ***rebuttable*** by an express or implied direction of Congress to the contrary or "by a clear incompatibility between state court jurisdiction and federal interests." *Gulf Offshore Co. v. Mobil Oil Corp.*, 453 U.S. 473 (1981).

5. **AMOUNT IN CONTROVERSY**

(a) General Rule: There is ***no amount required*** for actions that meet the "general" federal question jurisdiction language of Title 28 U.S.C. § 1331. Some "specific" grants of federal claim jurisdiction, e.g., Title 28 U.S.C. § 1335 (federal statutory interpleader—$500.00 or more) do require a stated amount. ***Diversity actions require an amount in excess of $75,000***, exclusive of interest and costs. The amount stated by the pleader "controls if the claim is apparently made in good faith. It must appear to a legal certainty that the claim is really for less than the jurisdictional amount to justify dismissal." *St. Paul Mercury Indem. Co. v. Red Cab Co.*, 303 U.S. 283 (1938). If the claimant seeks equitable relief, the majority rule is "that the jurisdictional amount is to be tested by the value of the object to be gained . . . ," e.g., as in *Glenwood Light & Water Co. v. Mutual Light, Heat & Power Co.*, 239 U.S. 121 (1915).

(b) Aggregation: If one plaintiff sues one defendant, the plaintiff may aggregate the claims even if they arise from completely different transactions or occurrences. For example, in a diversity action where the plaintiff sues the defendant for a $50,000 tort claim and a $26,000 contract claim, the two claims can be added together to arrive at the requirement of ***an amount in excess of $75,000***. In multi-party litigation (i.e., more than one plaintiff or defendant), ***aggregation is not permitted unless the claims are viewed*** by the substantive law ***as common and undivided as opposed to separate and distinct. Eagle v. American Tel. & Tel. Co.***, 769 F.2d 541 (9th Cir. 1985). An example of when aggregation should be permitted: One plaintiff sues three defendants to recover a tract of land valued at $76,000 and each defendant defends based on a common title source. J. Friedenthal, M. Kane & A. Miller, *Civil Procedure* § 2.9, p. 50 n. 7 (1985).

6. **PENDENT OR ANCILLARY ("SUPPLEMENTAL") JURISDICTION**

(a) A Starting Point: Every claim in federal court ***must be supported by an independent ground of subject matter jurisdiction*** (federal question, or diversity plus over $75,000) or the ***claim must be one*** that is ***permitted to use the discretionary*** basis of jurisdiction called pendent or ancillary jurisdiction. This discretionary device allows the court to hear such claims if they arise from the ***same transaction or occurrence*** as the underlying suit.

(b) Pendent Claims: If the plaintiff seeks recovery from the defendant on two claims, one with an independent ground of subject matter jurisdiction (e.g., federal question) and another with no independent ground (e.g., a state claim of $76,000 but no diversity), the federal court may hear the state claim, if "the state and federal claims . . . derive from a common nucleus of operative fact." *UMW v. Gibbs*, 383 U.S. 715 (1966). To be related by a ***common nucleus means to arise from the same transaction or occurrence***. Pendent claim jurisdiction is a doctrine of discretion. Factors relevant: Has the federal claim been dismissed by pretrial motion practice? Does the state claim substantially predominate? Does the federal claim involve a significant federal policy (e.g., raise the federal doctrine of preemption)? Would trying the claims together create the likelihood of jury confusion?

(c) Pendent Party: What if plaintiff has a federal claim against defendant X ***and a transactionally-related state claim against*** defendant Y, but ***there is no independent ground of subject matter jurisdiction*** (e.g., no diversity) to support the state claim against defendant Y? The following decisions show a ***trend toward the narrow exercise of pendent party jurisdiction: Finley v. US.***,—U.S.—, 109 S. Ct. 2003 (1989) (Despite ***exclusive*** jurisdiction granted federal courts by Federal Tort Claims Act, 28 U.S.C. § 1346(b), pendent party jurisdiction not permitted); *Owen Equip. & Erection Co. v. Kroger*, 437 U.S. 365 (1978) (Plaintiff's claim against third-party defendant cannot be supported by pendent party jurisdiction); *Aldinger v. Howard*, 427 U.S. 1 (1976) (Pendent party jurisdiction not permitted in litigation under the Civil Rights Act, 42 U.S.C. § 1983).

7. **REMOVAL**

(a) "The defendant's forum shopping: By Title 28 U.S.C. § 1441, a ***defendant has the option of removing a federal question action*** from state to federal court "without regard to the citizenship or residence of the parties." A defendant can only remove an action that could have originally been brought by the plaintiff in a federal court. Although § 1441(b) also permits the defendant to remove based upon diversity plus over $75,000 in amount claimed, ***diversity removal is proper "only if none of the parties*** in interest properly joined and served as ***defendants is a citizen of the State in which such action is brought.***" By § 1441(a), the presence of a ***fictitious defendant*** (John Doe) ***does not defeat diversity for removal.*** Section 1446(b) ***bars the removal of a diversity action beyond one year after it commenced*** in state court.

(b) The notice of removal: ***All co-defendants must join in the notice.*** *Ely Valley Mines, Inc. v. Hartford Accident & Indem.* Co., 644 F.2d 1310 (9th Cir. 1981). The removal notice is filed in the federal court and requires a statement of the grounds for removal. The notice must be signed pursuant to Rule 11 (Signing of pleadings, motions, and other papers; sanctions). Service of the notice (with state court documents appended) is required to all parties. Title 28 U.S.C. § 1446.

(c) The motion to remand: If the plaintiff believes that the removed ***claims*** lack proper ***subject matter jurisdiction***, a motion to remand will raise that issue for court resolution. A federal court has discretion under the doctrine of pendent claim Jurisdiction to ***remand*** a properly removed case to state court ***if all federal claims*** have been ***eliminated*** and only ***pendent state claims remain*** for litigation. *Carnegie-Mellon Univ. v. Cohill*, 484 U.S. 343 (1988).

(d) The significance of a separate and independent claim: By Title 28 U.S.C. § 1441(c), if a separate and independent claim has an independent ground of subject matter jurisdiction and that claim is joined with another claim with no independent ground, ***the entire case may be removed.*** What is a ***separate and independent claim***? Ask yourself to what extent the federal and the state claims involve different facts and evidence. The greater the factual and evidentiary difference, the more likely the federal claim is separate and independent thus permitting the state claim to remain in federal court.

(e) Exceptions to removal: By statute, Congress has expressly denied removal to Federal Employers' Liability Actions (28 U.S.C. § 1445(a) and to actions arising under state workers' compensation laws (28 U.S.C. § 1445(c).

(f) Notice of removal of a civil action or proceeding shall be filed within ***30 days*** after receipt by the defendant through service or within ***30 days*** after the service of summons upon the defendant if such initial pleading has been filed in court and is not required to be served on the defendant.

8. **PLEADING SUBJECT MATTER JURISDICTION**

Because federal courts are of ***limited*** jurisdiction, the ***plaintiff must plead in the complaint the basis of*** the court's ***subject matter jurisdiction***. Federal Rule 8(a)(1) requires "a short and plain statement of the grounds upon which the court's jurisdiction depends . . . ." If the defendant or the court, sua sponte, raises a subject matter jurisdiction issue, the claimant bears the burden of proof.

IV. PROCEDURAL DUE PROCESS

INTRODUCTION. ***By what method of service*** (e.g., personal, abode, mail, publication, or posting) is the plaintiff required or permitted ***to notify*** an opponent that an action has been initiated against him? ***At what point of litigation is the defendant entitled to notice of suit against her?*** How does the 14th Amendment Due Process Clause serve to protect the defendant on the matters of the ***quality of the service and the time when that service must be made***?

A. DUE PROCESS AND QUALITY OF NOTICE

1. **THE MULLANE STANDARD**

In *Mullane v. Central Hanover Bank & Trust Co.*, 339 U.S. 306 (1950), the Supreme Court says that ***constitutionally adequate notice*** under the 14th Amendment Due Process Clause is that "reasonably calculated, under all the circumstances, to apprise interested parties of the pendency of the action . . . [and] the means employed must be such as one desirous of actually informing the . . . [defendant] might reasonably adopt to accomplish it."

Obviously, personal service (hand-to-hand delivery) of the complaint and summons will satisfy the constitutional requirement. But when will ***substitute service*** meet the *Mullane* test of ***reasonableness***? Does *Mullane* apply to all actions (i.e., whether categorized as in personam, quasi in rem, or in rem)? The answer to the first question is best explored by looking to *Post-Mullane* decisions of the Supreme Court provided in the section, *infra*. The answer to the second question is "yes", the *Mullane* standard applies to all actions.

2. POST-MULLANE CASES

Walker v. City of Hutchinson, 352 U.S. 112 (1956) (Publication notice, in a condemnation proceeding against a landowner whose name was known, constitutionally inadequate); *Schroeder v. City of New York*, 371 U.S. 208 (1962) (Publication and posting notice on property, in a condemnation proceeding against landowner whose name and address readily ascertainable, constitutionally inadequate); *Greene v. Lindsey* 456 U.S. 444 (1982) (Posting notice, in forcible entry or detainer action against tenant, constitutionally inadequate since posted notices frequently removed before actual notice received and mail service could have been used); *Mennonite Bd. of Missions v. Adams*, 462 U.S. 791 (1983) (Publication and posting notice of sale of real property for tax nonpayment constitutionally inadequate as to mortgagee readily identifiable); *Tulsa Professional Collection Servs., Inc. v. Pope*, 485 U.S. 478 (1988) (Publication notice, to known or reasonably ascertainable creditor with claim against estate, constitutionally inadequate since alternative of mail service could provide inexpensive and efficient mechanism reasonably calculated to provide actual notice).

B. DUE PROCESS AND TIMING OF NOTICE

1. THE FUENTES STANDARD

In *Fuentes* v, *Shevin*, 407 U.S. 67 (1972), the Supreme Court says that before a provisional remedy (e.g., garnishment or attachment) is ***used to seize property***, the 14th Amendment requires notice and an opportunity to be heard "at a time when the deprivation can still be prevented." The Court did recognize that an extraordinary situation might exist to permit seizure on ***ex parte*** application: "There may be cases in which a creditor could make a showing of immediate danger that a debtor will destroy or conceal disputed goods." *Id.* at 93.

The 4-3 *Fuentes* holding appears on its face to have broad impact on prejudgment remedies. Since that 1972 case, however, the Supreme Court has decided additional cases that suggest *Fuentes* may not have the clout once thought. The section, *infra*, looks at the post-*Fuentes* decisions.

2. POST-FUENTES CASES

Mitchell v. W.T. Grant Co., 416 U.S. 600 (1974) (Property seizure, without notice or opportunity to be heard, upheld because judge (as opposed to clerk) permitted seizure only after presented with verified petition that person whose property seized could reclaim property immediately); *North Ga. Finishing, Inc. v. Di-Chem, Inc.*, 419 U.S. 601 (1975) (Property seizure, without notice or opportunity to be heard, constitutionally invalid because clerk permitted seizure on conclusory allegations and no provision for early hearing for person whose property seized to reclaim property); *Flagg Bros., Inc. v. Brooks*, 436 U.S. 149 (1978) (Property seizure by creditor, without notice or opportunity to be heard, upheld because seizure a self-help remedy that does not involve state action); *Lugar v. Edmondson Oil Co., Inc.*, 457 U.S. 922 (1982) (Property seizure, without notice or opportunity to be heard, constitutionally invalid because self-help remedy involved joint participation of state officers, therefore, state action).

To analyze whether the use of a provisional remedy passes constitutional muster, the following are relevant: (a) Did the party who caused the seizure post a bond? (b) Was the seizure permitted by a judge or a court clerk? (c) Were the moving papers verified? (d) Is the person whose property was seized entitled to an immediate hearing to reclaim the property? (e) Is an extraordinary situation involved?

C. SERVICE OF PROCESS

1. SERVICE BY WHOM

Federal Rule 4(c)(2)(A) permits service "by any person who is not a party and is not less than 18 years of age."

2. SERVICE TO AN INDIVIDUAL

Federal Rule 4(d)(1) permits service by: (a) personal delivery (b) abode service or (c) to an agent authorized by appointment or by law.

Federal Rule 4(c)(2)(C)(i) permits the plaintiff to borrow the forum-state's methods of service of process.

Federal Rule 4(c)(2)(C)(ii) permits mail service to be used but if the defendant does not acknowledge the mail service then follow-up service by another method must be utilized.

3. SERVICE TO A BUSINESS ENTITY

Federal Rule 4(d)(3) permits service by: (a) personal delivery to an officer or a managing or general agent or (b) to an agent authorized by appointment or by law.

Federal Rule 4(c)(2)(C)(i) permits the borrowing of forum-state methods.

Federal Rule 4(c)(2)(C)(ii) permits mail service with follow-up alternative service required if mail service is not acknowledged.

V. VENUE, TRANSFER, AND FORUM NON CONVENIENS

INTRODUCTION. Among those courts that are appropriate because personal jurisdiction and subject matter jurisdiction can be satisfied there, the plaintiff must also consider the law of ***venue*** (place) since it ***may further limit forum choice.*** Even if the plaintiff can satisfy the personal jurisdiction, subject matter jurisdiction, and venue requirements for a particular court, the ***action may qualify for transfer to another court.*** If transfer cannot be achieved because the alternative forum is the court of another country, then the ***forum non conveniens*** law may ***lead to dismissal*** of the action.

A. VENUE. Even if competency and subject matter jurisdiction requisites are satisfied, venue (the proper judicial district) requirements must also be met.

1. **DIVERSITY CASES**

   In federal court, where subject matter jurisdiction is based upon *diversity*, the action may be brought in the judicial district where:

   (a) ***any*** defendant resides (so long as all defendants reside in the same state);

   (b) where a substantial part of the acts or omissions on which the claim is based took place, or a substantial part of the property which is the subject of the action is located; or

   (c) where the defendants (apparently, all of them) are subject to personal jurisdiction when the case was commenced.

   (d) Note: Prior to December, 1990, venue in diversity cases was proper in a district where all plaintiffs resided. This choice has thus been eliminated.

2. **FEDERAL CLAIM CASES**

   In federal court, where subject matter jurisdiction is based upon a ***federal*** claim, the action may be brought in the judicial district where:

   (a) ***any*** defendant resides (so long as all defendants reside in the same state);

   (b) where a substantial part of the property which is the subject of the action is located; or

   (c) if (a) or (b) cannot be satisfied, then in any district where any defendant may be found.

3. **CORPORATE RESIDENCY**

   For purposes of venue, a corporate ***defendant*** resides in any judicial district in which, at the time the action is commenced, its contacts would be sufficient to subject it to personal jurisdiction if that district were a separate state. If there is no such district, the corporation resides in the district within it has the most significant contacts.

4. **WHERE A CORPORATE PLAINTIFF RESIDES**

   A corporate plaintiff ***resides only in the state of its incorporation***, and, if that state has more than one district ***also in*** the district where it has its ***principal office.***

5. **WHERE AN UNINCORPORATED ASSOCIATION RESIDES**

   Whether a ***plaintiff or defendant***, an ***unincorporated association resides in any state and district*** where it is ***doing business***.

6. **MEANING OF RESIDES**

   For venue purposes "***residence***" is the ***equivalent of "domicile."***

7. **MEANING OF WHERE THE CLAIM AROSE**

The most commonly used definition is "one that attempts to determine the 'weight of the contacts' with the various districts in which venue might lie." J. Friedenthal, M. Kane & A. Miller, *Civil Procedure* § 2.15, p. 83 (1985).

8. **VENUE FOR REMOVAL CASES**

When an action is removed from state to federal court, the proper venue is "the district court of the United States for the district and division embracing the place where such action is pending." Title 28 U.S.C. § 1441(a).

9. **CONSEQUENCE OF IMPROPER VENUE**

(a) ***If venue is improper***, the court can dismiss or "transfer such case to any district or division in which it could have been brought." Title 28 U.S.C. § 1406(a).

(b) The Supreme Court says that a § 1406(a) transfer is permitted even if the transferor court does not have personal jurisdiction over the defendant. *Goldlawr, Inc. v. Heiman*, 369 U.S. 463 (1962).

(c) Because of the *Erie* doctrine applicable to diversity cases, an action transferred pursuant to § 1406(a) is governed by the law of the state where the federal transferee court sits. *Martin v. Stokes*, 623 F.2d 469 (1980).

(d) A § 1406(a) transfer is permitted only if the transferee court would have had venue, personal jurisdiction, and subject matter jurisdiction on the date the complaint was filed in the transferor court. See *Hoffman v. Blaski*, 363 U.S. 335 (1960).

B. TRANSFER OF VENUE

1. **TRANSFER DESPITE PROPER VENUE**

Although the plaintiff may have laid proper venue, a federal court "for the convenience of parties and witnesses, in the interest of justice, . . . may transfer any civil action to any other district or division where it might have been brought." Title 28 U.S.C. § 1404(a).

2. **FACTORS RELEVANT TO TRANSFER DISCRETION**

The burden is on the party who makes a § 1404(a) transfer motion to show that there should be a transfer by reference to the following factors: (a) convenience of parties; (b) convenience of material witnesses; (c) availability of process to compel presence of unwilling witnesses; (d) relative ease of access to proof; (3) calendar congestion; (f) where material event occurred; and (g) deference, due, if any, to plaintiff's forum choice. *Connors v. Lexington Ins. Co.*, 666 F. Supp. 434 (E.D.NY 1987).

3. **TRANSFER LIMITATIONS AND IMPLICATIONS**

(a) A § 1404(a) transfer is permitted only if the transferee court would had venue, personal jurisdiction, and subject matter jurisdiction on the date the complaint was filed in the transferor court. *Hoffman v. Blaski*, 363 U.S. 335 (1960).

(b) The prevailing view is that a § 1404(a) transfer is permitted even if the transferor court does not have personal jurisdiction over the defendant. *Ellis v. Great Southwestern Corp.*, 646 F.2d 1099 (5th Cir. 1981); *Smith v. Morris & Manning*, 657 F. Supp. 180 (S.D.NY 1987).

(c) Because of the Erie doctrine applicable to diversity cases, an action transferred under § 1404(a) is governed by the law of the state where the transferor court sits; this rule applies whether transfer is by defendant's motion, *Van Dusen v. Barrack*, 376 U.S. 612 (1964), or plaintiff's motion, *Martin v. Stokes*, 623 F.2d 469 (6th Cir. 1980).

(d) Even if the parties have agreed to be bound by a forum-selection contract clause, a § 1404(a) transfer is not compelled if the statutory factors weigh against the private agreement of the parties. Moreover, because of the *Erie* doctrine principles laid down in *Hanna v. Plumer*, 380 U.S. 460 (1965), § 1404(a) controls in a diversity case despite a conflicting law of the state where the federal court sits. *Stewart Org., Inc. v. Ricoh Corp.* 108 S. Ct. 2239 (1988).

C. FORUM NON CONVENIENS (FNC)

1. HOW FNC RELATES TO VENUE AND TRANSFER OF VENUE

If the plaintiff has laid improper venue, a court can transfer the action to another federal court where venue is proper (Title 28 U.S.C. § 1406(a). Even if plaintiff's venue choice is proper, the case may be transferred to another more convenient federal court (Title 28 U.S.C. § 1404(a). If the alternative forum is not another federal court but a court in a foreign country, the common law doctrine of FNC steps in to fill the statutory void. ***FNC***, if successful, ***leads to dismissal or stay, but not to transfer.***

2. THE LANDMARK CASES

(a) *Gulf Oil Corp. v. Gilbert*, 330 U.S. 501 (1947): In this case the Supreme Court says that FNC applies (1) only if there is an alternative forum where personal jurisdiction, subject matter jurisdiction, and venue can be satisfied and (2) when the convenience factors identical to those under § 1404(a) point to a dismissal because of the availability of the more convenient alternative forum.

(b) *Piper Aircraft Co. v. Reyno*, 454 U.S. 235 (1981): In the course of this decision the Supreme Court says that (1) the possibility of a change in the substantive law may be given substantial weight only if the remedy in the alternative forum is so clearly inadequate or unsatisfactory as to be no remedy at all; (2) ordinarily, there is a strong presumption in favor of the plaintiff's choice of forum which may be overcome only when the convenience factors clearly point to trial in the alternative forum; (3) but, the presumption applies with less force when the plaintiff is from a foreign country.

3. FNC CONSEQUENCE

Ordinarily, if the defendant succeeds on an FNC motion, the plaintiff's action is ***dismissed***. A court, however, may ***condition dismissal*** on the defendant's agreement to submit to jurisdiction in the alternative forum.

VI. PRETRIAL MOTION PRACTICE

INTRODUCTION. By what method does the procedural system permit a party to raise preliminary issues about the nature of an opponent's claim or defense? Beyond the stage of preliminary matters, how does a party seek the resolution of a dispute without the need for trial? In the federal system, motion practice is the primary procedural tool that serves those functions.

A. RAISING PRELIMINARY OBJECTIONS

1. Federal Rule 12(b) provides for a motion to dismiss on the following grounds:

   (1) lack of subject matter jurisdiction;
   (2) lack of personal jurisdiction;
   (3) improper venue;
   (4) insufficiency of process;
   (5) insufficiency of service of process;
   (6) failure to state a claim; and
   (7) failure to join a party needed for a just adjudication.

   The above defenses or objections may also be raised in a responsive pleading; but, note that motion practice is usually the most expedient avenue to raise the issue for a ruling by the court. Rule 12(b) requires that motion practice be used ***"before pleading . . ."***

2. Federal Rule 12(g) requires a ***consolidation*** of defenses ***into one*** pre-pleading motion and failure to consolidate leads to waiver of the defense or objection unless provided otherwise by Rule 12(h).

3. Federal Rule 12(h) specifically describes what ***matters*** are ***waived*** or ***preserved*** by violating the ***consolidation*** requirement of Rule 12(g) or pleading requirements. The ***defense of*** lack of personal jurisdiction (12(b)(2)), improper venue (12(b)(3)), insufficiency of process (12(b)(4)), or insufficiency of service of process (12(b)(5)), ***is waived if omitted*** from the ***one pre-pleading motion*** permitted or, if no motion is made, ***if not included in a responsive pleading***. ***For example***, if a defendant makes a motion to dismiss for improper venue (12(b)(3)) and loses on the motion, the defendant cannot thereafter raise either by another motion or in the answer, the defenses of 12(b)(2), 12(b)(4), or 12(b)(5).

   Some defenses are preserved even though ***not consolidated*** into a single pre-pleading motion. The defense of failure to state a claim (12(b)(6)) and failure to join a party needed for a just adjudication (12(b)(7)) may be raised by a pleading subsequent to earlier motion practice or by a second motion following an earlier pleading. ***For example***, a defendant who makes a motion to dismiss for lack of personal jurisdiction (12(b)(2)) and loses on the motion, may thereafter raise either by a subsequent motion or in the answer, the defenses of 12(b)(6) and 12(b)(7). Note that, since 12(b)(6) and 12(b)(7) are defenses that reach beyond mere preliminary matters, they are preserved by Rule 12(h).

Finally, the defense of lack of subject matter jurisdiction (12(b)(1)) goes to the nature of the ***limited jurisdiction*** of a federal court, and that defense may be raised ***at any time on direct attack. For example***, if a defendant never raises either by motion or pleading, the defense of 12(b)(1), that defense may be raised for the first time by the defendant who appeals the judgment lost.

B. COLLATERAL ATTACK AND LACK OF PERSONAL JURISDICTION OR SUBJECT MATTER JURISDICTION

1. **PERSONAL JURISDICTION:** If the defendant never makes an appearance and a default judgment is taken, can the defendant ***collaterally attack*** the judgment for lack of personal jurisdiction when the judgment creditor begins a judgment enforcement proceeding? Yes, the defendant is entitled to a "day in court" on the question of personal jurisdiction. However, if the defendant loses on the personal jurisdiction issue, the default judgment stands. If the defendant uses Rule 12(b), makes a motion to dismiss for lack of personal jurisdiction, loses and then defaults, the issue of personal jurisdiction may not be raised by the defendant on ***collateral attack*** in a proceeding to enforce the judgment. The defendant had a "day in court" at the trial level. *Baldwin v. Iowa State Traveling Men's Ass'n*, 283 U.S. 522 (1931).

2. **SUBJECT MATTER JURISDICTION:** Will the defendant be permitted to ***collaterally attack*** a judgment on the ground that the court that rendered it lacked subject matter jurisdiction? If the judgment was taken by ***default***, the defendant is ***generally permitted to attack the judgment collaterally*** for lack of subject matter jurisdiction. *Restatement Second of Judgments § 65. If* the judgment is the result of a contested action (and, regardless of whether or not the issue of subject matter jurisdiction actually was raised), ***collateral attack is generally not permitted unless*** (1) the court acted in such plain excess of authority as to amount to an abuse of discretion; or (2) the court's exercise of jurisdiction amounts to a substantial infringement on the authority of another court or governmental agency; or (3) the court didn't have the capacity to determine the issue. *Restatement Second of Judgments* §§ *12, 69*. Obviously, it is a matter of the competing values of the ***validity*** of the judgment versus the ***finality*** of the judgment.

C. JUDGMENT ON THE PLEADINGS

After all the pleadings have been completed, Rule 12(c) permits any party to move for a judgment on the pleadings. Factual allegations in the pleading of the opposing party are taken as true and the moving party's pleading allegations, if denied, are taken as false. Because the courts are reluctant to deal summarily with a claim as pleaded, the motion will not be granted unless it appears beyond doubt that the claimant can prove no set of facts to support the claim. The only difference between a Rule 12(c) motion for judgment on the pleadings and a Rule 12(b)(6) motion to dismiss for failure to state a claim is that the Rule 12(c) motion is made at the close of the pleading stage rather than in the beginning (i.e., after the service of a complaint). A second use of Rule 12(c) is to test the adequacy of an affirmative defense. In this context, because the defendant has the burden of proof on an affirmative case, Rule 12(c) allows a plaintiff to ask the court to evaluate whether an affirmative case is adequately asserted and is consistent with law.

D. MOTION FOR A MORE DEFINITE STATEMENT

Rule 12(e) permits a motion for a more definite statement to be directed to an opponent's pleading that requires a responsive pleading. The motion is appropriate only if a pleading contains a claim that is "so vague or ambiguous" that a responsive pleading cannot reasonably be framed. Because federal pleading is so-called "notice" pleading, the courts are reluctant to grant the motion and its utility comes largely in those Rule 9 areas that require particularity of pleading (e.g., Rule 9(b)—allegations of fraud or mistake; Rule 9(g)—stating specifically items of special damage). If the court grants the motion, the pleader is required to amend the allegations to cure the pleading deficiency.

E. MOTION TO STRIKE

A Rule 12(f) motion to strike is appropriate to challenge redundant, immaterial, impertinent, or scandalous matter in a pleading or to test the sufficiency of an opponent's defense stated in a pleading. Unless it is clear that the portion of the pleading to which the motion is directed has no bearing on the subject matter of the litigation, and that its inclusion prejudice the movant, the motion to strike should be denied. The primary importance of the motion to strike is when it is used by a plaintiff to make a preliminary challenge to the legal sufficiency of a defense stated in the defendant's answer. Only if a defense is insufficient as a matter of law will it be stricken. A defense is insufficient as a matter of law if, on the face of the pleading, it is patently frivolous.

F. VOLUNTARY AND INVOLUNTARY DISMISSAL

1. **VOLUNTARY DISMISSAL:** Until service of an adverse party's answer or motion for summary judgment, Rule 41(a)(1)(i) permits a claimant to ***voluntarily dismiss*** by ***filing*** a notice of dismissal. The filing of the notice of dismissal automatically terminates the case. A claimant may also ***voluntarily dismiss***, pursuant to Rule 41(a)(1)(ii), ***by filing a stipulation*** signed by all parties.

   If it is too late to seek voluntary dismissal by filing a notice or stipulation as provided by Rule 41(a)(1), ***a motion for voluntary dismissal may be made*** under Rule 41(a)(2). The court will grant the motion unless the opponent will suffer prejudice. By "prejudice," is meant something other than the necessity the defendant might face of defending another action. That kind of disadvantage can be lessened by a condition that plaintiff pay the defendant's attorney fees and costs. But if defendant is likely to win the case, should it continue, reimbursement of fees and expenses cannot make the defense whole from the injury of being sued again.

2. **INVOLUNTARY DISMISSAL:** Rule 41(b) authorizes an ***involuntary dismissal for failure to prosecute*** or to comply with the Federal Rules of Civil Procedure or any order of court. If the claimant fails to use reasonable diligence in pursuit of a claim (e.g., after the close of pleadings makes no effort to move the case through the usual litigation stages), the court may dismiss the claim or impose financial sanctions upon an attorney who fails to prosecute a client's case. Unless otherwise specified by the court, an involuntary dismissal operates as an ***adjudication upon the merits***.

G. ENTRY OF AND JUDGMENT BY DEFAULT

1. **ENTRY OF DEFAULT:** If a party fails to plead or otherwise defend and that fact is brought to the clerk's attention, the clerk must enter the party's default. "Otherwise defend," as used in Rule 55(a)(1), includes attacks on the service or motions to dismiss, for example, that may prevent default apart from having complied with pleading requirements.

2. **JUDGMENT BY DEFAULT:** In certain circumstances, a ***default judgment*** can be entered by the clerk following a ***prior entry of default***. Rule 55(b)(1) ***limits the clerk's authority to situations*** when the claim is for an amount susceptible to reliable computation, ***the defendant has never appeared, and*** the defendant is not an infant or incompetent.

   When the default situation exceeds the limitations of the clerk, the default judgment must be handled by the court. Court rendered default judgments under Rule 55(b)(2) require that the defendant be served with written notice of application for judgment at least three (3) days prior to the court's decision on the matter. ***If the defendant has ever appeared***, the notice of application is automatically required.

   Rule 54(c) provides that a ***default judgment is limited to the amount requested in the pleading*** for affirmative relief. A court has discretion to set aside a default judgment. Exercise of that discretion entails consideration of (1) whether the default was willful and (2) whether a set-aside would prejudice the opposing party. The Supreme Court says in *Peralta v. Heights Med. Center, Inc.*, 485 U.S. 80 (1988) that it is a due process denial to require a defendant, ***who was not served properly***, to show as a condition for set-aside that there is a meritorious defense on the merits.

H. SUMMARY JUDGMENT

Under Rule 56(a), a party seeking relief may move for a summary judgment after the expiration of twenty (20) days from the action's commencement or after service of a summary judgment motion by the adverse party.

By Rule 56(b), a party defending against a claim may move for summary judgment. A defendant ***may make the motion*** with or ***before filing an answer***.

While a motion for judgment on the pleadings (Rule 12(c)) and a motion to dismiss for failure to state a claim (Rule 12(b)(6)) focus on the content of pleadings, a ***summary judgment motion*** permits the movant to draw ***attention to matter outside the pleadings*** (e.g., evidence gained by discovery or affidavit practice).

A summary judgment motion calls for a determination of whether or not there is a genuine issue of material fact. Said simply, are there any facts which give rise to a triable issue? What is a material fact has meaning only in the context of the substantive law of claims and defenses. A genuine issue exists when there is a bona fide factual dispute. The standard to determine if a genuine issue of material fact exists is whether, viewing the evidence and the inferences that can be drawn therefrom in the light most favorable to the opposing party, the moving party is entitled to prevail as a matter of law.

The burden of establishing the nonexistence of a triable issue is on the moving party. This burden has the following two components: (1) the initial burden of production, that, if satisfied, then shifts to the party opposing the motion; and (2) the ultimate burden of persuasion that always remains on the moving party.

The court should not determine whether the ultimate burden of persuasion has been satisfied until the moving party has discharged its initial burden of production. The manner in which the initial burden can be made depends upon which party will bear the burden of persuasion on the issue at trial. If the moving party bears the burden of persuasion at trial, that party must support its motion with the kind of credible evidence that would entitle it to a directed verdict if not controverted at trial. At this point, the burden of production shifts to the party opposing the motion to produce evidentiary materials that show a triable issue.

If the burden of persuasion at trial would be borne by the party opposing the motion, the moving party can satisfy the burden of production ***by relying solely*** on "the pleadings, depositions, answers to interrogatories, and admissions on file, together ***with affidavits, if any***" to show (1) that the party opposing the motion has no evidence to support the issue ***or*** (2) that the opponent's evidence is insufficient on the issue. There is no requirement that the moving party support its motion with evidence tending to ***negate*** an essential element of an opposing party's claim. If the moving party meets its burden of production, then the party opposing the motion must come forward with evidentiary materials, beyond the mere pleadings, although the evidence need not be produced in a form that would be admissible at trial. *Celotex Corp. v. Catrett*, 477 U.S. 317 (1986).

VII. THE ERIE DOCTRINE

INTRODUCTION. Federal subject matter jurisdiction based upon diversity has been a part of the limited authority of the inferior federal courts since their creation by Congress in the Judiciary Act of 1789. In 1842, the Supreme Court held that, in a diversity case with a claim based upon state law, a federal court should apply federal substantive law to the state claim unless that claim involved state legislative law or matters of local custom or usage. *Swift v. Tyson*, 41 U.S. (16 Pet.) 1. The holding of *Swift* controlled until it was overruled by the landmark decision of *Erie Railroad Co. v. Tompkins*, 304 U.S. 64 (1938). In *Erie*, the Supreme Court said that ***state substantive law applies in a diversity case***. *Erie* means that the ***substantive law of a state includes its decisional law***. Since the *Erie* decision, the Supreme Court has decided a series of cases that are designed to help in the analysis of the difference between substantive and procedural law. If an issue is one of substance, state law controls; but, if the matter involves procedure, federal law controls even in a diversity case where the source of the right sued upon is state law. ***The Erie doctrine is a constitutional law mandate that applies to diversity cases.***

A. THE STATUTORY BACKDROP

1. RULES OF DECISION ACT (RDA)

Title 28 U. S.C. § 1652 says: "The laws of the several states, except where the Constitution or treaties of the United States or Acts of Congress otherwise require or provide, shall be regarded as rules of decision in civil actions in the courts of the United States, in cases where they apply."

From *Erie* (1938) to, but not including *Hanna* (1965), all of the important Supreme Court cases are about the meaning of the word "laws" in the Rules of Decision Act. The important RDA cases follow, *infra.*

2. **RULES ENABLING ACT (REA)**

Title 28 U.S.C. § 2072(a) authorizes the Supreme Court to prescribe rules of practice, procedure, and evidence for the federal courts; but, § 2072(b) is a limitation because it says that "such rules shall not abridge, enlarge or modify any substantive right."

Since *Hanna* (1965), there are two important Supreme Court cases that also use its approach to analyze an *Erie* problem. The REA cases follow, *infra.*

3. **RULES OF DECISION ACT (RDA) CASES**

(a) *Erie Railroad Co. v. Tompkins*, 304 U.S. 64 (1938). (State decisional law must be applied to a state claim in order to serve twin aims: avoid forum shopping and the inequitable administration of the law. The forum shopping that concerned the Court was choosing a federal court over a state court for the litigation of a state claim. The inequity to which the Court referred was the out-of-state plaintiff going to a defendant's home state and therein suing in a federal court and reaping a benefit from that court's application of federal rather than state law. Held: The duty of a landowner to a person upon the land is an issue of substantive law and therefore state law applies.)

(b) *Klaxon Co. v. Stentor Elec. Mfg. Co.*, 313 U.S. 487 (1941). (Federal courts are required by *Erie* to apply the conflict of laws principles of the state where the federal court sits.)

(c) *Palmer v. Hoffman*, 318 U.S. 109 (1943). (*Erie* requires the application of state law on burden of proof.)

(d) *Guaranty Trust Co. v. York*, 326 U.S. 99 (1945). (Under *Erie*, a state law is one of substance if not to apply it would lead to a different outcome in federal court from what would occur in state court. Held: A state statute of limitations is a substantive law applicable to a state claim litigated in federal court.)

(e) *Cohen v. Beneficial Indus. Loan Corp.*, 337 U.S. 541 (1949). (In a shareholder's derivative action, the "outcome-determinative" test of *Guaranty Trust* requires that a federal court apply a state law calling for the plaintiff to post a security bond for costs and fees.)

(f) *Ragan v. Merchants Transfer Co.*, 337 U.S. 530 (1949). (The "outcome-determinative" test obligates a federal court to use the state law regarding the tolling of the state statute of limitations.)

(g) *Woods v. Interstate Really Co.*, 337 U.S. 535 (1949). (A state law that defines whether a foreign corporation qualifies to use the courts of a state is "outcome-determinative" and must be followed by a federal court.)

(h) *Bernhardt v. Polygraphic Co. of Am.*, 350 U.S. 198 (1956). (A federal court cannot allow arbitration where a state court would disallow it.)

(i) *Byrd v. Blue Ridge Rural Elec. Coop.*, 356 U.S. 525 (1958). (Although a state law may have the potential of producing a difference in outcome, it does not apply in federal court if there is a strong federal countervailing policy—particularly, when the state law is not "outcome-determinative" in the ultimate sense. Held: Federal judge-jury function prevails over a conflicting state law that allocates the factual determination to a state judge.)

(j) *Walker v. Armco Steel Corp.*, 446 U.S. 740 (1980). (Since Federal Rule 3 does not speak to tolling of a statute of limitations, the federal court must use the state's tolling law as previously held by *Ragan* (1949). The Supreme Court says in a *Walker* footnote (n. 9): "This is not to suggest that the Federal Rules of Civil Procedure are to be narrowly construed in order to avoid a 'direct collision' with state law. The Federal Rules should be given their plain meaning. If a direct collision with state law arises from that plain meaning, then the analysis developed in *Hanna v. Plumer* [, 380 U.S. 460 (1965)] applies.")

4. **RULES ENABLING ACT (REA) CASES**

(a) *Hanna v. Plumer*, 380 U.S. 460 (1965). (If a Federal Rule of Civil Procedure is in direct collision with state law, the F.R.C.P. controls unless the Rule violates the Rules Enabling Act (by abridging, enlarging or modifying a substantive right) or the U.S. Constitution. Held: Rule 4(d)(1), which permits abode service, applies despite a conflicting state service law that requires personal service.)

(b) *Burlington Northern R. Co. v. Woods*, 480 U.S. 1 (1987). (The *Hanna* analysis also applies to the Federal Rules of Appellate Procedure. The Supreme Court says in a *Burlington* footnote (n. 3): "Article III of the Constitution, augmented by the Necessary and Proper Clause of Article 1, §8, cl. 18, empowers Congress to establish a system of federal district and appellate courts and, impliedly, to establish procedural Rules governing litigation in these courts. In the Rules Enabling Act, Congress authorized this Court to prescribe uniform Rules to govern the 'practice and procedure' of the Federal District Courts and Courts of Appeals . . . . Though *Hanna* . . . involved a conflict between state law and a Federal Rule of Civil Procedure, its analytical framework provides the test for the validity of Federal Rules of Appellate Procedure as well, since these Rules were also prescribed pursuant to the Rules Enabling Act.")

(c) *Stewart Org., Inc. v. Ricoh Corp.*, 108 S. Ct. 2239 (1988). (*Hanna* provides a major part of the analytical framework when a federal statute is "sufficiently broad" to cover the point in dispute. In *Stewart*, the Supreme Court says: "[W]hen the federal law sought to be applied is a congressional statute, the first and chief question . . . is whether the statute is "sufficiently broad to control the issue before the Court '. . . This question involves a straightforward exercise in statutory interpretation to determine if the statute covers the point in dispute . . . . If the . . . Court determines that a federal statute covers the point in dispute, it proceeds to inquire whether the statute represents a valid exercise of Congress' authority under the

Constitution." Held: Title 28 U.S.C. § 1404(a) (Transfer of venue) applies despite a state law that looks unfavorably upon contractual forum-selection clauses.)

5. **AN ERIE FORMULA: CHOOSING BETWEEN THE RDA AND THE REA LINES OF ANALYSIS**

   (a) Does the issue arise in a diversity case with recovery sought under state law?

   (b) Is there a conflict between state law (that would be applied if the case were in state court), and federal law?

   (c) What is the source of the conflict? Federal case law? A Federal Rule of Civil Procedure? A Federal Rule of Appellate Procedure? An Act of Congress?

   (d) If the conflict is between state law and federal case law or principles, an *Erie* analysis based upon the holdings of the RDA cases from *Erie* (1938) through *Walker* (1980) is appropriate.

   (e) If the conflict is between state law and a Federal Rule of Civil Procedure or a Federal Rule of Appellate Procedure or An Act of Congress, an *Erie* analysis based upon the holdings of the REA cases from *Hanna* (1965) through *Stewart* (1988) is appropriate.

VIII. PLEADINGS

INTRODUCTION. Pleadings are the paper work that begin litigation. The federal system looks to the pleadings to provide ***notice*** to an opponent of the nature of a claim or defense. In general, federal pleadings do not provide the detail that will later be sought by the discovery process. It is essential, however, that we know what pleadings are required and the content of those pleadings, and how the pleadings can be amended.

A. PLEADINGS ALLOWED

Federal Rule 7(a) calls for the following pleadings: ***complaint***; ***answer***; ***reply to an answer that contains a counterclaim***; ***answer to a cross-claim if the answer contains a cross-claim***; ***a third-party complaint*** if a person is added for the purpose of seeking from that added party ***indemnity or contribution***; and a ***third-party answer to a third-party complaint.***

B. CLAIM FOR RELIEF

In general, a claim for relief is made when the pleader asks for money damages, injunctive relief, or declaratory relief. The plaintiff seeks affirmative relief in a complaint; a defendant seeks affirmative relief by interposing a counterclaim against an opposing party; a defendant seeks affirmative relief by making a cross-claim against a co-party defendant; and a party claimed against may, by becoming a third-party plaintiff, make a third-party complaint against someone outside the lawsuit and seek indemnity or contribution from that third-party defendant.

C. THE COMPLAINT

1. A complaint, counterclaim, cross-claim, and third-party claim share in common the aim of seeking relief. Within the pleading of the claim that seeks that objective, there

must be three components. First, a statement of the grounds for subject matter jurisdiction; second, a statement of the claim; and third, a demand for judgment that grants relief.

2. Rule 8(a)(1) requires a "short and plain statement of the grounds upon which the court's jurisdiction depends . . . ." The purpose of alleging **subject matter jurisdiction** is to recognize that a federal court is ***limited*** by the United States Constitution, Article III, and statutes enacted thereunder, ***to specified kinds of dispute***. Here, of course, we're talking about a claim based upon a **federal question or** a claim based upon ***diversity plus*** an ***amount*** in controversy ***exceeding*** $75,000.

3. Rule 8(a)(2) requires a "short and plain statement of the claim showing that the pleader is entitled to relief . . . ." The "notice philosophy" embodied in (a)(2) is best exemplified by case decisions where the sufficiency of the pleader's statement is challenged by a Rule 12(b)(6) motion to dismiss for failure to comply with the Rule. For example, in *Conley v. Gibson*, 355 U.S. 41 (1957), the Supreme Court says that "a complaint should not be dismissed for failure to state a claim unless it appears beyond doubt that the plaintiff can prove no set facts in support of his claim which would entitle him to relief . . . . [T]he Federal Rules of Civil Procedure do not require a claimant to set out in detail the facts upon which he bases his claim."

   Ordinarily, the remedy for noncompliance with Rule 8(a)(2) is ***dismissal with leave to amend***; but if the pleader makes no progress by amendment, a court is likely to dismiss with prejudice.

4. Rule 8(a)(3) requires "a demand for judgment for the relief the pleader seeks." The Rule is designed to permit the pleader to demand whatever legal or equitable relief is alternatively or cumulatively available. Different and inconsistent legal theories may be pleaded. Indeed, Rule 54(c) says that, ***except in default judgment cases***, "every final judgment shall grant the relief to which the party in whose favor it is rendered is entitled, ***even if the party has not demanded such relief in the party's pleadings***."

D. PLEADING PARTICULAR MATTERS

Federal Rule 9 does require detailed pleading in certain areas and, therefore, that Rule stands as an exception to the basic pleading commands of Rule 8. The most important instances of a burden of ***particular pleading*** are with the ***following topics: capacity to sue***; ***fraud or mistake***; ***conditions precedent***; and ***special damage***.

1. CAPACITY TO SUE

If a defendant wishes to contest the plaintiff's capacity to sue, it is the defendant's pleading responsibility to point out in what manner the plaintiff lacks capacity. If the defendant does not specifically challenge capacity, in an answer or by motion practice, lack of capacity is waived unless the capacity issue deprives the court of subject matter jurisdiction.

2. FRAUD OR MISTAKE

An allegation of fraud or mistake should be sufficient in detail if it states the time, place, and nature of the activities and circumstances constituting fraud or mistake thereby giving the defendant an opportunity to prepare an answer from the allegations. Failure of the pleader to meet this requirement renders a pleading vulnerable to a Rule 12(b)(6) motion to dismiss for failure to state a claim or a Rule 12(e) motion for a more definite statement.

3. CONDITIONS PRECEDENT

Although Rule 9 places a minimal pleading burden on the party whose claim is conditioned on the performance or occurrence of certain events (i.e., the performance or occurrence may, as usual, be pleaded generally), the ***denial*** of performance or occurrence of conditions precedent ***must be pleaded*** with particularity. If a defendant makes ***only a general denial***, there may be a ***waiver*** of trial on the issue of the performance of conditions precedent or the performance may be deemed admitted.

4. SPECIAL DAMAGE

Actual or compensatory damages are subclassified as general or special and pleaded according to the label. Traditionally, general damages are defined as those which necessarily result from an act or omission and those damages need not be pleaded with particularity; whereas, special damages are those which are not the inevitable result of an injury and that type of harm must be pleaded with specificity. In a personal injury case, it would be ordinary if a jurisdiction were to classify pain and suffering as general damages while classifying medical expenses, repairs to property, and loss of earnings or income as special damages. Failure to plead special damages may lead to the inadmissibility of a pleader's special damage evidence.

E. THE ANSWER

Rule 8(b) says that an answer is a pleading in which the defendant ***admits, denies, or makes a non-positive denial*** (i.e., without knowledge or information sufficient to form a belief); ***states defenses***; ***and makes a claim for affirmative relief such as a counterclaim or cross-claim***.

In response to the complaint, the defendant must decide the aptness of making a general denial to each and every allegation made by the plaintiff. The ***general denial***, which supplies the least responsive information to the plaintiff, is ***appropriate only*** when the defendant intends ***to deny all*** of the plaintiff's ***allegations including*** those pertaining ***to subject matter jurisdiction***.

The nonpositive denial (e.g., "Defendant alleges that she is without knowledge or information sufficient to form a belief as to the truth of the allegations contained in paragraph 2 of the complaint.") is inappropriate if an admission or denial could be made were the defendant to consult a public record or exert a reasonable effort to learn the facts.

Two very ***critical aspects of the answer involve*** its use to state a ***counterclaim or cross-claim and*** to make ***affirmative defenses***. As will be noted in the topic **"IX. JOINDER,"** *infra*, a ***defendant must state a compulsory counterclaim in the answer and may state a permissive counterclaim or a crossclaim by answer***. Of primary importance is the ***defendant's obligation to allege affirmative defenses***. For example, if the defendant believes the ***statute of limitations*** has run on plaintiff's claim or the claim is unenforceable because of the ***statute of frauds***, those defenses must be stated ***in*** the ***defendant's answer***.

At what risk is the defendant if there is an improper denial or an omission of a compulsory counterclaim or affirmative defense? An ***ineffective denial*** leads to an ***admission***, an omitted ***compulsory counterclaim*** or ***affirmative defense is waived unless*** the court permits the defendant to ***amend*** the answer.

F. AMENDING PLEADINGS

1. "MATTER OF COURSE" AMENDMENT

Federal Rule 15 (a) permits a party to amend a pleading ***once*** at any time ***before a responsive pleading is served***. In other words, motion practice and court involvement are not required for the plaintiff to amend the complaint before the defendant serves an answer.

2. "LEAVE" AMENDMENT

(a) Before trial: By ***motion practice***, a party may seek the court's permission to amend a pleading ***after a responsive pleading has been served***. For example, after the defendant serves an answer, the plaintiff must seek court approval to amend. The federal courts follow a very liberal policy ***permitting amendment in order to reach the merits*** of the entire dispute between parties.

(b) During trial: If ***evidence*** is ***objected*** to at trial ***on the ground*** that it is ***not within*** the issues raised by the ***pleadings***, the ***court permits amendment*** where to do so will ***facilitate the presentation of the merits*** of the action.

(c) After trial: Even after trial, a court is authorized by Rule 15(b) to permit pleadings to be amended to reflect the issues that have been impliedly tried by the consent of the parties. Since this type of amendment may, if granted, increase the affirmative relief to be awarded, the court ***searches*** the trial ***record for indications that*** the party contesting the amendment ***received actual notice of the unpleaded issues and had*** an adequate ***opportunity to litigate***. The clearest ***indication of*** a party's ***implied consent*** to try an issue ***lies in failure to object to evidence or*** in the ***introduction of evidence relevant to a new issue*** not raised by the pleadings.

3. "RELATION BACK" AMENDMENT

(a) Adding a new claim: If a party learns of an additional claim (even though the statute of limitations has run against that claim), an amendment of the original pleading will be permitted as long as the new claim and an original claim arise from the same conduct, transaction, or occurrence. By the authority of Rule 15(c), the amendment ***relates back to the date of the original pleading and prevents the use of the statute of limitations defense***.

(b) Adding a new party: An amendment to an original pleading to add a party, and state a claim against the added party, will relate back to the date of the original pleading if: (1) the new claim against the new party arises from the same conduct, transaction, or occurrence as that set forth in an original claim against an original party; ***and*** (2) ***before the statute of limitations expired, the new party had actual notice that an action had been started***; and (3) ***also, within the statutory period***, the new party ***knew or should have known that***, but for a mistake concerning the identity of the proper party, ***a claim would have been made against the new party.*** In *Schiavone v. Fortune*, 477 U.S. 21 (1986), the Supreme Court makes it very clear that ***unless the new party actually knows of the action before the expiration of the statute of limitations, there can be no relation back.***

4. **THE *ERIE* DOCTRINE AND RELATION BACK TO ADD A PARTY**

Under California law, Cal. Civ. Proc. Code § 474, the plaintiff may sue a person described as a "Doe" defendant, and, upon discovery of the true name of the person, substitute by amendment the real name in place of the "Doe". By Cal. Civ. Proc. Code 583.210, a plaintiff has three years to make the substitution and serve process to the real defendant. In effect, the "Doe" procedure extends the applicable statute of limitations three years past commencement of the action.

What happens if a federal diversity complaint contains the California "Doe" practice allegation ("against Does I-X"), and, after the running of the state statute of limitations, the plaintiff seeks to use California law to amend to substitute a real person who had no actual knowledge of the suit before the statute expired? Federal Rule 15(c) would not permit the amendment to relate back because of lack of actual notice during the statutory period. A California state court would allow the amendment as long as service to the real person to be substituted is made within three years after suit began. As to this *Erie* problem, the Ninth Circuit says the ***federal court must apply California law because it involves the state statute of limitations.*** *Lindley v. General Elec. Co.*, 780 F.2d 797 (9th Cir. 1986), *cert. denied*, 476 U.S. 1186 (1986).

G. TRUTH IN PLEADING

Federal Rule 11 requires the attorney to sign "every ***pleading***, motion, and other paper" prepared for the client. The attorney's signature is a certification that the pleading is ***supported by a reasonable inquiry into the facts and*** "is warranted by existing law or a good faith argument for the extension, modification, or reversal of existing law, ***and*** that it is not interposed for any improper purpose . . ."

A violation of Rule 11 ***need not be based upon subjective*** bad faith. An attorney is in violation of Rule 11 if he or she signs a pleading without having conducted a ***reasonable inquiry into whether the pleading is frivolous, legally unreasonable, or without factual foundation***. Reasonableness is measured by an objective standard. If the Rule is violated, the court ***must*** impose an appropriate ***sanction on the attorney, the client, or both***. The sanction may include having to pay an opponent's reasonable attorney's fee. *Unioil, Inc. v. E.F. Hutton & Co.*, 809 F.2d 548 (9th Cir. 1986).

A complaint that is found to be well-grounded in fact and law cannot be sanctioned as harassing, regardless of the attorney's subjective intent. *Hudson v. Moore Business Forms, Inc.*, 836 F.2d 1156 (9th Cir. 1987).

Procedural due process requires notice of the misconduct and opportunity to be heard in defense before imposition of a Rule 11 sanction. *Tom Growney Equip., Inc. v. Shelley Irr. Dev., Inc.*, 834 F.2d 833 (9th Cir. 1987).

IX. JOINDER

INTRODUCTION. If one plaintiff asserts a single claim against one defendant, and that is the entire scope of the lawsuit, there is no issue raised about joinder of claims and parties. Seldom is litigation that simple. Modern joinder provisions are constructed to foster a complete resolution of all claims, involving all of the players to the same transaction or occurrence, that raise common issues of law or fact. ***Joinder rules repeatedly sound the theme of transactional relationship. Running parallel*** with the transactional ***analysis is a cardinal rule of the federal system: Every claim against each party must be supported by an independent ground of subject matter jurisdiction*** (i.e., federal question, or diversity plus an amount in controversy exceeding $75,000) ***or by the discretionary principles of ancillary or pendent subject matter jurisdiction***. (see **"III. SUBJECT MATTER JURISDICTION,"** *supra.*)

A. JOINDER OF CLAIMS

Federal Rule 18 ***permits a party to join as many claims as the party has against an opposing party***. There is no requirement that the claims be transactionally related since the goal in joinder of claims is to achieve a complete resolution of the dispute between the parties. For example, in a diversity case where one plaintiff sues one defendant on two unrelated claims (one for $80,000 and the other for $76,000), the plaintiff may join the two claims in a single lawsuit. If the joinder would lead to jury confusion or other prejudice, Rule 42(b) permits the court to sever the claims for separate trial.

Although joinder of claims is expressed in ***permissive terms, joinder is compelled when failure to join could result in splitting a cause of action*** (see, **"XIV. BINDING EFFECT"**, *infra*). For example, if plaintiff has suffered both personal injury and property loss as a result of an auto mobile collision, the applicable law of res judicata may say that the plaintiff has one cause of action for recovery on both harms. In that situation, the plaintiff ***must seek relief, in a single lawsuit, for the personal injury and property loss***.

B. COUNTERCLAIMS

1. **PERMISSIVE COUNTERCLAIM:** Rule 13(b) ***permits*** a party claimed against to seek relief from the opposing party. A ***permissive counterclaim*** is one that is ***not transactionally related*** to an opposing party's claim. For example, in a diversity case where the plaintiff seeks $80,000 breach of contract damages, the defendant may state a permissive counterclaim in the answer for $76,000 in tort damages that are totally unrelated to plaintiff's claim.

2. **COMPULSORY COUNTERCLAIM:** Rule 13(a) ***requires*** a party claimed against to seek transactionally-related relief from the opposing party.

A counterclaim arises out of the same transaction or occurrence as an opposing party's claim if: (1) there is a logical relationship between the claim and the counterclaim; ***or*** (2) the claim and counterclaim raise common issues of fact and law; ***or*** (3) the claim and counterclaim involve the use of evidence common to both; ***or*** (4) res judicata would prevent the defendant from asserting the claim in a subsequent action.

If a defending party ***fails to include a compulsory counterclaim*** in an answer, it is ***waived*** and ***can not be brought by a separate suit***.

C. CROSS-CLAIMS

Rule 13(g) ***permits*** a party to seek transactionally-related relief from a co-party. Whereas counterclaims apply to opposing parties (and compulsory counterclaims ***must be asserted***), ***cross-claims are permissive*** and ***may be asserted only if transactionally related***. For example, plaintiff, a passenger in a car driven by D1, is injured when D1's car collides with one driven by D2; and, since D1 and D2 are made co-party defendants by plaintiff's suit against them, D2 may, in an answer to plaintiff's complaint, seek relief from D1 for personal injury or property damage suffered in the collision that gave rise to plaintiff's action. Even if D2 has no claim against D1 for personal injury or property damage, D2 may by cross-claim seek indemnity or contribution from D1 in the event plaintiff wins a judgment against D2.

D. ADDING AN ADDITIONAL PARTY TO RESPOND TO A COUNTERCLAIM OR CROSS-CLAIM

Rule 13(h) ***permits*** a party to add someone outside the lawsuit to respond to a counterclaim or crossclaim being asserted against someone already a party to the action. For example, plaintiff sues defendant for personal injury and property loss suffered in a three-car collision; defendant responds to plaintiff with an answer that contains a counterclaim for property damage to defendant's car, and defendant, using Rule 13(h), adds to the action the third auto driver who becomes, along with plaintiff, a counterclaim defendant to the original defendant's counterclaim.

E. JOINDER OF PARTIES

1. PERMISSIVE JOINDER

Rule 20 permits multiple parties plaintiff to join in one action as long as ***each*** seeks relief on at least ***one*** claim that arises from the same transaction or occurrence ***and*** presents a common question of law or fact. And, by the same concept, one plaintiff may join several defendants in a single action as long as ***each*** defendant is claimed against on at least ***one*** claim that arises from the same transaction or occurrence ***and*** presents a common question of law or fact.

In multiple-party and multiple-claim joinder, there is an important guide to remember: Join parties first and then join claims.

Suppose that A, B, and C sign promissory Note X in P's favor. Note X is now in default. In a completely unrelated transaction, C is indebted to P on Note Y. Note Y is in default. How many lawsuits must P start to recover on both notes? First, to Rule 20P can join A, B, and C because P has a claim against each that meets the transactional and commonality test. Now, to Rule 18—since P knows that C is targeted as one of the defendants on Note X, P may join a second claim against C on Note Y. P needs to begin only one action.

2. NECESSARY AND INDISPENSABLE PARTIES

One of the important defensive tools is the Rule 12(b)(7) motion to dismiss for failure to join an indispensable party. Under Rule 19, someone outside the lawsuit may have an interest in the action and ought for the sake of complete relief in a single suit be joined to the fray. However, if joinder is impossible because the presence of the outsider would destroy subject matter jurisdiction, the ***action may proceed*** without that person ***if*** a court views the ***outsider as only a necessary party***. On the other hand, ***if*** joinder is impossible and the court finds the ***outsider to be indispensable, the entire action must be dismissed***.

If joinder of the outsider is impossible, the following factors are relevant to determine whether the absent person is necessary or indispensable: (1) prejudice to present parties or the outsider; (2) extent to which prejudice can be mitigated by protective measures; (3) adequacy of remedy without the outsider; and (4) availability of an alternative forum where joinder of the outsider can be achieved. Relatively few suits are dismissed for failure to join an indispensable party. ***The courts are reluctant to dislodge the plaintiff if there appears to be no other alternative forum where complete joinder is possible.***

Another relevant perspective about Rule 19 is whether the outsider's interest is more like that of a plaintiff or a defendant. For example, suppose that A and B sign promissory Note X in P's favor. Note X is in default in the amount of $125,000. P, domiciled in California, brings a federal suit in Arizona against A who is an Arizona domiciliary. A makes a motion to dismiss the action on the ground that B, domiciled in California, is an indispensable party. B's joinder is impossible because it will destroy subject matter jurisdiction. Will A's defense suffer prejudice by B's absence? Is B prejudiced by being absent from the *P v. A* suit? If there is prejudice, can the court shape P's relief to alleviate the problem? Can P get adequate relief without B? If P's action is dismissed, is there another forum where P could join the defendants A and B? What if B is not amenable to personal jurisdiction in Arizona and A is not subject to personal jurisdiction in California? Do the personal jurisdiction problems eliminate the state courts as sites for the litigation where complete joinder can be achieved?

Most courts that analyze the absence of a joint obligor do not find that person indispensable. Of course, if the obligor will not destroy subject matter jurisdiction, joinder is generally ordered because more complete relief can be achieved by the presence of the obligor not named originally as a defendant.

Suppose that D signs promissory Note Y in favor of A and B. Note Y is in default in the amount of $125,000. A, domiciled in California, brings a federal suit there against D, an Arizona domiciliary, who is subject to personal jurisdiction in California. D makes a Rule 12(b)(7) motion on the argument that B is an indispensable party plaintiff. Joinder is impossible because B's domicile is Arizona. Is B an indispensable obligee who has the same interest at stake as plaintiff A? Is a California state court an alternative forum where, if B is subject to personal jurisdiction there and California's indispensability law is identical to Federal Rule 19, B's Joinder can be forced? Might this lead a federal court to dismiss A's action?

F. IMPLEADER

Any party in a defensive position hopes that there is a basis upon which ***to seek indemnity or contribution***. In the event the person against whom such a claim may be asserted is not already a party, ***impleader*** or third-party practice ***is used to add that person to the suit***. By permitting the defendant to implead an outside person "who is or may be liable" to the defendant "for all or part of the plaintiff's claim," Federal Rule 14 is designed to accelerate into the main action the secondary indemnity or contribution claim that arises in consequence of the action originally instituted. The defendant becomes a third-party plaintiff by serving a third-party complaint upon the third-party defendant. ***Even an original plaintiff who is counterclaimed against can use impleader to seek indemnity or contribution on the counterclaim.***

After a third-party defendant has been impleaded, the original plaintiff may assert a transactionally related claim against the third-party defendant. Such a claim puts the third-party defendant in a defensive position to the original plaintiff. In that situation, the third-party defendant is obligated to obey the compulsory counterclaim rule and assert any transactionally related claim back against the original plaintiff.

Once impleaded, a third-party defendant may claim first in time by asserting a transactionally related claim against the original plaintiff. Now the original plaintiff is in a defensive position to the third-party defendant. In that role, the original plaintiff is mandated to follow the compulsory counterclaim rule and assert any transactionally related claim back against the third-party defendant.

If a party impleads two third-party defendants for indemnity or contribution, those two parties are co-parties and either may cross-claim against the other for transactionally related relief.

G. INTERPLEADER

If a person holds a "stake" in property that is subject to conflicting demands by two or more claimants, the interpleader action is an appealing procedural device. The "stakeholder" may bring those claimants into court to decide the matter in a single action thus, by taking the offensive, the stakeholder avoids the possibility of multiple suits. The first stage of interpleader, i.e., the point at which the court determines whether the prerequisites for interpleader exist, is reached by a pleading requesting interpleader relief. If the court determines that interpleader is appropriate on the facts, the first stage ends. A stakeholder who has no interest in the stake is discharged after depositing the property with the court. Generally, the stakeholder is entitled to recover costs and reasonable attorney's fees. In the second stage, the adverse claimants make their claims to the stake. If the stakeholder is itself an interested party to the property, it remains in the suit to present its claim along with the other parties.

In *New York Life Ins. Co. v. Dunlevy*, 241 U.S. 518 (1916), the Supreme Court said that an interpleader action is ***in personam*** and therefore ***personal jurisdiction is required over all adverse claimants to the stake***. Because this period of personal jurisdiction history requires a *Pennoyer-**type*** presence (personal service on a defendant inside the territorial limits of the state), the state courts were severely handicapped in offering interpleader relief when any adverse claimant was a nonresident. Congress rose to the occasion by providing the Federal Interpleader Act of 1917. That Act is called federal ***statutory interpleader*** and it is now embodied in Title 28 U.S.C. §§ 1335, 1397, and 2361. The Federal Rules of Civil Procedure went into effect in 1938 and Federal Rule 22 also contains what is called ***rule interpleader***. The two interpleader avenues have separate requirements that are unique to each. It's an "all or nothing" proposition, i.e., the elements of one are not interchangeable with the elements of the other.

1. **STATUTORY INTERPLEADER**

   (a) Subject matter jurisdiction (28 U.S.C. §1335): (1) A ***stake of $500.00 or more***; and (2) at least ***two adverse claimants domiciled in different states***. For example, P, domiciled in California and holding a stake worth $25,000, is faced by A, domiciled in Arizona, and B, domiciled in California, each claiming the property. Since A and B are domiciled in different states, ***P has the minimal diversity required for statutory interpleader even though P is domiciled in the same state as one of the adverse claimants***.

   (b) Venue (28 U.S.C. § 1397): "[I]nterpleader . . . may be brought in the . . . district in which one or more of the claimants reside."

   (c) Personal jurisdiction (28 U.S.C. § 2361): Because § 2361 gives a federal court nationwide service of process authority, a federal court has personal jurisdiction over any adverse claimant residing in the United States.

   (d) Injunctive relief (28 U.S.C. § 2361): The stakeholder would not achieve very much if, during or after an interpleader action, suits about the stake are brought by adverse claimants. Section 2361 permits the federal court to enter an order restraining the adverse claimants "from instituting or prosecuting any proceeding in any State or United States court affecting the property, instrument or obligation involved in the interpleader action . . . ."

2. **RULE 22 INTERPLEADER**

   (a) Subject matter jurisdiction: Rule interpleader requires a traditional subject matter jurisdiction basis, i.e., ***federal question*** under Title 28 U.S.C. § 1331 ***or diversity plus a stake exceeding $75,000*** under Title 28 U.S.C. § 1332.

   (b) Venue: The venue requirements for Rule interpleader are found in the general venue provisions of Title 28 U.S.C. §§ 1391(a) and (b). Since most Rule interpleader actions are founded upon diversity, venue under § 1391(a) is where the stakeholder resides, where all the adverse claimants reside, or where the adverse claims arose.

   (c) Personal Jurisdiction: Rule interpleader is governed by the personal jurisdiction requirements of Federal Rule 4. To the extent that Rule 4(e) permits a state's long-arm statute to be borrowed and Rule 4(c)(2)(C)(i) allows the use of state methods of service of process, the potential personal jurisdiction grasp of Rule interpleader is to the limits of the 14th Amendment Due Process Clause.

   (d) Injunctive relief: The source of injunctive relief for Rule interpleader is found in an exception to the federal anti-injunction statute ("A court of the United States may not grant an injunction to stay proceedings in a State court ***except*** . . . where necessary in aid of its jurisdiction . . . ." Title 28 U.S.C. § 2283.)

   Because of the relative flexibility of ***statutory interpleader, Rule interpleader*** is usually ***relied upon only when the minimal diversity requirements of statutory interpleader cannot be satisfied***.

In Rule 22 diversity interpleader and in statutory interpleader, the substantive law of the state where the federal court sits, including the state's conflict rules, apply. ***Griffin v. McCoach***, 313 U.S. 498 (1941).

H. INTERVENTION

The purpose of intervention is to enable a person outside an action to enter the suit to present an interest or a claim or defense relevant to the issues presented by the existing parties.

Intervention can contribute to judicial economy and provide protection to a nonparty from having its interest adversely affected by the litigation conducted without that person's participation.

In the federal system, ***a distinction is drawn between intervention of right*** (Federal Rule 24(a)) and permissive intervention (Federal Rule 24(b)).

1. INTERVENTION OF RIGHT

Rule 24(a) has four requirements: (a) timely application; (b) the applicant must have a protectable interest relating to the property or transaction involved in the suit; (c) the applicant's interest must be subject to impairment or impediment; and (d) that interest must be inadequately represented by existing parties to the suit.

(a) Timely application: Consider (1) the length of time during which the applicant actually knew or reasonably should have known about an interest in the case before making an application to intervene; (2) the extent of prejudice that existing parties may suffer by an applicant's delay in seeking intervention; and (3) the extent of prejudice that the applicant may suffer if the application to intervene is denied.

(b) Protectable interest: What is required is that the interest be one that the substantive law recognizes as belonging to or being owned by the applicant. Typically, a traditional property interest is involved. For example, D signs promissory Note Y in favor of A and B. Note Y is in default in the amount of $125,000. A, domiciled in California, brings a federal suit there against D, an Arizona domiciliary, who is subject to personal jurisdiction in California. B, domiciled in California, makes an application to intervene of right in the *A v. D* suit. As co-obligee with A, doesn't B have a protectable interest at stake?

What about an interest not as translatable to monetary terms?

Suppose the Federal Park Board (FPB) passes a regulation that forbids the planting in a federal park of any tree that sheds its leaves in fall or produces fruits or nuts during any season of the year. The Squirrel Lovers (SL) are outraged; pursuant to congressional authority given exclusively to a federal court to grant injunctive relief in actions involving federal park management, the SL organization brings suit in federal court to enjoin the FPB regulation. The Autumn Color Committee (ACC) seeks to intervene as a plaintiff. Does the ACC have a protectable interest sufficient to intervene of right? There would probably be a split of authority on this. To some courts, the ACC interest would be too indirect or insubstantial. Others would view the "interest" test primarily as a practical guide to disposing of lawsuits and find ACC's application compatible with an efficient use of the courts for the expression of broad public interests.

(c) Impairment or impediment of interest: The question here is not one of res judicata or collateral estoppel. Only parties who are named and served are bound by the outcome of prior litigation. ***The question is whether the result in the existing suit would put an applicant's interest to the risk of practical disadvantage.*** If the existing suit involves the disposition of real or personal property, there may be a risk that the property will be conveyed by the winning party. In *Atlantis Dev. Corp. v. United States*, 379 F.2d 818 (5th Cir. 1967), the court held that the stare decisis effect on an applicant's interest was sufficient.

(d) Inadequate representation: The burden is on the applicant. The Supreme Court says the burden should be treated as minimal and is satisfied if the applicant shows that representation of the applicant's interest "may be" inadequate. *Trbovich v. UMW*, 404 U.S. 528 (1972). Consider whether (1) the interests of a present party are such that it will undoubtedly make all of the applicant's arguments; (2) a present party is willing to make such arguments; and (3) the applicant will offer a perspective to the proceedings that existing parties do not have.

2. **PERMISSIVE INTERVENTION**

Rule 24(b) has three requirements: (a) timely application; (b) the applicant's claim or defense and the main action must have a question of law or fact in common; and (c) the intervention must not unduly delay or prejudice the existing parties to the action.

(a) Timely application: The same factors considered, *supra*, in regard to intervention of right are relevant to permissive intervention. However, an application is more likely to be denied on timeliness grounds if it is permissive because of the potential for delay of the main action.

(b) Common question of law or fact: There must be commonality between an applicant's claim or defense and the present suit. For example, P sues D for personal injury resulting from a fire allegedly caused by a defective product. P's insurer, A, paid P's property damage caused by the fire and A is subrogated in the amount of payment to the rights of P against D. A seeks permission to intervene. Does A's claim against D share a question of law or fact in common with P's claim against D?

(c) Court discretion: Permissive intervention is addressed to the discretion of the trial court. Consider (1) the complexity of the existing action and the complexity of the applicant's claim or defense; (2) the length of time the main action has been pending and (3) how much the present parties will be delayed by the addition of the applicant's claim or defense.

I. JOINDER AND PENDENT OR ANCILLARY JURISDICTION

1. JOINDER DEVICES GENERALLY ALLOWING USE OF P/A JURISDICTION

(a) Compulsory counterclaims, Rule 13(a).
(b) Cross-claims, Rule 13(g).
(c) Adding additional parties to respond to a compulsory counterclaim or a cross-claim, Rule 13(h).
(d) Impleading a third-party defendant or a third-party defendant's claim against an original plaintiff, Rule 14.
(e) Joinder of claims, Rule 18.
(f) Rule interpleader, Rule 22.
(g) Intervention of right, Rule 24(a).

2. JOINDER DEVICES NOT PERMITTING USE OF P/A JURISDICTION

(a) Permissive counterclaims, Rule 13(b).
(b) An original plaintiff's claim against a third-party defendant impleaded by the original defendant, Rule 14.
(c) Necessary or indispensable parties, Rule 19.
(d) Joinder of parties, Rule 20.
(e) Permissive intervention, Rule 24(b).

J. CLASS ACTIONS

1. NATURE

A class action is representative litigation whereby one or more members of a class sue or defend for themselves and all other members of the class who are similarly situated.

2. CONJUNCTIVE REQUIREMENTS

(a) Ascertainable group: Unless the group can be defined or described by some characteristic, there is no ascertainable class.

(b) Named party: The person named to represent the class must be a member of the group.

(c) Numerosity: The class must be so numerous that the conventional joinder of parties approach is impracticable. A class of twenty persons would not ordinarily be large enough. To certify such a small group (and not join each as a named party), comes at the cost of permitting each to have a day in court by counsel of individual choice.

(d) Commonality: While it is not required that each question of law or fact be common to every member of the class, at least one question must be common. Otherwise, there is very little utility to the class action device.

(e) Typicality: The typicality requirement connects the representative party to the class, and demands that the representative's claims or defenses typify those of the larger group.

(f) Adequacy of representation: The court must examine the adequacy of the representative party, the attorney for the class, and the class itself. Does the representative party have a real stake in the litigation? Is class counsel qualified, experienced and generally able to conduct the proposed action? Is the class troubled with internal conflict?

3. **DISJUNCTIVE REQUIREMENTS**

If the ***preceding conjunctive prerequisites are satisfied***, the court must then ***determine whether the case is appropriate for any of the following categories***.

(a) Federal Rule 23(b)(1)(A): This type of class action is labeled "***incompatible standards of conduct***." Would individual suits put the party opposing the class at risk of not being able to comply with one individual judgment without violating the terms of another? For example, Chemco builds a chemical plant on the outskirts of a residential neighborhood. The residents contend that the noxious fumes emanating from the plant constitute a nuisance. Individual actions might result in inconsistent decisions about the measures Chemco may be required to take.

(b) Rule 23(b)(1)(B): This category is known as the "***impaired interest standard***." Would individual suits jeopardize the rights of some members of the class? If the individual claims of the class exceed a limited fund to satisfy the claims, there is a risk that individual suits could exhaust the fund and leave some of the members of the class with impaired interests. In short, too many individuals are chasing too few dollars to satisfy the totality of the claims. The Ninth Circuit takes the position that Rule 23(b)(1)(B) prohibits class certification of mass tort actions for compensatory or punitive damages unless the record establishes that separate punitive damage claims necessarily will affect later claims. *In re Northern Dist. of Cal. Dalkon Shield IUD Prods. Liab. Litig.*, 693 F.2d 847 (9th Cir. 1982), *cert. denied*, 459 U.S. 1171 (1983). Subsection (b)(1)(B) is also not intended to remedy possible stare decisis or other precedential effect of the judgment on the merits of individual claims. *Alsup v. Montgomery Ward & Co.*, 57 F.R.D. 89 (N.D. Cal. 1972). The primary purpose of the "impaired interest standard" category ***is to facilitate class certification when the class members have interests in a common organization, fund or contract.***

(c) Rule 23(b)(2) describes a kind of class action that bears the name "***equitable relief standard***." There are two important considerations here to address. First, the ***primary relief sought must be injunctive or declaratory***. Second, the ***defendant must have acted or refused to act on grounds generally applicable to the class***. Money damages cannot be the predominant relief sought by the class. Suppose that the State Teachers' Retirement System (STRS) uses sex-based mortality tables to calculate the value of retirement benefits. Class certification is sought for a group of teachers who believe that use of the tables is a violation of Title VII of the Civil Rights Act and of the Equal Pay Act. The class complaint seeks to enjoin STRS from using sex-segregated actuarial tables; asks the court to order the defendant to equalize pension benefits for the class; and demands that STRS be required to make retroactive payments for the period of alleged unlawful discrimination. Has STRS engaged in conduct generally applicable to the class? Does the class seek injunctive or declaratory relief? Do the money damages inherent in the retroactive relief make certification inappropriate under Rule 23(b)(2)? Should the court view the money damages as merely incidental to the primary claim for injunctive relief to prohibit use of the sex-based mortality tables? See *Probe v. State Teachers' Retirement System*, 780 F.2d 776 (9th Cir. 1986), *cert. denied*, 476 U.S. 1170 (1986).

(d) Rule 23(b)(3) is called the ***"money damages"*** class action. Certification under subdivision (b)(3) is permitted ***if questions of law or fact common to the members of the class predominate over any questions affecting only individual members, and a class action is superior to other available methods of adjudication***. The ***predominance*** requirement turns on whether there is an essential common factual link between class members and the defendant for which the law provides a remedy. Whether a class action is superior requires (1) an informed consideration of alternative available methods of adjudication of each issue, (2) a comparison of the fairness to all whose interests may be involved between the alternative methods and a class action, and (3) a comparison of the efficiency of adjudication of each method. There are two possible alternatives to a class action: (1) a test case, and (2) an action by named plaintiffs with a liberal right of intervention for those similarly interested and its variant, a multiplicity of individual suits by those persons who would otherwise be members of a class.

Mass tort situations have usually failed the class action certification criteria because the damage issues are unique to each individual.

4. **NOTICE**

A Rule 23(b)(3) "money damages" class action ***requires individual notice, at least by ordinary mail, to each member of the class***. The usual rule is that the named representative must initially bear the cost of notice to the class. *Eisen v. Carlisle & Jacquelin*, 417 U.S. 156 (1974). If the class action succeeds, the cost of notice may be deducted from the class recovery or the cost may be awarded to the class as a prevailing party in the suit.

The ***Rule 23(b)(3) class action notice must include the following*** information: (a) the court will exclude anyone from the class if the member requests exclusion (i.e., "opts-out"); (b) the judgment, whether or not favorable, will bind all class members who do not request exclusion; and (c) any member, who does not seek exclusion, may enter an appearance.

There is no requirement of mandatory notice to members of a class certified under Rule 23(b)(1)(A), (b)(1)(B), or (b)(2). The reason no notice is required is because those types of classes are thought to be more cohesive than a class certified under Rule 23(b)(3).

5. **SUBJECT MATTER JURISDICTION**

A federal class action requires a traditional basis of ***subject matter jurisdiction***, i.e., ***federal question, or diversity*** plus an amount in controversy exceeding $75,000. ***Diversity*** subject matter jurisdiction is ***measured by the domicile of the representative party***. In ***diversity class actions, every member of the class must have a claim exceeding $75,000***, *Zahn v. International Paper Co.*, 414 U.S. 291 (1973), ***unless the claims*** spring from a ***common and undivided*** interest. See **"III. SUBJECT MATTER JURISDICTION, 5. AMOUNT IN CONTROVERSY,"** *supra*.

6. **PERSONAL JURISDICTION**

To bind the members of a defendant class to a judgment, personal jurisdiction must be achieved over the named representative of the defendant class.

In a Rule 23(b)(3) "money damages" plaintiff class, members of the class can be bound to the judgment outcome even without forum minimum contacts as long as the class members receive the mandatory notice required in subdivision (b)(3) actions. *Phillips Petroleum Co. v. Shutts*, 472 U.S. 797 (1985).

7. **VENUE**

The ***general venue requirements*** of Title 28 U.S.C. § 1391 ***apply*** unless a special venue provision is made applicable to the nature of the claim involved in the class action. Courts look to the residence of the representative party for determining whether venue is proper.

8. **STATUTE OF LIMITATIONS**

The commencement of a class action suspends the applicable statute of limitations as to all asserted members of the class who would have been parties had the suit been permitted to continue as a class action. *American Pipe & Constr. Co. v. Utah*, 414 U.S. 538 (1974). Once the statute has been tolled, it remains so for all members of the putative class until class certification is denied. At that point, class members may file their own suits or seek to intervene in the pending action. *Crown, Cork & Seal Co. v. Parker*, 462 U.S. 345 (1983).

9. **BINDING EFFECT**

A class action judgment is binding (res judicata and collateral estoppel) on all class members unless an individual elects to "opt-out" from a Rule 23(b)(3) class.

A collateral attack on a class action judgment may be successful if it appears that the representative party did not adequately protect the interest of the class. *Gonzales v. Cassidy*, 474 F.2d 67 (5th Cir. 1973).

10. **CLASS ACTION SETTLEMENT**

Rule 23(e) ***requires court approval for the dismissal or compromise*** of a class action and notice of the proposed dismissal or compromise ***must be given to all class members*** in a manner determined by the court. The purpose of this Rule is to ensure that the representative party fulfills his or her fiduciary duty to the class. The court will not approve a settlement or voluntary dismissal that is unfair to the class.

The court's ***inquiry*** into a settlement or voluntary dismissal ***differs before and after class certification.*** Before certification, a voluntary dismissal will not have res judicata or collateral estoppel impact on class members and the court does not need to perform the kind of substantive oversight required when reviewing a post-certification settlement binding upon the class. The court's role in precertification voluntary dismissal or settlement is to determine whether the members of the putative class must be given notice. What circumstances may require pre- certification notice? What if there is reason to believe that the named party appended class allegations in an attempt to get favorable individual settlement? Should notice be required here as a deterrent to an abusive plaintiff? What if members of the putative class have refrained from filing suit because of actual knowledge that a class action has been filed? The likelihood of prejudice, resulting from reliance on the class action filing, compounded by a short period remaining on the statute of limitations, is a strong argument that pre-certification notice must be given to the putative class. *Diaz v. Trust Territory of Pacific Islands*, 876 F2d 1401 (9th Cir. 1989).

X. DISCOVERY

INTRODUCTION. If the primary purpose of federal pleadings is to provide notice to the parties, the facts will not be stated in much detail. The facts surrounding an action come to light through the use of discovery. There are specified discovery ***devices*** that are designed to ***elicit information within a permissible scope of discovery***. In addition to understanding discovery devices and scope, it is important to appreciate that ***discovery is generally initiated by the parties***. The court gets involved when there is a discovery dispute and the voluntary effort of the parties cannot solve the breakdown. To keep the parties from using discovery to abuse and harass, ***there are ways for the court to impose sanctions that relate to costs and attorney's fees*** and also sanctions that have an impact on the ***merits of the action***.

A. DISCOVERY DEVICES

1. DEPOSITIONS UPON ORAL EXAMINATION, RULES 30, 45

Depositions permit the direct questioning of a party or witness under oath. If a party, the deposition is scheduled by a notice of deposition served on all counsel. Non-parties must be brought by subpoena. In the federal system, a non-party cannot be compelled to travel more than 100 miles from the edge of the district in which the case is pending (the bulge), but they can be compelled to testify in the district in which they reside or are found. Audiovisual depositions can be taken if the procedural requirements are met. Depositions of corporations are permitted, and the corporation must designate one or more persons whose answers bind the corporation and who must have completed a reasonably diligent investigation.

2. DEPOSITIONS ON WRITTEN QUESTIONS, RULE 31

A rarely used procedure now that telephonic depositions can be taken, this mechanism allows a list of written questions to be propounded and answers taken under oath.

3. INTERROGATORIES, RULE 33

Interrogatories are written questions that must be answered in writing under oath by the defendant. In general, the number of interrogatories is limited. Corporate parties must engage in reasonable investigation and the interrogatories must be signed by a corporate officer with the authority to bind the corporation.

4. **PRODUCTION OF DOCUMENTS AND THINGS AND ENTRY UPON LAND FOR INSPECTION AND OTHER PURPOSES, RULE 34**

Parties can be required to produce all documents, both paper and electronic, relevant to any claim or defense. The same result can be obtained by subpoena from non-parties. To the extent that physical evidence is at issue, such evidence must be produced for inspection. Finally, for those cases in which the condition of land is relevant, Rule 34 can be used for that purpose.

5. **REQUESTS FOR ADMISSION, RULE 36**

A party can propound factual requests to another party that must be admitted or denied under oath. Any request that is admitted is deemed established for all purposes in the litigation. Unlike many discovery techniques, failure to respond automatically causes the request to be deemed admitted.

B. DISCOVERY SCOPE

1. **RELEVANCE**

Only information "relevant to the subject matter involved in the pending action" is open to discovery. "Relevant" is construed broadly to encompass any matter that bears on, or that reasonably could lead to other matter that could bear on, any issue that is or may be in the case.

It is ***not necessary that information*** sought by discovery ***be admissible in evidence at trial.*** Information is open to discovery it if appears reasonably calculated to lead to admissible evidence.

The scope of discovery is particularly enhanced by Rule 26(a)'s reference to "the identity and location of persons having knowledge of any discoverable matter." Those people are discoverable even though they will not be called for trial testimony.

2. **PRIVILEGE**

Privileged matter is ***not*** discoverable. A privilege may arise because of the law of evidence or constitutional principles.

Occasionally, information is protected from discovery even though it is not technically privileged matter. Relevancy may be overcome by a stronger policy consideration. For example, even though disinterment and autopsy may be relevant to the issue of suicide, the courts are reluctant to permit that discovery because of the emotional distress that may be caused to survivors.

3. **INSURANCE**

Rule 26(b)(2) makes insurance agreements discoverable where the insurance is extended by a person in that business. Although discovery may be had about the nature of coverage and policy limits, that information is seldom admissible at trial.

4. **NET WORTH**

Information about a defendant's financial status is ***not ordinarily permitted. When a plaintiff seeks punitive damages***, however, the ***defendant's financial status becomes relevant and discovery is allowed.***

5. **WORK PRODUCT**

Rule 26(b)(3) establishes ***a qualified immunity*** from discovery ***for the work product of an attorney***. Work product includes material prepared in anticipation of litigation or for trial.

Attorney ***work product is discoverable if*** the court can be ***convinced that the information is essential to the party's case and there are no other reasonable means to obtain the information***. Even when there is the required showing of substantial need and inability to obtain the information without undue hardship, ***any writing that reflects an attorney's impressions, conclusions, opinions, or legal research or theories is absolutely immune from discovery.***

6. **EXPERTS**

Without the necessity of a ***motion, limited discovery about expert trial witnesses is permitted.*** Under Rule 26(b)(4), a party may use an interrogatory to receive a summary of the grounds for the opinions held by the opponent's testifying experts. ***Through the use of motion practice, courts routinely permit*** further discovery. The additional discovery normally comes by deposing an opponent's testifying expert and gaining access to testifying expert reports by use of a subpoena duces tecum.

Retained experts, who are not expected to be called as trial witnesses, are subject to discovery ***only upon a special showing***. The ***party seeking information about non-testifying experts must show*** that there is ***no practical alternative means to gain the discovery.***

No discovery is contemplated for non-retained informally consulted experts.

7. **PROCEDURAL ASPECTS OF DISCOVERY**

(a) Motion to compel: If a party's discovery request is met with no response or by an evasive or incomplete answer, a motion to compel may be used so that the court can determine the merits of the discovery breakdown.

(b) Protective order: Upon motion by a party or by the person from whom discovery is sought, the court may determine the extent of permissible discovery. The grounds for a protective order are: annoyance, embarrassment, oppression, or undue burden or expense.

C. DISCOVERY SANCTIONS

1. **RULE 26(f)**

Upon motion by a party, the court must call a discovery conference. Part of the purpose of the conference is to establish, by court order, a plan and schedule for discovery. If a party or a party's attorney fails to participate in good faith in the framing of a discovery plan, the ***court may***, after opportunity for hearing, ***impose an expense sanction*** (reasonable costs and attorney's fees).

2. **RULE 26(g)**

   Every ***request for discovery or response or objection thereto, must be signed*** by the attorney. The signature constitutes a certification (1) that there has been a reasonable inquiry into the facts and law; (2) that the request, response or objection is not interposed for the purpose of harassment, unnecessary delay, or needless increase in the cost of litigation; and (3) it is not unreasonable or unduly burdensome or expensive. If a certification is made in violation of Rule 26(g), the court ***must impose upon the attorney or client or both an appropriate sanction***. The sanction may include an order to pay reasonable costs and attorney's fees.

3. **RULE 11**

   When an attorney signs a discovery motion (including points and authorities in support of or opposition to the motion), Federal Rule 11 applies. See **"VIII. PLEADINGS, G. TRUTH IN PLEADING,"** *supra*.

4. **RULE 37(b)**

   If a party *fails to obey an order to provide or permit discovery* (including a discovery conference order under Rule 26(f)), the court is ***authorized to impose a sanction that has impact on the merits*** of the action. The ***court may enter an establishment order*** (i.e., certain matters must be taken as established), a ***preclusion order*** (i.e., the sanctioned party is precluded from supporting or opposing claims or defenses or prohibited from introducing matters in evidence), ***or an order of default judgment***.

   In lieu of or in addition to merits sanctions, ***the court must order*** the attorney or client or both to pay an ***expense sanction*** (reasonable costs and attorney's fees).

5. **RULE 37(d)**

   Although the court may not have entered an order regarding discovery, merits and expense sanctions may still be imposed for flagrant discovery abuse.

XI. JURY TRIAL

INTRODUCTION. Right to jury trial in a civil action is governed by the meaning of the Seventh Amendment to the United States Constitution. The Seventh Amendment is not applicable to the states and therefore the federal system and the states often have very different views about the jury trial right. When a right to jury exists, there is, of course, a body of law that governs jury selection. Moreover, the right to jury trial may be lost by failing to make a timely demand.

A. RIGHT TO JURY TRIAL

1. GENERAL PRINCIPLES

(a) *Beacon Theatres, Inc. v. Westover*, 359 U.S. 500 (1959). (When some claims are legal (i.e., for money damages) and others are equitable, there is a right to jury trial on the legal issues that cannot be lost through prior court-trial determination of the equity issues.)

(b) *Dairy Queen, Inc. v. Wood*, 369 U.S. 469 (1962). (When both legal and equitable relief are sought, the right to jury trial may not be lost by characterizing legal issues as incidental to equity issues and trying the entire action to the court.)

(c) *Katchen v. Landy*, 382 U.S. 323 (1966). (Bankruptcy proceedings are inherently proceedings in equity and, when a bankruptcy issue requires summary disposition, there is no right to jury trial.)

(d) *Ross v. Bernhard*, 396 U.S. 531 (1970). (When money damages are sought in a shareholder's derivative action, there is a right to jury trial to the same extent the corporation itself would have had that right had it brought the action. Whether issues are legal or equitable depends upon (1) the characterization of the action in the courts of England in 1791; (2) the nature of the relief sought (i.e., legal or equitable); and (3) the practical abilities and limitations of juries. Of these factors, the first, requiring extensive and possibly abstruse historical inquiry, is obviously the most difficult to apply.)

2. FEDERAL STATUTORY ACTIONS

If Congress chooses, it may confer a statutory right to jury trial in circumstances where that right is not required by the Seventh Amendment. But what if Congress creates a statutory claim and says nothing in the statute about jury trial? Moreover, what if the statute that creates the claim expressly negates jury trial? The following cases explore the Seventh Amendment analysis on the questions just raised.

(a) *Curtis v. Loether*, 415 U.S. 189 (1974). (The Seventh Amendment applies to actions enforcing statutory rights. If the statute creates legal rights and remedies enforceable in an action for damages in the ordinary law courts, there is a right to jury trial. Held: Because the statute authorizes an action for actual and punitive damages (i.e., traditional relief offered in the courts of law), the Seventh Amendment requires a jury trial at the demand of any party.)

(b) *Pernell v. Southall Realty*, 416 U.S. 363 (1974). (In a statutory action for repossession of real property, there is a Seventh Amendment right to jury trial because the action involves a right protected at common law.)

(c) *Atlas Roofing Co. v. Occupational Safety & Health Review Commission*, 430 U.S. 442 (1977). (The Seventh Amendment is not violated when Congress creates a new cause of action in the federal government for civil penalties enforceable in an administrative agency where there is no jury trial, because public rights are being litigated in a specialized forum.)

(d) *Tull v. United States*, 481 U.S. 412 (1987). (The Seventh Amendment guarantees a right to jury trial on the liability phase of an action brought by the federal government to seek a civil penalty and injunctive relief, because the penalty is in the nature of punitive damages. However, Congress has not violated the Seventh Amendment by authorizing the court to fix the amount of the penalty because penalty assessment is not a fundamental element of jury trial.)

(e) *Granfinanciera, S.A. v. Nordberg*,——U.S.——, 109 S. Ct. 2782 (1989). (If a claim that is legal in nature asserts a public right (i.e., even one brought by a private party yet closely integrated into a public regulatory scheme), the Seventh Amendment does not entitle the parties to a jury trial if Congress assigns its adjudication to an administrative agency or specialized court of equity. But Congress cannot eliminate a party's Seventh Amendment right to jury trial by relabeling a cause of action to which it attaches and placing exclusive jurisdiction in an administrative agency or a specialized court of equity. Held: A person who has not submitted a claim against a bankruptcy estate has a right to jury trial, when sued by the bankruptcy trustee to recover an allegedly fraudulent conveyance, even though Congress has designated fraudulent conveyance actions as "core proceedings" tried to the court.)

3. **ACTIONS AGAINST THE UNITED STATES**

The Seventh Amendment gives no right to jury trial in suits against the United States. There is a right to jury trial when the United States is sued only if a statute expressly provides. *Lehman v. Nakshian*, 453 U.S. 156 (1981).

4. **THE ERIE DOCTRINE AND RIGHT TO JURY TRIAL**

In a ***per curiam*** opinion the Supreme Court says that ***state law does not apply*** to determine whether an action is legal or equitable for the purpose of deciding whether there is a right to jury trial. "The right to a jury trial in the federal courts is to be determined as a matter of federal law in diversity as well as other actions." *Simler v. Conner*, 372 U.S. 221 (1963).

B. JURY SELECTION

1. **VOIR DIRE**

The federal jury is selected by the voir dire process. Federal Rule 47 permits the court to conduct the examination and to refuse the attorneys the opportunity to question ***directly*** the prospective jurors. The court, however, ***must permit supplemental direct questioning by the attorneys or itself submit to the prospective jurors the additional questions raised by the attorneys***. The purpose of the voir dire is to explore germane factors that might expose a basis for challenge, whether for cause or peremptory.

2. **CHALLENGES FOR CAUSE**

Based upon the questions and responses at voir dire, the attorneys will ask the court to excuse any juror who exhibits bias. The matter is for the court to determine. Challenges for cause are divided generally into three categories: ***general disqualification*** (e.g., someone who has been convicted of a felony and whose civil rights have not been restored); ***implied bias*** (e.g., a person related to a party within the fourth degree); and ***actual bias*** (e.g., a prospective juror whose response indicates that he or she will not act impartially).

3. **PEREMPTORY CHALLENGES**

In civil cases, Title 28 U.S.C. § 1870 says that each party is entitled to three peremptory challenges. Traditionally, no reason need be given to challenge peremptorily. You may recall that, ***in criminal cases,*** *Batson v. Kentucky*, 476 U.S. 79 (1986), ***applies***. In *Batson*, the Supreme Court says that it is a violation of the Equal Protection Clause for a peremptory challenge to be exercised by the prosecution against prospective jurors solely because they and the defendant are of the same race. In 1992, *Batson* was expanded in *Georgia v. McCollum* to prohibit racially based peremptory challenges made by the defendant as well. Furthermore, in *Edmondson v. Leesville Concrete Co.*, 59 LW 4574 (1991), the same rule was extended to civil cases and applied to both plaintiff and defendant. The Court held a private litigant in a civil case may not use peremptory challenges to exclude jurors on account of race. In sum, race-based exclusion of jurors violates the Equal Protection Clause of the Fourteenth Amendment.

C. JURY DEMAND AND WAIVER

Federal Rule 38(b) requires that a written demand for a jury trial be ***served within ten days after service of the last pleading directed to such issue***. If the only relevant pleadings in a case are the complaint and the answer, the demand for a jury trial must be served not later than ten days after service of the answer.

Failure to make a timely demand for a jury trial leads to waiver. Upon motion, however, the court has the discretion to grant relief. The federal courts have not been uniform in the exercise of their discretion. ***Compare*** *Parrot v. Wilson*, 707 F.2d 1262 (11th Cir. 1983), *cert. denied*, 464 U.S. 936 (1983) (Trial court should grant jury trial in absence of strong and compelling reasons to contrary) ***with*** *Bank Bldg. & Equip. Corp. of Am. v. Mack Local 677*, 87 F.R.D. 553 (E.D. Pa. 1980). (Mere inadvertence, oversight, or lack of diligence will not justify relief from belated jury request.)

XII. TRIAL AND POST-TRIAL MOTIONS

INTRODUCTION. Not every case goes to the trier of fact. An action may not have been submitted to the jury because of the grant of a directed verdict. In a court-tried case, the directed verdict counterpart is called a motion for involuntary dismissal. Even if a jury verdict is rendered, it may not control because a judgment notwithstanding the verdict (JNOV) is granted. In a trial to the court, the most closely related device to the JNOV is the motion to amend the judgment. The directed verdict and JNOV motions have the single purpose of testing the sufficiency of the evidence. Apart from the issue of evidence sufficiency, a judgment based upon jury or non-jury factual resolution may fall by the wayside because of a successful motion for new trial.

A. DIRECTED VERDICT (JURY TRIAL)

1. TIMING OF THE MOTION

The directed verdict motion (or judgment as a matter of law as it is now called in federal court) may be appropriate at an early stage (after the opening statement of opposing counsel), middle stage (at the close of an opponent's evidence), or late stage of trial (at the close of all the evidence). If the motion is made before the close of all the evidence and denied, as a precautionary measure, it should be renewed at the close of all evidence in order to fulfill a condition precedent to making a later motion for judgment notwithstanding the verdict.

2. STANDARD FOR MEASURING MOTION

The ***motion tests whether there is sufficient evidence to raise an issue for the jury***. The standard is often phrased in the following manner: Viewing the evidence in the light most favorable to the nonmoving party, and giving that party the benefit of all legitimate inferences that can be drawn from the evidence, would reasonable minds differ on the conclusion to be reached? The trial judge is not supposed to pass on either the weight or the credibility of the evidence. If all reasonable people would arrive at the same conclusion on the evidence presented, the verdict should be directed.

B. MOTION FOR INVOLUNTARY DISMISSAL (COURT TRIAL)

The major difference here is with the role of the judge. Since the court itself is trying the facts, the judge must determine the credibility and weight of the evidence. Moreover, the judge makes no special inferences in favor of the nonmoving party. Obviously, the judge has far greater leeway in testing the sufficiency of the evidence in a non-jury case than that available in a jury trial.

C. JUDGMENT NOTWITHSTANDING THE VERDICT (JNOV) (JURY TRIAL)

1. TIMING OF THE MOTION

A party who has moved for a directed verdict at the close of all the evidence, may move for a JNOV, not later than ten days after entry of judgment. A motion for JNOV is the same as a directed verdict motion except that the former is made after the jury has rendered its verdict.

2. STANDARD FOR MEASURING MOTION

The ***purpose of the motion is to test the sufficiency of the evidence supporting the jury's verdict***. The standard is identical to the one stated for directed verdict, supra.

D. MOTION TO AMEND THE JUDGMENT (COURT TRIAL)

In the federal system the party who loses the decision in a case tried to the court, may ask the judge to reverse the judgment because the evidence is insufficient to support the court's conclusion. This motion is made infrequently and, when used, seldom succeeds. The judge, as trier of fact, has determined the facts from the evidence and applied the law to those facts. One would not expect a reversal of position in such a short period of time (i.e., ten days after entry of judgment).

E. MOTION FOR JUDGMENT NOTWITHSTANDING THE FAILURE OF THE JURY TO AGREE

Both California (Cal. Civ. Proc. Code § 630(f)) and the federal system (Federal Rule 50(b)) permit either party to make a motion for judgment when the jury has been discharged without having rendered a verdict. The standard governing the motion is identical to the one used for directed verdict, *supra*.

F. MOTION FOR NEW TRIAL

A new trial motion is generally made as a form of alternative relief to a motion for judgment notwithstanding the verdict (JNOV).

1. GROUNDS FOR NEW TRIAL

The usual grounds are:

(a) Errors of law, in particular, trial rulings on the admissibility of evidence and jury instructions;

(b) misconduct by judge, attorney or jury;

(c) newly discovered evidence;

(d) excessive or inadequate damages; and

(e) verdict against the weight of the evidence.

The first four grounds above speak to procedural matters during trial while the last one on the list goes to the question of the evidence presented during trial.

2. SUPPORTING THE NEW TRIAL MOTION

A new trial motion may be supported by affidavits or even witness testimony at a hearing on the motion.

If jury misconduct is a ground for new trial, the evidence offered to support the motion must be of an ***objective nature***. The affidavit of a juror is admissible to impeach a jury verdict to the extent that the affidavit contains statements made, or conduct, conditions, or events relied upon as constituting jury misconduct; but, an affidavit is ***not admissible to the extent it recites the impact of such matters on the subjective reasoning process of individual jurors***. In short, the ***scope of inquiry is what happened, not what effect.***

3. VERDICT AGAINST THE WEIGHT OF EVIDENCE

Although, in a jury-tried action, the trial court does not weigh the evidence on a directed verdict or judgment notwithstanding the verdict motion, ***it is free to do so on a new trial motion when the ground in support thereof is that the verdict is against the weight of the evidence***. The judge is not required to take the view of the evidence most favorable to the verdict and the judge may grant the new trial even though there is substantial evidence to support the verdict.

4. **PARTIAL NEW TRIAL**

A partial new trial on liability alone may be granted when the damages are liquidated. A partial new trial on damages alone may be granted where liability is clear on the evidence properly admitted. Because issues of liability and damages are often closely intertwined, a partial new trial is usually not appropriate.

5. **CONDITIONAL NEW TRIAL**

If a new trial limited to the issue of damages would be proper, the court may grant the new trial subject to a condition.

(a) Remittitur: If the ground for granting a new trial is excessive damages, the court may grant the motion subject to the condition that it is denied if the plaintiff consents to a reduction in the amount of the judgment.

(b) Additur: In ***federal courts, additur is not permitted.*** *Dimick v. Schiedt*, 293 U.S. 474 (1935). ***California state courts permit its use.*** Cal. Civ. Proc. Code § 662.5(a).)

G. MISTAKE IN JUDGMENT

In addition to correction of substantive errors, the rules also permit a motion to amend a technical error in any final judgment (Federal Rule 60). A motion under that rule is limited to corrections of technical errors. Even though the case is closed, the court retains jurisdiction to make such correction for a motion that is made within the one year time limit.

XIII. APPEAL

INTRODUCTION. After reasonable efforts to gain relief from the trial court, economic resources and other considerations may make an appeal the next feasible procedural step. Appeal in the federal system is subject to the basic principle that only final judgments may be taken to the appellate court. This basic rule is modified by a few other principles that, when available, provide an avenue for appeal even though the underlying action has not yet gone to final judgment. Thus, interlocutory orders are sometimes appealable. If there is subject matter jurisdiction (appealability) to support the appeal, what is the scope of review (reviewability) on appeal?

A. APPEALABILITY

1. **THE FINAL JUDGMENT RULE**

By Title 28 U. S.C. § 1291, Congress has given to the federal courts ***subject matter jurisdiction over appeals from all final decisions of the federal district trial courts***. This statute is the source of the final judgment rule. A final judgment is generally defined as one that disposes of all issues as to all parties.

2. **INTERLOCUTORY ORDER REGARDING INJUNCTIVE RELIEF**

By Title 28 U.S.C. § 1292(a)(1), Congress has given to the federal courts ***subject matter jurisdiction over appeals from an interlocutory order of*** the trial court ***that grants, denies, continues, modifies, or dissolves an injunction***.

A trial court order ***denying a motion to stay*** or dismiss ***an action*** when a similar suit is pending in state court is ***not appealable as an order denying injunctive relief*** under § 1292(a)(1). *Gulfstream Aerospace Corp. v. Mayacamas Corp.*, 485 U.S. 271 (1988).

3. **TRIAL JUDGE CERTIFICATION OF INTERLOCUTORY ORDER**

By Title 28 U.S.C. § 1292(b), Congress permits a trial judge to certify an order for appeal when he or she believes the order (1) involves a controlling question of law as to which there is substantial ground for difference of opinion ***and*** (2) that an immediate appeal from the order may materially advance the termination of the litigation. Following the written certification, the party who seeks appeal must apply to the federal court of appeals for it to accept the matter. The court of appeals is vested with the sole discretion to grant or deny the application.

4. **APPEAL OF INTERLOCUTORY ORDER BY EXTRAORDINARY WRIT**

By Title 28 U.S.C. § 1651, Congress permits the federal courts of appeals to issue extraordinary writs. Therefore, a party may petition the appellate court to issue a writ of mandamus thereby permitting an appeal.

Whether a writ should issue is determined by the following five general guidelines: (1) does the petitioner have other adequate means to attain relief such as direct appeal of the final judgment; (2) does the petitioner face harm that is not correctable on appeal; (3) is the trial court's order clearly erroneous as a matter of law; (4) is the court's order an oft repeated error or one that manifests persistent disregard for the Federal Rules of Civil Procedure; and (5) does the court's order raise important issues of first impression. *In re Cement Antitrust Litigation*, 688 F.2d 1297 (9th Cir. 1982).

5. **MULTI-CLAIM OR MULTI-PARTY JUDGMENT**

By Federal Rule 54(b), when a ***final decision*** has been reached on ***at least one of the claims*** in a multi-claim or multi-party case, the trial judge may direct the entry of a final judgment as to that claim by a finding on the record that there is no reason to delay judgment on that claim until the entire case is resolved. Rule 54(b) thus permits the rendering of a separate judgment on the claim that becomes appealable despite the fact that at least one other claim is still pending for decision.

The Supreme Court says that the discretion of the trial judge under Rule 54(b) should be given substantial deference and that the court of appeals should disturb the trial court's assessment only if it can say that the judge's conclusion was clearly unreasonable. *Curtiss-Wright Corp. v. General Elec. Co.*, 446 U.S. 1 (1980).

6. **THE COLLATERAL ORDER DOCTRINE**

If the trial judge renders an interlocutory order that (1) conclusively determines that disputed question; (2) resolves an important issue completely separate from the merits of the action; and (3) is effectively unreviewable on appeal from a final judgment, the requirements for an appeal by the federal case-created collateral order doctrine are fulfilled. *Firestone Tire & Rubber Corp. v. Risjord*, 449 U.S. 368 (1981).

Suppose the judge enters an interlocutory order denying the defendant's motion to dismiss an action on the basis of a contractual forum-selection clause. Can the defendant appeal the order on the argument that it meets the definition of the collateral order doctrine? No, says the Supreme Court in *Lauro Lines v. Chasser,—U.S.—,* 109 S. Ct. 1976 (1989). The opinion finds that the order fails to satisfy the third requirement of the collateral order test since the issue does not involve an asserted right the legal and practical value of which would be destroyed if it were not vindicated before trial.

Suppose the court enters an order denying the defendant's motion to transfer venue (Title 28 U.S.C. § 1404(a)) to another federal district court, basing the denial on the ground that the defendant's attorney obviously had ignored the holding of *Hoffman v. Blaski.* Moreover, the judge then enters an order fining the attorney $5,000 for violating Rule 11. Can the attorney appeal the order using the collateral order doctrine? A Rule 11 order of sanction on a nonparty is held to satisfy the three elements of the doctrine. See *Sanko S.S. Co., Ltd. v. Galin*, 835 F.2d 51 (2d Cir. 1987); *Optyl Eyewear Fashion Int'l Corp. v. Style Cos., Ltd.*, 760 F.2d 1045 (9th Cir. 1985).

B. REVIEWABILITY

Although an appellant may want the appeals court to review all errors alleged to have occurred at the trial court level, there are some restrictions on what is reviewable. Are the errors on the record of the trial court proceeding? Did the appellant object to the error at a time when the court had an opportunity to correct it? Is the error harmless? Errors that do not affect substantial rights are disregarded in deference to finality and the realistic limits on the attention that the judicial machinery can pay to any single action.

XIV. BINDING EFFECT

INTRODUCTION. When litigation ends, what has been won and lost? The party who prevails has the obvious victory of succeeding on a claim or a defense at the expense of the losing party. But might there be more at stake? Can the plaintiff come back to court to increase the amount of relief previously won against the defendant? Can the former defendant become a plaintiff and sue the earlier opponent in an effort to reap affirmative relief from a successful defense in the first action? The body of law that addresses these questions is traditionally referred to as *res judicata and collateral estoppel.* In tune with the times, those defenses are known respectively as *claim preclusion and issue preclusion.*

A. RES JUDICATA (CLAIM PRECLUSION)

1. ELEMENTS

Res judicata ***precludes relitigation of an earlier claim*** if the ***previous action*** was ***determined on its merits by a court with proper subject matter and personal jurisdiction.*** Preclusion ***applies to*** claims that were ***actually litigated and*** to those that ***should have been litigated.*** The previous action is ***binding on the parties and those in privity*** with them. ***Res judicata or claim preclusion operates as a defense that is waived by failure to raise it.***

2. **DEFINITION OF CLAIM**

The definition of a claim or cause of action differs with the territory. One definition honored by time is that a plaintiff has as many causes of action as there are primary rights invaded by the defendant. In the federal system, the meaning for the word "claim" is influenced by the *Restatement Second of Judgments* § 24. The Restatement takes the view that the word "claim" embraces all of the remedial rights of a plaintiff that arise from a transaction of occurrence or series thereof.

Suppose plaintiff suffers both personal injury and property loss as a result of an automobile collision. Under a primary rights analysis, it may be that plaintiff has two causes of action because two primary rights are allegedly invaded (i.e., the right to protection from personal injury and a similar right as to property). The Restatement analysis leads to a conclusion of one claim because both injuries arose from the same occurrence.

3. **SPLITTING A CLAIM**

(a) ***Merger:*** If the plaintiff wins a judgment on a part of the total harm suffered, and in a second suit seeks recovery on the remaining loss, the defendant will argue ***merger***. If the jurisdiction views the plaintiff as having only one cause of action for ***all*** affirmative relief, the plaintiff's rights (including relief that might have been sought in the first suit) ***merged*** in the first judgment. ***Merger*** is the term applied to a ***winner who splits a cause of action***.

(b) ***Bar:*** If the plaintiff loses in a first action and seeks, by subsequent litigation, to recover for other injury, the defendant will argue ***bar***. If the jurisdiction describes the plaintiff as having only one cause of action for ***all*** affirmative relief, the first judgment ***bars*** the second suit. ***Bar*** is the term applied to a loser who splits a cause of action.

B. COLLATERAL ESTOPPEL (ISSUE PRECLUSION)

1. **ELEMENTS**

Collateral estoppel ***precludes relitigation of an issue that was actually litigated and necessary to the final decision in a previous case***.

2. **NONMUTUAL COLLATERAL ESTOPPEL**

As with res judicata (claim preclusion), ***collateral estoppel*** (issue preclusion) ***cannot be used against someone who was not a party to the previous action***. It would be a violation of due process to bind a nonparty or anyone not in privity with a party since that person has not had a "day in court" to litigate the issue.

Can a nonparty to a previous suit use collateral estoppel against someone who was a party? Both California and the federal system have adopted nonmutual collateral estoppel.

(a) Defensive nonmutual collateral estoppel: Collateral estoppel may be used ***defensively*** (as a "shield") by one who was not a party to the first action against one who was a party. For example, A, the driver of a car, is involved in a collision with B, the driver of a truck owned by B's employer C. Employee B was acting within the scope of employment. A sues B to recover for A's personal injury and property damage. A loses and then sues C for the same relief. C can bind A to the earlier judgment through the use of ***defensive*** collateral estoppel.

(b) Offensive nonmutual collateral estoppel: Collateral estoppel may be used ***offensively*** (as a "sword") by one who was not a party to the first action against one who was a party. The use of estoppel offensively, however, involves several more considerations. Could the second-action plaintiff have easily joined in the earlier action? Was the second-action defendant in an offensive or defensive position in the earlier action? If a defendant in the first action, was he or she sued for small or nominal damages? Might that reduce the incentive to defend vigorously in the first action? Was the defendant in the first action forced to defend in an inconvenient forum and therefore was unable to engage in full scale discovery or call witnesses? These factors are important because the courts know that the offensive use of collateral estoppel may increase rather than decrease the total amount of litigation. If the second-action plaintiff could always use offensive estoppel, then a potential plaintiff has every incentive to adopt a "wait and see" attitude in the hopes that the first action by another plaintiff will result in a favorable judgment. See *Parklane Hosiery Co. v. Shore*, 439 U.S. 322 (1979).

3. **COLLATERAL ESTOPPEL FROM PRIOR CRIMINAL PROCEEDING**

(a) Acquittal: The general rule is that a prior acquittal does not have collateral estoppel impact on a subsequent civil proceeding. The usual criminal law burden of proof is beyond a reasonable doubt whereas, in a civil action, the ordinary burden is by a preponderance of the evidence. Failure to establish the criminal burden does not mean that it cannot be proven by reference to the civil burden of proof.

(b) Conviction: If the defendant has been convicted of a crime that has an element common to an issue in a subsequent civil proceeding, the conviction may have collateral estoppel impact in the civil case. Two considerations are relevant: Was the conviction for an offense that would have motivated the defendant to fully defend? Did the conviction follow from a fair trial?

4. **COLLATERAL ESTOPPEL FROM PRIOR ADMINISTRATIVE PROCEEDING**

A prior administrative decision may lead to collateral estoppel in subsequent civil litigation. Apply the following question to the facts: Did the administrative agency act in a judicial capacity and resolve disputed issues of fact properly before it which the parties have had an adequate opportunity to litigate? *People v. Sims*, 32 Cal. 3d 468, 651 P.2d 321, 186 Cal. Rptr. 77 (1982).

QUESTION BY QUESTION CAPSULE OUTLINE

1. Subject Matter Jurisdiction
2. Subject Matter Jurisdiction
3. Venue
4. Subject Matter Jurisdiction
5. Removal
6. Subject Matter Jurisdiction
7. Statutory Interpleader
8. Service of Process
9. Indispensable Party
10. Third Party Claims, Ancillary Jurisdiction
11. Pendent Jurisdiction
12. Collateral Attack Upon Default Judgment
13. Subject Matter Jurisdiction
14. Pleadings
15. Subject Matter Jurisdiction
16. Class Actions
17. Removal
18. Third Party Claims, Counterclaims
19. Amendments to Pleadings
20. Joinder of Claims, Joinder of Parties
21. Subject Matter Jurisdiction, Venue
22. Res Judicata
23. Counterclaims, Ancillary Jurisdiction
24. Discovery, Work Product Privilege
25. Voir Dire Examination
26. Remittitur
27. Subject Matter Jurisdiction

28. Class Actions
29. Class Actions
30. Personal Jurisdiction
31. Counterclaims, Ancillary Jurisdiction
32. Cross-Claims, Ancillary Jurisdiction
33. Collateral Estoppel
34. Class Actions
35. Personal Jurisdiction
36. Joinder of Parties
37. Third Party Claims
38. Removal
39. Statutory Interpleader
40. Jury Trials
41. Removal, Forum Non Conveniens
42. Indispensable Party, Third Party Claims
43. Removal, Forum Non Conveniens
44. Pleadings
45. Pleadings
46. Personal Jurisdiction
47. Venue, Removal
48. Intervention
49. Right to Jury Trial
50. Venue
51. Discovery, Work Product Rule
52. Summary Judgment
53. Summary Judgment
54. Default Judgment, Collateral Attack Upon Default Judgment

55. Quasi-In-Rem Jurisdiction
56. Removal
57. Subject Matter Jurisdiction
58. Counterclaims, Third Party Claims
59. Amendments to Pleadings
60. Amendments to Pleadings
61. Venue
62. Class Actions, Notice
63. Discovery, Work Product Privilege
64. Removal
65. Class Actions, Subject Matter Jurisdiction
66. Indispensable Party
67. Collateral Estoppel
68. Intervention
69. Third Party Claims
70. Discovery
71. Subject Matter Jurisdiction
72. Collateral Estoppel
73. Class Actions
74. Intervention, Ancillary Jurisdiction
75. Statutory Interpleader
76. Directed Verdict
77. Directed Verdict
78. Directed Verdict, Judgment Notwithstanding the Verdict
79. Indispensable Party
80. Intervention
81. Presumptions

82. Presumptions
83. Cross-Claims
84. Third Party Claims, Ancillary Jurisdiction
85. Collateral Estoppel, Right to Jury Trial
86. Subject Matter Jurisdiction
87. Discovery
88. Discovery
89. Discovery
90. Class Actions
91. Discovery
92. Discovery
93. Full Faith and Credit
94. Collateral Estoppel
95. Subject Matter Jurisdiction
96. Notice
97. Personal Jurisdiction
98. Indispensable Party
99. Summary Judgment
100. Collateral Estoppel

Question 1 is based on the following fact situation.

Paul, a State District Attorney, files a complaint in the proper U.S. District Court seeking to enjoin a pro-communist rally. He alleges the rally is being held without a license, in violation of a state statute. Paul asserts federal question jurisdiction by alleging that the defendants have publicly claimed immunity for such rallies on First Amendment grounds. Denton, the group leader, files an FRCP 12(b)(1) motion to dismiss for lack of subject matter jurisdiction. He alternatively claims immunity from prosecution under the First Amendment as an affirmative defense.

1. Denton's motion should be:

(A) Granted, because there is no subject matter jurisdiction.
(B) Granted, because Denton has asserted a First Amendment defense.
(C) Denied, because there is "federal question" subject matter jurisdiction.
(D) Denied, because Paul's claim involves the U.S. Constitution.

Question 2 is based on the following fact situation.

Paula and Pete were hit by a truck driven by an employee of the D Corporation. The accident occurred in California, where Paula and Pete were living at the time. D's headquarters are in Florida, but its principal place of business is in Michigan. It is incorporated in Dela ware. After the accident, Paula and Pete moved to Miami, Florida, where they planned to retire.

After moving, they contacted a lawyer who filed suit against D in the appropriate U.S. District Court where Paula and Pete lived, alleging diversity jurisdiction. The suit alleged that each plaintiff had suffered personal injuries in excess of $75,000. D moved to dismiss the case for lack of subject matter jurisdiction.

2. D's motion should be:

(A) Granted, because the plaintiffs were citizens of California when they were injured.
(B) Granted, because D's headquarters are in Florida.
(C) Denied, because diversity subject matter jurisdiction exists.
(D) Denied, because D is a citizen of Delaware only.

Question 3 is based on the following fact situation.

3. P files suit in the U.S. District Court in Nevada alleging a federal claim (i.e., racial discrimination against him occurring in Texas). The defendant is a citizen of California, and all of the witnesses live in Texas. P lives in Nevada. The defendant moves to change the venue to California, or alternatively, to Texas.

(A) The action may be transferred to California, only.
(B) The action may be transferred to California or Texas.
(C) The action must be dismissed, since it was commenced in an improper forum.
(D) It is discretionary with the court whether to retain the action or transfer it to California or Texas.

Question 4 is based on the following fact situation.

Priscilla filed suit against Derek for recovery of a shipment of cargo lost at sea. The suit was filed in a court of general jurisdiction in State

A. Derek was personally served at his home in State B. He has no contacts with State A. Derek made a general appearance in the State A court and filed a demurrer to the complaint. The demurrer was overruled and the case proceeded to trial, where Priscilla prevailed. You may assume that Priscilla's claim is in admiralty, which is within the exclusive jurisdiction of the federal courts. On appeal Derek asserted (1) lack of personal jurisdiction; and (2) lack of subject matter jurisdiction.

4. Derek should:

   (A) Prevail on both (1) and (2)
   (B) Prevail on (1) only
   (C) Prevail on (2) only
   (D) Lose on both (1) and (2)

Question 5 is based on the following fact situation.

Plaintiff, a citizen of State A, filed suit against Defendant in a State A court, alleging a claim based upon a federal statute. Defendant, also a citizen of State A, filed a petition for removal to the federal court which encompasses the judicial district in which the state court is located.

5. Should the action be removed?

   (A) No, because the action could not have originally been brought in the U.S. District Court to which removal has been requested.
   (B) Yes, because Plaintiff's action arises under a U.S. Statute.
   (C) Yes, because state courts, even those of general jurisdiction, do not have subject matter jurisdiction over federal claims.
   (D) No, because Defendant is a citizen of State A.

Question 6 is based on the following fact situation.

Acme became involved in a labor dispute with the Steamroller's Union (the entity which ordinarily supplied workers for Acme's plant). Acme commenced an action against Steamroller's Union ("Union") in the appropriate U.S. District Court, claiming $75,000 in damages as a consequence of Union's conduct in harassing and intimidating non-union workers in violation of the National Labor Relations Act and applicable state law. Acme is an Indiana corporation and Union (an unincorporated association) has members who are domiciled in every state, except New York and New Jersey. Union answered by denying Acme's allegations and filing a $15,000 counter-claim (which asserted that Acme had deliberately made false accusations about Union to the local papers for the purpose of obtaining favorable press coverage).

6. If Union moves to dismiss for lack of subject matter jurisdiction, it should

   (A) Prevail, because there is no diversity.
   (B) Prevail, because Acme has not claimed monetary damages in excess of $75,000.
   (C) Lose, because subject matter jurisdiction is satisfied.
   (D) Lose, because a state claim has been asserted in a federal court.

Question 7 is based on the following fact situation.

Bank is a Missouri Corporation. Bank has a savings account in the name of one of its customers, Harvey Hunt, who was domiciled in California. Harvey recently died. In his will, Harvey left the entire account (in the specific amount of $7,000) to his nephew Sam, a citizen of Texas. On the same day that Sam showed up to claim the money, Jay appeared at Bank and presented a notarized agreement signed by Harvey assigning the entire bank account to Jay. Jay is a citizen of New York. Bank filed for a statutory interpleader action in the U.S. District Court for the judicial district of California in which it is located.

7. Which of the following statements is correct?

   (A) The case should be dismissed because the citizenship of Sam will be imputed to Harvey, and so diversity of citizenship will be lacking.
   (B) Although there is complete diversity between adverse parties, the case lacks the necessary amount in controversy, and so it should be dismissed for lack of subject matter jurisdiction.
   (C) The case would be subject to a motion to dismiss under Rule 12(b)(3) because venue in a statutory interpleader action would be proper only in a district where one of the claimants resides.
   (D) Both A and B.

Question 8 is based on the following fact situation.

In a state court of general jurisdiction, Pete sued the Big Time Corporation for personal injuries he received in an auto collision with a truck driven by a Big Time truck driver. Doris was the President of Big Time when the accident occurred. Pete personally served Big Time Corporation by handing the summons and complaint to Doris the day before she retired. In the excitement of her retirement, Doris neglected to deliver the papers to anyone else at Big Time. A default was entered against Big Time. Other than service upon Doris, Big Time never received notice of the pending lawsuit prior to the entry of a default judgment. Big Time now moves to quash service of process. You may assume that applicable state law pertaining to service of process is identical to the Federal Rules of Civil Procedure.

8. Which of the following statements is probably correct?

   (A) Service should be quashed because Big Time Corporation did not receive actual notice of the pending lawsuit.
   (B) Service should be quashed because Doris was not an officer of Big Time at the time an answer was due.
   (C) Service should be quashed because the summons and complaint was served by Pete.
   (D) Big Time's motion should be denied.

Question 9 is based on the following fact situation.

Plaintiff, a citizen of California, sues The Bank of Nevada ("Bank") in the U.S. District Court for the District of Nevada. Bank has its only place of business in Nevada. Plaintiff seeks an order directing Bank to deliver the proceeds of a savings account in the amount of $85,000 to her. She alleges an agreement between her and Krooke, also a California citizen, whereby they each deposited an equal amount of money in the account, to be held solely in the name of Krooke. She further alleges that Krooke has asked Bank to split the account equally and to deliver a pass-book to her, but that Bank refused to do this. The Bank answers by alleging that it refused to make the transfer because Krooke claims that plaintiff assigned her interest in the account to him as repayment for a loan. Bank makes a motion to dismiss for failure to join Krooke as a party. At a hearing on this issue, the court orders joinder of Krooke and then dismisses for lack of complete diversity.

9. Which of the following statements is correct:

   1. Plaintiff will not be barred from refiling the action in a state court since the dismissal on the grounds provided in FRCP 12(b)(7) does not constitute an adjudication on the merits.
   2. The court should not have required the joinder of Krooke because it destroyed diversity.
   3. The court should not have dismissed the action because it has pendent jurisdiction over Plaintiff's claim against Krooke.
   4. The court should not have dismissed the action because there was diversity between Plaintiff and Bank.

   (A) 1 only
   (B) 2 only
   (C) 1 and 4
   (D) 2 and 3

Question 10 is based on the following fact situation.

P, a citizen of Idaho, brings a multimillion dollar diversity action for wrongful death in the proper U.S. District Court against his wife's employer, D Construction Company, a Washington corporation. He alleges that D negligently allowed the scaffolding to collapse while his wife was walking beneath it. D impleads the manufacturer of the scaffolding, T, alleging that it would have a right to indemnity from T as a consequence of the latter's negligent manufacture of the equipment in question. T is an Idaho corporation. P was granted leave to file an amended complaint alleging negligent manufacture against T. Thereafter, T moved to dismiss P's action against it for lack of subject matter jurisdiction.

10. Which of the following statements is correct?

    (A) The motion should be denied because of the pendent jurisdiction doctrine.
    (B) The motion should be denied because of the ancillary jurisdiction doctrine.
    (C) The motion should be granted because diversity is lacking.
    (D) The motion should be granted because there is diversity between P and D.

Question 11 is based on the following fact situation.

P, a citizen of California, filed an action in the U.S District Court in Los Angeles against D, a Texas corporation, and Z, a New York corporation, alleging that (1) they were engaged in a conspiracy to fix prices in violation of the Sherman Act, 15 U.S.C. 1, and (2) that his actual damages from the conduct of the defendants was $73,000. P further alleged in a second cause of action that D is wrongfully withholding $1,000 which P paid to D as a deposit for a computer which was not delivered.

11. Which of the following statements is correct?

    1. The action should be dismissed by the District Court since the value of the aggregated claims do not meet the amount in controversy requirement.
    2. The district court may exercise pendent jurisdiction over the second cause of action only if it arises from a common nucleus of operative facts with the first cause of action.
    3. The federal court has subject matter jurisdiction because there is complete diversity of citizenship between all plaintiffs and defendants.

    (A) 1 only
    (B) 2 only
    (C) 3 only
    (D) None

Question 12 is based on the following fact situation.

P brings an action against D in a state court of general jurisdiction in California. P is a Citizen of California. D is a citizen of New York. P alleges that D has infringed upon a patent recently granted to P by the U.S. Patent and Trademark Office. P seeks $75,000 in damages and an injunction barring D from further acts of infringement. Patent infringement matters are within the exclusive jurisdiction of the federal courts. D is personally served with a copy of the summons and complaint when his airplane lands at Los Angeles International Airport on a brief stopover. The flight was bound for Hawaii. D fails to answer the complaint and P obtains a default judgment. P then seeks to enforce the judgment in a New York state court.

12. Which of the following statements is correct?
    1. The Court in California did not have subject matter jurisdiction over the action, so P's judgment is not entitled to Full Faith and Credit from a New York court.
    2. Even assuming *Shaffer v. Heltner* does not alter the traditional rule that service of process within a state is a valid means of obtaining personal jurisdiction over a defendant, the California state court never obtained personal jurisdiction over D since he does not reside in California (and so the judgment is not entitled to Full Faith and Credit from a New York court).
    3. By failing to appear, D waived his right to object to subject matter and personal jurisdiction.

    (A) 1 only
    (B) 2 only
    (C) 3 only
    (D) None

Question 13 is based on the following fact situation.

P, a citizen of Arizona, was injured in an automobile accident in New Mexico. The driver of the other vehicle is D, a citizen of Texas. New Mexico is a comparative negligence state and the law of New Mexico would apply to this action. P knows that D's damages are $50,000. P brings her action in the only U.S. District Court in Arizona, alleging in good faith that she has incurred damages in the total amount of $75,000.

13. Which of the following statements is correct?
    1. Venue is not proper.
    2. The federal court lacks subject matter jurisdiction because the claim does not meet the amount in controversy requirement.
    3. The federal court has subject matter jurisdiction because the parties are diverse and P's claim satisfies the amount in controversy requirement.

    (A) 1 only
    (B) 2 only
    (C) 3 only
    (D) 1 and 2

Question 14 is based on the following fact situation.

Packer, a New York citizen, purchased a mountainside home in Lake Tahoe, Nevada, from Denton. Packer asked Denton if the latter was sure that the land on which the home is situated was geologically sound. Denton (aware that there was a major fault under the home) nevertheless responded to Packer's question in a positive manner. Two months after Packer occupied the house, it collapsed. Packer brings an action for fraud against Denton in the appropriate U.S. District Court. The complaint alleges that "Denton fraudulently induced the plaintiff to enter into the purchase agreement for the house and land." Denton moved for a more definite statement under FRCP 12(e).

14. Which of the following statements is correct?
    1. The motion should be granted, since the FRCP requires that circumstances constituting fraud must be stated with particularity.
    2. The motion should be denied, since the FRCP requires only that the pleader give a short, plain statement of the claim for relief.
    3. The motion should be denied, if the complaint is adequate under Nevada law.

    (A) 1 only
    (B) 2 only
    (C) 3 only
    (D) None

Question 15 is based on the following fact situation.

D, a Michigan corporation, sells its automobiles through independent dealers. D's principal place of business is Detroit. Each dealer has a separate dealership agreement which they executed with D at the time they are appointed to be a dealer. Their agreements entitle them to sell all automobiles manufactured by D in their areas. This year, D has produced a new sports car which is a radical departure from its previous automobiles. D decides that it will not sell this car to its existing dealers, but instead will enter into agreements with new dealers to handle the new sports car line. Twelve dealers in California jointly file actions for breach of contract and an injunction against D in the appropriate U.S. District Court. D moves to sever the actions.

15. Which of the following statements is correct?
    1. The motion should be granted, because there is no diversity since plaintiffs are all citizens of the same state.
    2. The motion should be denied, because plaintiffs are compelled to join their actions if their claims arise out of the same transaction or series of transactions.
    3. The motion should be granted, if (a) the court finds that the claims arise out of the same transaction or series of transactions, and (b) there are common issues of law and fact to all of the claims.

    (A) 1 only
    (B) 2 only
    (C) 3 only
    (D) None

Question 16 is based on the following fact situation.

North America Insurance Company ("NAIC"), an Illinois corporation with its principal place of business in New York, is sued by five of its policyholders in a class action which alleges that NAIC overcharged them and 2,000 other persons in their states for automobile insurance. The action seeks a refund of the overcharges. The plaintiffs in the action are Adams ("A"), a citizen of Arizona; Baron ("B"), a student who is domiciled in Arizona, but is attending law school in California; Collins ("C"), a citizen of Colorado; Dante ("D"), a citizen of Delaware; and, Ellwood ("E"), a citizen of Florida. The amounts of the overcharges claimed by the named plaintiffs are: A, $15,000; B, $10,000; C, $50,000; D, $29,000; and E, $14,000.

16. Which of the following statements is correct?

    1. The federal court lacks subject matter jurisdiction over the action since the diversity requirement is not met.
    2. The federal court must dismiss the action because the claim of each of the representative's fails to meet the amount in controversy requirement.
    3. The federal court has subject matter jurisdiction, since the aggregate claims of the class representatives meet the amount in controversy requirement.

    (A) 1 only
    (B) 2 only
    (C) 3 only
    (D) None

Question 17 is based on the following fact situation.

P, a citizen of New York brings an action against D, in the U.S. District Court in New York (the judicial district in which P lives). D is a citizen of Michigan. The action alleges $80,000 in damages and is based on an alleged breach of contract by D to manufacture equipment for P's restaurants. Subsequently, D brings an action against P for $76,000 in a New York court of general jurisdiction for personal injuries suffered by D when he slipped on a banana peel while at P's restaurant in New York three weeks before the parties were initially introduced. P seeks to remove the state court action to the proper U.S. District Court.

17. Which of the following statements is correct?

    1. D's action may *not* be removed.
    2. Assuming the state court action meets applicable subject matter jurisdiction requirements, it could be removed to the appropriate U.S. District Court in New York.
    3. D was *not* required to assert his action in the original federal court litigation initiated by P, since it did not arise out of the same transaction or occurrence as P's action.

    (A) 1 only
    (B) 2 only
    (C) 2 and 3
    (D) 3 only

Question 18 is based on the following fact situation.

Able, a Colorado citizen, is injured when her car is hit by Chance, also a Colorado citizen. Chance is a minor who was served drinks illegally at a bar located in Wyoming owned by Baker, a Wyoming citizen. Able brings an action in the only U.S. District Court in Colorado against Baker, alleging negligence and the breach of a statutory duty by the latter. Thirty days after answering, Baker files a motion seeking leave to file a third-party claim (i.e., an impleader action) against Chance, based entirely upon Chance's (1) unpaid bar bill, and (2) failure to pay for a used car which Baker had sold to Chance.

18. Which of the following statements is correct?

    1. The motion will be denied because Baker's claim does not assert that Chance may be liable to Baker on all or part of Able's claim.
    2. If the court finds that Baker may properly implead Chance, then Chance will probably be allowed to assert any claim he has against Baker.
    3. Chance cannot be made a party to the action by Baker because that would destroy diversity subject matter jurisdiction.

    (A) 1 only
    (B) 2 only
    (C) 1 and 3
    (D) 1 and 2

Question 19 is based on the following fact situation.

Pat, a citizen of New York, filed a federal diversity action against Dan, a citizen of Arizona, for personal injuries and property damage suffered in an automobile collision in Arizona. The action was commenced in the only U.S. District Court in Arizona the day before the applicable statute of limitations expired. The action also named Roger as a defendant. He was a passenger in the car with Dan at the time of the accident. The complaint alleged that Roger (also an Arizona citizen) was the registered owner of the car. Process was served on Roger under FRCP 4(c) by leaving a copy of the summons and complaint with Roger's father, Richard, at their home in Phoenix. Richard read the entire complaint to his son. One year later (and three months before the trial), Pat amends the complaint to change the name of the owner of the car to Richard (Pat having just discovered that Richard is the owner of the vehicle and that Arizona has a statute which makes the owner of a car liable for the negligent driving of a bailee with permission). The court dismissed the amended complaint as being barred by the Arizona statute of limitations.

19. Which of the following statements is probably correct?

    1. The amended complaint should relate back to the original complaint, because service of process was physically delivered to Richard.
    2. The amended complaint should relate back to the original complaint, because it arose out of the same transaction or occurrence set forth in the original pleading.
    3. The amended complaint should not be allowed, since the state statute of limitation had expired.

    (A) 1 only
    (B) 2 only
    (C) 3 only
    (D) 1 and 2

Question 20 is based on the following fact situation.

Paul, a citizen of Ohio, was involved in a three-car auto collision with Peter and Mary. Paul sued Peter and Mary in the only U.S. District Court in Maine. The defendants were citizens of the latter state. Paul's action against each defendant was for personal injuries in the amount of $75,000 and property damage in the amount of $5,000.

20. Which of the following statements is correct?

    1. Paul might be permitted to assert a $1,000 breach of contract action against Mary.
    2. Peter might be permitted to assert a $12,000 breach of contract action against Mary.
    3. Paul's action should be dismissed because no single claim satisfies the "amount in controversy" requirement.

    (A) 1 only
    (B) 2 only
    (C) 1 and 2
    (D) 1 and 3

Question 21 is based on the following fact situation.

Railroad Corporation brings a class action in the U.S. District Court for the Eastern District of Ohio against the members of the United Railroad Fireman's Union ("Union"). The class action complaint names as the class representatives the four officers of Union. Railroad is a Pennsylvania corporation, which has its principal place of business in New York. Union is an unincorporated association which has its headquarters in Ohio, the place where the major portion of Union's administrative work is performed. All of the officers of Union are citizens of Pennsylvania. The membership of Union includes railroad employees who reside in Michigan, Pennsylvania and Ohio. The action asserts that members of Union destroyed railroad property in Pennsylvania during a strike.

21. Which of the following statements is correct?

    1. Venue is proper in Ohio because that is where the union is doing business, and would therefore be considered its residence.
    2. The action cannot be brought in a U.S. District Court, unless it is based upon a federal claim.
    3. Since this is an action involving an unincorporated labor organization, it is outside of the subject matter jurisdiction of federal courts.

    (A) 1 only
    (B) 2 only
    (C) 3 only
    (D) 1 and 2

Question 22 is based on the following fact situation.

John owns Riverdale, a palatial residence. Bill owns the adjoining residence. One day Matt, Bill's butler, started a fire on Bill's estate to burn some excess rubbish. Unfortunately, the fire got out of control, and burned down John's residence. It also caused considerable damage to the rest of Riverdale. John sustained some injuries and was hospitalized for ten days. John files an action against Bill, in which he seeks damages in excess of $300,000 for property loss caused by the fire.

22. If John obtains a judgment against Bill, which of the following statements is correct?

    (A) Bill cannot sue Matt.
    (B) Any action by John against Matt is barred.
    (C) The judgment against Bill would not be binding upon Matt in a subsequent lawsuit by John against Matt.
    (D) John's claim against Bill for personal injuries is not barred by normal res judicata principles because that action was not litigated in the *John v. Bill* lawsuit.

Question 23 is based on the following fact situation.

Acme became involved in a labor dispute with the Steamroller's Union (the entity which ordinarily supplied workers for Acme's plant). Acme commenced an action against Steamroller's Union ("Union") in the appropriate U.S. District Court, claiming $80,000 in damages as a consequence of Union's conduct in harassing and intimidating non-union workers in violation of the National Labor Relations Act and applicable state law. Acme is an Indiana corporation and Union (an unincorporated association) has members who are domiciled in every state, except New York and New Jersey. Union answered by denying

Acme's allegations and filing a $90,000 counterclaim (which asserted that Acme had deliberately made false accusations about Union to the local papers for the purpose of obtaining favorable press coverage).

23. If Acme moves to dismiss Union's counterclaim for lack of subject matter jurisdiction, it should:

(A) Lose, if Union's counterclaim is mandatory in nature.
(B) Prevail, if Union's counterclaim is permissive in nature.
(C) Prevail, since Acme has asserted a state cause of action.
(D) Lose, because diversity does not exist.

Questions 24-26 are based on the following fact situation.

Paul was injured while operating a drill press manufactured by Manco. Paul properly commenced an action against Manco in the appropriate U.S. District Court. Prior to trial, Paul sought discovery of a report which had been made to Manco by Brown, a claims investigator for Manco. Brown had inspected the machine and investigated the circumstances of the accident immediately thereafter. The machine was subsequently destroyed in a fire and Brown has retired (leaving no forwarding address).

In selecting the jury, the judge conducted the voir dire, but refused Manco's request that the judge ask the members of the jury panel whether any of them were prejudiced against corporations. A verdict was returned in favor of Paul for $75,000. Manco moved for a new trial. The trial judge agreed to grant a new trial, unless Paul accepted a reduction in the verdict from $75,000 to $25,000. Paul agreed to the reduction under protest. Paul then appealed. He asserted as error the trial court's order granting a new trial, unless he accepted a reduction in the verdict from $75,000 to $25,000.

24. Paul's request for Brown's report should be:

(A) Granted, because tangible items prepared in anticipation of litigation or trial are not discoverable.
(B) Granted, even if prepared in anticipation of litigation or trial, provided Paul can show that there is a substantial need for the information and he is otherwise unable to obtain it without undue hardship.
(C) Denied, because it was apparently prepared at Manco's request (rather than at the instigation of Manco's attorney).
(D) Denied, if Manco procured the report at the suggestion of its legal counsel.

25. The trial judge's refusal to comply with Manco's request at the voir dire was:

(A) Correct, because the question was irrelevant to the issues of the case.
(B) Correct, because Manco could have exercised a peremptory challenge against the potential juror.
(C) Erroneous, because prejudice against a party is a proper subject for inquiry at the voir dire.
(D) Erroneous, because when the trial judge conducts the voir dire, he/she must ask any questions requested by counsel.

26. Plaintiff's appeal from the order of remittitur should be:

    (A) Successful, since the court's order violated Paul's Seventh Amendment right to a trial by jury upon the issue of damages.
    (B) Successful, unless the trial court abused its discretion in ordering a new trial if Paul had not agreed to the lessened sum.
    (C) Unsuccessful, because Paul elected to accept the remittitur.
    (D) Unsuccessful, because the Seventh Amendment does not apply to damage issues.

Questions 27-29 are based on the following fact situation.

Ten College students in State X filed a class action in U.S. District Court. The complaint requested that five specifically named state officials, the defendants, be enjoined from enforcing the state's flag desecration statute which was alleged to be unconstitutional. The class which the plaintiffs sought to represent was all college students in State X. The defendants filed motions requesting that:

1. The complaint be dismissed on the grounds that the court lacked subject matter jurisdiction.
2. The court deny certification of the class.

27. The defendants' motion to dismiss for lack of subject matter jurisdiction should be:

    (A) Denied, because a First Amendment claim is involved.
    (B) Denied, only if there is diversity of citizenship between the plaintiff/representatives, on the one hand, and the defendants, on the other hand, and the amount claimed by each member of the plaintiff class satisfies the "amount in controversy" requirement.
    (C) Granted, because no specific assertion has been made that each plaintiff has suffered damages in excess of $75,000.
    (D) Granted, if any member of the plaintiff class and any defendant are citizens of the same state.

28. The defendants' strongest argument to deny certification of the plaintiff class would probably be that:

    (A) The "numerosity" element is absent.
    (B) The plaintiffs have failed to allege that each member of the prospective class will suffer damages in excess of $75,000.
    (C) The representatives do not adequately represent the interests of the entire class.
    (D) It would be impossible to individually notify each member of the proposed class by mail.

29. Assuming the court refused to certify the class:

    (A) The plaintiffs could immediately appeal the court's decision.
    (B) The plaintiffs could not appeal immediately, but would be obliged to try the action on the merits as a non-class action.
    (C) The plaintiffs would waive any right to appeal if they elected to first try the case on its merits.
    (D) The court would be obliged to dismiss the case.

Questions 30-32 are based on the following fact situation.

Arnold and Bates, citizens of State Z, are plaintiffs in an action brought in the United States District Court in State X against Manco, a State Y corporation, and Storeco, a State X corporation. Manco's office and plant are located in State Y. At no time has Manco had an office or salesmen in State X. Storeco's sole place of business is in State X.

The complaint alleges that each of the plaintiffs sustained serious personal injuries when a blade broke on an electric lawn-mower while the equipment was being demonstrated by a clerk in Storeco's store in State X. Each plaintiff requested damages in the sum of $80,000. The mower had been manufactured by Manco and shipped to Roe in State Z. Roe had a contract with Manco to act as exclusive distributor of Manco products in eleven states, including States X and Z.

Process was served personally on the president of Manco at Manco's office in State Y and on the president of Storeco at its office in State X. Thereafter the following occurred:

1. Manco moved to dismiss the action on the ground that the court had no jurisdiction over it.
2. Storeco filed a counterclaim against Arnold for $74,000 alleged to be due for merchandise previously sold to Arnold.
3. Manco filed a cross-claim against Storeco for $12,000 alleged to be due for merchandise previously sold by Manco to Storeco.

30. The U.S. District Court can assert personal jurisdiction over Manco:

(A) If State X has an appropriate long-arm statute and the assertion of personal jurisdiction would comport with due process.
(B) If the assertion of personal jurisdiction would comport with due process (there being nationwide service of process in actions commenced in federal court).
(C) If the amount in controversy exceeds $75,000, exclusive of interest and costs.
(D) If process was served upon Manco in accordance with both federal and State X law.

31. A motion to strike Storeco's counterclaim should be:

(A) Dismissed, because there is ancillary jurisdiction.
(B) Dismissed, because Arnold has implicitly consented to personal jurisdiction by commencing an action in State X.
(C) Granted, because the amount owed to Storeco is only $74,000.
(D) Granted, because Storeco's counterclaim is compulsory.

32. A motion to strike Manco's cross-claim against Storeco should be:

(A) Granted, because the cross-claim is unrelated to the plaintiff's action.
(B) Granted, because there is no ancillary jurisdiction with respect to this action.
(C) Denied, if the court believes that Manco's action will not confuse or divert the jury with respect to the original claim.
(D) Denied, because there is diversity subject matter jurisdiction with respect to Manco's cross-claim against Storeco.

Question 33 is based on the following fact situation.

You may assume that this jurisdiction has abandoned the "mutuality rule" pertaining to collateral estoppel. Paul is the executor of the estate of Carol. Paul files an action on behalf of the estate in the applicable state court against Doris (Carol's nurse) alleging that Doris converted Carol's money. Although Doris was authorized to deposit funds into Carol's account at the local bank ("Bank"), Paul claims that Doris also withdrew funds for her own use. At trial, the jury found that Carol had made an inter vivos gift to Doris of the money in question. Thereafter, Paul commenced an action against Bank in the applicable U.S. District Court, alleging that the withdrawals by Doris were not authorized by Carol, and therefore Bank had breached its contractual relationship with Carol.

33. Which of the following statements is correct?
    1. There will be no collateral estoppel from the first case because that action was not commenced in a federal court.
    2. Bank should be able to use the factual determination in favor of Doris in the first case as a shield to the claims of Paul in the second action.
    3. Since Carol and Bank are in privity, Paul will be bound by the issues determined in the first case.

    (A) 1 only
    (B) 2 only
    (C) 3 only
    (D) None

Question 34 is based on the following fact situation.

On behalf of herself and the 92 specific students in her class, P brought an FRCP 23(b)(2) class action against D, claiming that D had arbitrarily assigned final grades in a law school course by drawing names and numbers from two different hats. P sought declaratory relief and an injunction, forcing the teacher to withdraw the original grades and submit a new set based upon actually having read the students' papers. While P was a citizen of State X, all of her classmates and D were citizens of State Y. The suit was filed in a U.S. District Court in State Y, which entered a judgment for D after the jury found that P had failed to prove that D did not read the exams. The judgment was affirmed on appeal.

Thereafter, X, one of the students in the class who had received a grade of 65, brought an action against D in a state court in State X, seeking $75,000 in damages for D's alleged failure to actually read X's exam, as a result of which X received his lowest grade in law school.

34. Which of the following statements is correct?
    1. The judgment rendered in the first action is entitled to Full Faith and Credit in the present suit, even if the U.S. District Court had lacked subject matter jurisdiction.
    2. The U.S. District Court lacked subject matter jurisdiction because members of the plaintiff class and D were citizens of the same state (State Y).
    3. Assuming the federal court had subject matter jurisdiction, D can preclude X from seeking to prove that D failed to read the exams, even though X's action seeks to recover monetary damages (rather than injunctive relief).

    (A) 1 alone
    (B) 2 alone
    (C) 3 alone
    (D) None

Question 35 is based on the following fact situation.

P and D had an automobile accident in State X. P, a citizen of State Y, sued D, a citizen of State X, in a State Y court of general jurisdiction. P also attached real property belonging to D in State Y, pursuant to a State Y statute. (You may assume that the attachment was proper.) The land had recently been inherited by D. D was personally served with process at his home in State X. You may assume *Hess v. Pawloski*, 274 U.S. 352 (1927), is no longer "good" law.

35. Which of the following statements is correct?

    1. If State Y has a typical non-resident motorist statute, there is an adequate basis for obtaining personal jurisdiction over D.
    2. Even in the absence of a long-arm statute most courts would probably hold that the attachment of D's property, coupled with notice of suit by personal service, is sufficient to assert personal jurisdiction over D.
    3. Unless D makes an appearance, he will have waived any objection to the court's assertion of personal jurisdiction over him.

    (A) 1 alone
    (B) 2 alone
    (C) 3 alone
    (D) None

Question 36 is based on the following fact situation.

P, who had been employed by D, was fired when D learned that P, who was unmarried, was living with Q. P sued D in the appropriate U.S. District Court, seeking $60,000 for breach of their employment contract, $15,000 for violation of a federal civil rights statute, and $6,000 for damages which D had caused to P's car after P had loaned it to D earlier that year. Q also sued D in the action, claiming $8,000 in damages as a result of P's wrongful termination, since she is now obliged to pay their entire apartment rental herself. Prior to his discharge, P contributed one-half of the rental amount. P and Q are both citizens of State X, while D is a citizen of State Y.

36. Which of the following statements is correct:

    1. The Federal Rules of Civil Procedure do *not* allow all of the claims of P and Q to be joined together in a single action.
    2. A U.S. District Court would *not* have subject matter jurisdiction over Q's claim.
    3. If P failed to assert the claim for damages to his car in this action, it would be barred.

    (A) 1 alone
    (B) 2 alone
    (C) 3 alone
    (D) None

Question 37 is based on the following fact situation.

In a three-car collision, P's car was rear-ended by D, who was in turn rear-ended by E. P brought an action against D in the U.S. District Court in the state in which P was domiciled. P sought to recover $80,000 for damages to his Mercedes. D filed a counterclaim against P, seeking $852 for damages to his Volkswagen. D also filed two claims against E, the driver behind him, one seeking $80,000 in the event that D was liable to P, and the other seeking $852 for the damages caused to D's Volkswagen. P and D are both citizens of State X; E is a citizen of State Y. Judgment was entered for P against D, but all of the other claims were found to be without merit.

E has now filed a lawsuit against P and D in the U.S. District Court in X, seeking $1 million for personal injuries suffered in the earlier auto accident. P and D have each counterclaimed, seeking $1 million for their own personal injuries, and have filed similar crossclaims against each other.

37. Which of the following statements is correct?
    1. The court in the initial action lacked subject matter jurisdiction.
    2. Apart from any possible subject matter jurisdiction problems in the prior suit, E could have filed any claim arising out of the prior accident which he/she had against P.
    3. Apart from any possible subject matter jurisdiction problems in the prior suit, P and D may not assert their claims against each other in the present action.

    (A) 1 alone
    (B) 2 alone
    (C) 3 alone
    (D) All

Question 38 is based on the following fact situation.

P brings an action against D, E and F, asserting (1) infringement of copyright, and (2) breach of contract. Copyright actions are exclusively within the subject matter jurisdiction of federal courts. All of the claims arose from the defendants' having produced a television show based upon a script which P had written for them. P seeks to recover $75,000 apiece from the defendants. All of the parties are citizens of California.

38. Which of the following statements is correct?
    1. If this action were filed in a California state court, the defendants could *not* have it removed to federal court.
    2. If this action were filed in federal court, dismissal for lack of subject matter jurisdiction would be required.
    3. If this case goes to trial in a state court, and judgment is entered against P, P will have waived any lack of subject matter jurisdiction by failing to assert it before or during trial.

    (A) 1 alone
    (B) 2 alone
    (C) 3 alone
    (D) None

Question 39 is based on the following fact situation.

P, the publisher of a magazine, announced that D was the winner of a $5,000 prize for the best poem of the month. Before P had awarded the prize to D, however, P received a letter from E. E claimed that he had written the poem and D's entry was stolen from either him or F, E's agent. P, who is a citizen of State X, brought a statutory interpleader action in the appropriate U.S. District Court against D and E, seeking a declaratory judgment as to which of them was entitled to the prize money. D is a citizen of State Y, and E is a citizen of State X.

39. Which of the following statements is correct?
    1. The federal court lacks subject matter jurisdiction over this action.
    2. Apart from any possible subject matter jurisdiction problems, E may file a claim in this action against his agent, F, a citizen of State X, seeking $5,000 from F in the event that the prize money is awarded to D.
    3. Venue would be proper in either State X or Y.

    (A) 1 alone
    (B) 2 alone
    (C) 3 alone
    (D) None

Question 40 is based on the following fact situation.

Plaintiff, a citizen of Arizona, sued Defendant, a citizen of the state of Washington, in the U.S. District Court in Arizona for breach of contract, seeking $77,000 in damages. Defendant answered by denying that a contract was even formed. Plaintiff and Defendant each stipulated that the jury would consist of eight persons. Trial was held, and seven jurors voted in favor of Plaintiff. One juror voted for Defendant. The jurors then deliberated on the amount of damages and rendered a verdict in favor of Plaintiff for $18,500. Defendant appealed the ruling.

40. On which of the following grounds would Defendant be most likely to prevail on appeal?

    (A) The ruling was defective because rendered by less than twelve jurors.
    (B) The ruling was defective because based on a non- unanimous vote.
    (C) The court did not have subject matter jurisdiction, because the verdict was not in excess of $75,000.
    (D) The court lacked personal jurisdiction.

Question 41 is based on the following fact situation.

An automobile accident occurred in State Y involving P, Q and a vehicle driven by an employee of D. The car in which P and Q were riding was a Mercedes which they had purchased together for $79,000 (P contributing $40,000 towards the purchase price, and Q the remaining $39,000). The car was destroyed in the collision. P and Q are citizens of State X, and D is a corporation organized under the laws of State Z, with its principal place of business in Y. It does business in all 50 states. One year after the accident, P and Q sued D to recover a total of $79,000 in damages for the loss of their car.

41. Which of the following statements is correct?
    1. If this suit was properly commenced in a state court in State Y, D could **not** have the action removed to a federal court.
    2. If this action was filed in the U.S. District Court in State W, D could probably successfully have the action transferred to a U.S. District Court in State Y; but the federal court in State Y would have to apply the statute of limitation which the U.S. District Court in State W would have applied.
    3. Subject matter jurisdiction does not exist because neither P nor Q had invested a sum in excess of $75,000 in the car.

    (A) 1 alone
    (B) 2 alone
    (C) 3 alone
    (D) None

Question 42 is based on the following fact situation.

T, a citizen of Texas, is trustee of a trust set up by G, also a citizen of Texas. The beneficiaries, A, B and C, are citizens of New Jersey. The terms of the trust provide that the res is to be invested only in "community businesses." X persuades T to buy real estate for the trust, knowing that such a purchase would probably violate its terms. X, a citizen of Texas, had convinced T that the land was very valuable, but X actually knew that it was worthless. T bought the real estate for the trust for $78,000. A and B sued T in the only U.S. District Court in New Jersey for violating the terms of the trust. You may assume that a decision in this action would, under New Jersey res judicata principles, be binding upon C.

42. Which of the following statements is true?

(A) The court could probably order C to be joined as an involuntary plaintiff.
(B) Personal jurisdiction and venue requisites aside, if (1) T impleads X on the basis that the latter defrauded the former, and (2) the court determines that the fraud is distinct from the issue of T's breach of his fiduciary duties to the trust beneficiaries, the court would be obliged to dismiss the *T v. X* claim.
(C) Personal jurisdiction and venue requisites aside, if T properly impleaded X, the plaintiffs could *not* assert a claim against X for $78,000 since X was impleaded by T.
(D) None.

Question 43 is based on the following fact situation.

An automobile accident occurred in State Y involving P, Q and a vehicle driven by an employee of D. The car in which P and Q were riding was a Mercedes which they had purchased together for $79,000 (P contributing $75,000 towards the purchase price, and Q the remaining $4,000). The car was destroyed in the collision. P and Q are citizens of State X, and D is a corporation organized under the laws of State Z, with its principal place of business in Y. It does business in all 50 states. One year after the accident, P and Q sued D to recover a total of $79,000 in damages for the loss of the car.

43. Which of the following statements is correct?

1. If this suit was properly commenced in a state court in State X, D could *not* have the action removed to a federal court.
2. If this action was filed in the U.S. District Court in State W, D could probably successfully have the action transferred to a U.S. District Court in State Y; but the federal court in State Y would have to apply the statute of limitation which the U.S. District Court in State W would have applied.
3. Subject matter jurisdiction does *not* exist because neither P nor Q had invested a sum in excess of $75,000 in the car.

(A) 1 alone
(B) 2 alone
(C) 3 alone
(D) None

Questions 44-45 are based on the following fact situation.

Phil was driving his car in San Diego, California, when he was involved in an accident with Dowd. Phil lives in San Diego. Dowd is a citizen of Alabama, but the registered owner of the car which Dowd was driving is Ellwood (a citizen of Kentucky). Phil filed an action against Dowd in the appropriate U.S. District Court in California. The complaint contained a proper subject matter jurisdiction allegation.

44. The complaint alleged only that there was a collision between the cars driven by Phil and Dowd, and that the former suffered personal injuries and property damage in the amount of $80,000. If Dowd filed a motion to dismiss for failure to state a claim upon which relief could be granted, the court would probably:

(A) Overrule the motion, without leave to amend.
(B) Grant the motion, with leave to amend.
(C) Overrule the motion, since Phil's complaint fails to identify the legal theory upon which his claim is predicated.
(D) Grant the motion, but only if the applicable statute of limitation under California law had expired.

45. The complaint contained a proper subject matter jurisdiction allegation and asserted that (1) the collision was caused by Dowd's negligence in driving into the rear of Phil's car while Phil was lawfully stopped at a red light, or (2) alternatively, the collision was caused by Dowd's negligence in driving through a red light and into Phil while the latter was lawfully driving through an intersection. Phil alleged personal injuries and properly damages in excess of $80,000. If Dowd filed a motion to dismiss for failure to state a cause of action upon which relief can be granted, the court would probably:

(A) Grant the motion, on grounds of inconsistency.
(B) Grant the motion, since Phil has pleaded a legal conclusion (i.e., that Dowd was negligent in his conduct).
(C) Overrule the motion, since alternative grounds for relief are permissible under the FRCP.
(D) Overrule the motion, but require Phil to strike one of the inconsistent claims.

Question 46 is based on the following fact situation.

P is a citizen of New York who works in New Jersey. D and E are citizens of New Jersey who work in that state. One day, D borrowed E's car, advising the latter that he intended to use it to pick up his sister in Trenton (the capital of New Jersey). However, D drove to New York to take a new girlfriend to Coney Island (which is in Brooklyn, New York). Unfortunately, D became involved in a traffic accident with P while driving in New York City. P brought an action against E in the proper U.S. District Court in New York for personal injuries and property damages in the amount of $85,000. A New York statute permits an action against the owner of a motor vehicle where he/she loaned the car to the person who was driving it when the incident occurred.

46. If E makes an FRCP 12(b)(2) motion to dismiss the action for lack of personal jurisdiction, he should:

(A) Prevail, since the assertion of personal jurisdiction over him would probably violate due process.
(B) Prevail, unless New York had a long-arm statute which specifically authorized service of process upon an out-of-state citizen in circumstances such as these.
(C) Lose, because federal courts have nationwide service of process,
(D) Lose, because New York law specifically extends liability to E in circumstances such as these.

Question 47 is based on the following fact situation.

P is incorporated in State X, but has its principal place of business in State Z. P corporation is licensed to do business in every state, except W. P filed an action against D Insurance Company and E. D is a corporation existing under the laws of State Y, where it has its principal place of business. D also does business in States X and Z. E, a natural person, is a citizen of Ontario, Canada. P's claim against E arises out of a fire occurring at P's plant in State X. P's claim against D is for breach of contract, based upon D's refusal to pay P the proceeds under a fire insurance policy which P had purchased from D. Both claims are for $100,000.

47. Which of the following statements is correct?
    1. If this action were filed in the U.S. District Court for State Z, subject matter jurisdiction would exist and venue would be proper.
    2. If this action was properly commenced in a State W court, the defendants could remove the action to the appropriate U.S. District Court, even though the action could not have been commenced in a U.S. District Court in State W.
    3. P's joinder of D and E in one action is *not* proper, since P is asserting two distinct causes of action.

    (A) 1 alone
    (B) 3 alone
    (C) 1 and 2
    (D) None

Question 48 is based on the following fact situation.

P suffered personal injuries of a permanent nature in an auto accident with D and E. D and E were each driving separate cars. P's insurance company, X, paid P the maximum limit of $100,000 under the policy. Having collected from her insurance company, P then brought an action against D in the proper U.S. District Court, seeking $500,000 for her personal injuries. You may assume that the "collateral source" rule is in effect in this jurisdiction (i.e., a plaintiff's recovery in tort from a defendant is *not* diminished by any insurance or other collateral sources which reimbursed the former for all or any portion of his/her damages). P is a citizen of State X, and D and E are citizens of State Y.

48. Which of the following statements is correct?
    1. D may object to P's bringing this action on the ground that the insurance company, rather than P, is the real party in interest (under the insurance agreement X is subrogated to P's rights to the extent that P's claim against D is paid by X).
    2. If D contends that the accident was caused exclusively by the negligence of E, D may implead E seeking to recover $78,000 from the latter for the damages which E caused to D's car.
    3. Whether or not D files a claim against E, E may intervene as of right as a defendant and file actions for her damages against both P and D.

    (A) 1 and 2 only
    (B) 2 and 3 only
    (C) 3 only
    (D) None

Question 49 is based on the following fact situation.

Delbert liked to cut across Pat's land on his way to law school. Pat, however, disliked Delbert because the latter had become somewhat arrogant since he had made the Law Review. When Pat asked Delbert to cease utilizing the shortcut, he responded that his time was "extremely valuable" and therefore it was "private necessity" that he continue to traverse Pat's land. Pat instituted an action against Delbert in the appropriate U.S. District Court, demanding that the latter be enjoined from utilizing her land. You may assume that competency and jurisdictional requisites are satisfied. Although her real property had not been injured by Delbert's constant encroach ments, she also requested nominal monetary damages.

49. Which of the following statements is correct?

    (A) Delbert is entitled to a jury trial with respect to the trespass issue.
    (B) Delbert is not entitled to a jury trial on the trespass claim, since the primary relief Pat is seeking is an injunction.
    (C) As a consequence of the "clean-up doctrine," the court, in its discretion, may decide both the legal and equitable issues.
    (D) There is no right to a jury trial because trespass was not a "suit at common law" under the Seventh Amendment.

Question 50 is based on the following fact situation.

P, a citizen of State X, and Q, a citizen of State Y, sued D, a citizen of State Z for breach of contract occurring in State Z. The action was filed in the U.S. District Court in State Y, and D was *improperly* served. Upon learning of the suit, D made a successful motion to transfer the case to the U.S. District Court in State Z.

50. Which of the following statements is correct?

    1. The federal court properly transferred the action to State Z.
    2. The federal court in State Y should have dismissed the action because venue in the U.S. District Court in State Y was improper.
    3. The federal court in State Y should have denied D's motion to transfer the case since he was improperly served.

    (A) 1 alone
    (B) 2 alone
    (C) 3 alone
    (D) None

Questions 51-53 are based on the following fact situation.

E, a State X corporation, designed a building for Smith, a citizen of State Y, six years ago. Part of that building collapsed last year, causing damages in excess of $80,000.

Smith has filed an action against E in the U.S. District Court in State X, alleging that his damages resulted from the negligent design of the building. E filed an answer denying negligence and asserting as an affirmative defense that the statute of limitation for negligence is two years.

At the time the building was being constructed, Jones, an attorney and member of E's board of directors, who occasionally handled legal matters for E, prepared and sent the following memorandum to the president of E:

> "I have been informed by Tom Withers, an architect who used to work for E, that the materials being used by the contractor, Builder Corp., in constructing the building are substandard."

Smith filed a timely motion for the pre-trial production of the Jones memorandum. The motion was denied.

Smith filed a timely motion for summary judgment, relying on an affidavit made by Withers which set forth facts consistent with Jones' memorandum. E also filed a motion for summary judgment, accompanied by an affidavit that the building had been constructed six years ago. Both motions were denied.

51. If E asserted the work product privilege in response to Smith's motion for production of Jones's memorandum:

    (A) E should prevail, because Jones was an attorney.
    (B) E should prevail, because it reflects Jones' Impressions about E's potential liability.
    (C) Smith should prevail, because it is relevant to his action.
    (D) Smith should prevail, if Jones is not representing E in the present action.

52. Smith's motion for summary judgment was properly denied because:

    (A) Based upon Withers' affidavit, genuine issues of fact remain as to the negligence of E.
    (B) Withers' affidavit did not address E's affirmative defense.
    (C) Because of the reason set forth in Choice (B), but not Choice (A).
    (D) Because of the reasons set forth in Choices (A) and (B).

53. E's motion for a summary judgment was:

    (A) Improperly denied, because the building was constructed six years ago.
    (B) Improperly denied, because Smith failed to file a responsive affidavit.
    (C) Properly denied, because the accident occurred only recently.
    (D) Properly denied, if E has the burden of proof with respect to its statute of limitation defense.

Question 54 is based on the following fact situation.

P and D were involved in a car accident in Texas. P is a citizen of State X and D is a citizen of New York. D owned several apartment houses in California, and kept a summer home in that state. You may assume that the State X service of process statute is similar to FRCP 4. P sued

D in a State X court of general jurisdiction. P served D by sending, via first class mail, the summons and complaint to D in New York. D received these documents, but failed to respond to them. P then obtained a default judgment.

54. If P sought to enforce the judgment in New York:

    (A) The judgment should be given Full Faith and Credit by a New York court, since D had actually received the summons and complaint.
    (B) D may collaterally attack the judgment for insufficient service of process.
    (C) The judgment should be given Full Faith and Credit because a default judgment is usually deemed to be "on the merits."
    (D) Choices (A) and (C) are correct, but not (B).

Question 55 is based on the following fact situation.

P commenced an action against D in a State X court of general jurisdiction. D is a citizen of State Z and P is a citizen of State X. D owned a boat which he kept at a pier in Houston, Texas. Pursuant to Texas law, P obtained an attachment against D's boat. When properly served with notice of the attachment, D moved to quash it. The boat is probably worth $20,000. P's action is for breach of contract and alleges damages in the amount of $15,000.

55. Which of the following statements is correct?

    (A) The attachment should be quashed, if a Texas court could not constitutionally assume personal jurisdiction over D.
    (B) Pre-judgment attachments are, per se, unconstitutional.
    (C) If D's motion was denied, P could apply all of the proceeds from sale of the boat to his/her obligation.
    (D) Choices (A) and (B) are correct, but not (C).

Question 56 is based on the following fact situation.

P, a citizen of Utah, was involved in an auto accident with D, a citizen of Minnesota. The accident occurred in Utah. Pursuant to the applicable Utah long-arm statute, P sued D in a Utah state court of general jurisdiction for $80,000. P also named C as a defendant. C was D's insurer. Pursuant to Utah law, this type of action was permissible. C is incorporated in Delaware and has its principal place of business in Utah.

56. D's petition to remove the case to the applicable U.S. District Court should be:

    (A) Granted, because D is not a citizen of Utah.
    (B) Denied, because C's principal place of business is Utah.
    (C) Denied, if C joins in the petition.
    (D) Granted, because the amount in controversy requirement is satisfied.

Question 57 is based on the following fact situation.

P commenced an action for copyright infringement against D, claiming that the latter had plagiarized portions of a book which the former had written. The action was properly commenced in the U.S. District Court in New York (the state in which D was domiciled). Federal courts have exclusive jurisdiction over copyright claims. P's complaint also included a claim for unfair business practices, as permitted by New York law. After the trial had commenced (but before a verdict was rendered), it was proven by D that P had failed to file his copyright with the appropriate federal agency. As a consequence, no claim for copyright infringement under federal law could be successfully asserted. However, it was still possible for P to obtain a favorable verdict with respect to the unfair business practices claim.

57. The U.S. District Court:

    (A) Must dismiss the entire action, since federal subject matter jurisdiction is lacking.
    (B) May, in its discretion, dismiss the action or hear the state law claim.
    (C) Should remand the action to a state court of general jurisdiction which is within the judicial district in which the U.S. District Court is located.
    (D) Should never have permitted P to assert a state law claim, since federal courts have exclusive jurisdiction over copyright claims.

Question 58 is based on the following fact situation.

Dr. Dumb, a citizen of State A, performed emergency surgery upon Pam, a citizen of State B, for which he charged $3,000. Pam was injured during the surgery and she thereafter filed a negligence lawsuit against Dr. Dumb in the appropriate U.S. District Court in State A for $85,000. Dr. Dumb impleads Insurance Co., a corporation incorporated in State B and doing business in States A and B, for payment on his malpractice insurance policy if Pam should win her lawsuit.

58. Which of the following causes of action may be joined?

    1. A $1,000 counterclaim by Dr. Dumb against Pam for damage done when Pam, angry at the results of the operation, broke Dr. Dumb's office window, if the counterclaim is deemed to be permissive in nature.
    2. A claim by Pam against Insurance Co. for the non- payment of a claim of $80,000 on a car insurance policy she maintained with Insurance Co. when her car was stolen, if Insurance Co.'s principal place of business is in State A.

    (A) 1
    (B) 2
    (C) Both
    (D) Neither

Question 59 is based on the following fact situation.

A properly commenced a diversity action in the applicable U.S. District against B. A claimed that he and B had entered into a valid contract, that the latter had repudiated the agreement, and that as a consequence A had sustained economic losses in the amount of $90,000. B answered by denying the existence of a contractual agreement. At trial, B attempted to introduce evidence that A had made an anticipatory repudiation of the alleged agreement prior to the time that B's performance was due. If this assertion were correct, B would have an affirmative defense to A's action (even if a valid contract had been formed).

59. Assuming A made a timely objection to the introduction of B's evidence pertaining to anticipatory repudiation:

    (A) His objection must be sustained, because the evidence is outside the pleadings.
    (B) The evidence may be admitted, in the discretion of the court.
    (C) The objection must be sustained, because amendments to pleadings cannot be made after trial has been commenced.
    (D) The evidence must be admitted, since it is relevant to B's defense (if it is admitted, however, A is entitled to a continuance to meet such evidence).

Question 60 is based on the following fact situation.

The State X Rules of Civil Procedure are basically equivalent to the FRCP. Paul sued Donna in a State X court, alleging that, at Donna's home, Donna hit Paul on the head with a hammer, and that Paul suffered injuries in the amount of $15,000.00. Donna moved to dismiss the case, but her motion was denied. Paul then amended his complaint to add as damages the lost wages resulting from having to miss work. Donna answered by denying that she hit Paul, and, as an affirmative defense, claimed that she hit Paul because he was attacking her. Paul then moved for summary judgment based on an affidavit signed by his cousin, Bill, stating that Paul had told him that Donna struck Paul out of jealousy (rather than because Paul was attacking her).

60. Which of the following statements is correct?

    (A) Donna's motion to dismiss should have been granted, since Paul did not state his legal theory.
    (B) Donna's pleadings are defective because they are inconsistent, answering that she did not hit Paul and also stating as a defense the reason why she had hit Paul.
    (C) Paul's amendment is permissible, even without leave of the court,
    (D) Paul's summary judgment motion should be granted because it was supported by an affidavit.

Question 61 is based on the following fact situation.

X, a citizen of Oregon, sued Y, a large Colorado corporation doing business only in Colorado. The action asserted that Y had failed to provide training, support and service for a $76,000 computer system which Y had sold to X. X sued Y in the U.S. District Court in Oregon. Although the contract was accepted and signed in Colorado, there was a provision which stipulated that in the event of litigation, Y could be sued by X in Oregon. Y moved for transfer of the action to the U.S. District Court in Colorado, claiming that its training, support and service personnel, who would be witnesses, are domiciled in Colorado. The Colorado damage remedies are more favorable to Y than the corresponding rules in Oregon.

61. Which of the following statements is correct?

    1. Transfer of the action will probably be granted.
    2. If Y's motion is granted, the law of Oregon regarding damages will be applied.
    3. The provision stipulating that Y would stand trial in Oregon is unconstitutional if Y did not have "minimum contacts" with Oregon.

    (A) 1 only
    (B) 2 only
    (C) 3 only
    (D) None

Question 62 is based on the following fact situation.

Daleon Motors, a Delaware corporation which has its principal place of business in Michigan, created the Daleon automobile. Approximately 3,000 of these vehicles were sold before it was discovered that the brake lining was defective. As a consequence, the car became virtually undrivable after about 500 miles. Paul, a citizen of Rhode Island, purchased a Daleon automobile in that state. He commenced an FRCP 23(b)(3) class action against Daleon on behalf of all of the purchasers of automobile in the U.S. District Court for Rhode Island, contending that the plaintiff class is entitled to return of the purchase price for fraud (Daleon Motors had advertised its car as being the "safest" in the world). Each Daleon car had cost $79,000. After Paul commenced the action, Daleon claimed that its offices had been broken into and its records of Daleon purchasers destroyed. Paul personally knows of two other purchasers of Daleon cars. One is a citizen of New Mexico and the other is a citizen of Delaware.

62. Which of the following statements is correct?

    1. Daleon could successfully make a motion to dismiss the class action, since at least one of the purchasers is a citizen of Delaware.
    2. Notice to the prospective class by publication in the major newspapers throughout the country will probably be permissible (except that mailing to the two known buyers will be required).
    3. Notice to the class may be dispensed with in light of the suspicious destruction of the names and addresses of prospective class members while such data was within Daleon's possession.

    (A) 1 only
    (B) 2 only
    (C) 3 only
    (D) None

Question 63 is based on the following fact situation.

P sued Amusement Co. for injuries sustained when she fell while getting off a ferris wheel at the Amusement Co.'s park. The lock holding the seat had prematurely broken open. At P's suggestion, her boyfriend immediately took pictures of the broken lock. Since the park was still open, Amusement Co. hired a locksmith to replace the lock that same afternoon. In doing the work, the locksmith had to completely disassemble the broken lock. P's attorney hired an expert locksmith to prepare a report and testify at trial regarding the defective nature of the lock. Amusement Co. moved to discover the report prepared by P's expert and the pictures taken by P's boyfriend of the broken lock. P claims both the pictures and the report are covered by the work product privilege.

63. Which of the following statements is correct?

    (A) Amusement Co. may not view the pictures or the report.
    (B) Amusement Co. may view the pictures and obtain the report.
    (C) Amusement Co. may view the pictures but not obtain the report.
    (D) Amusement Co. may not view the pictures, but may obtain the report.

Question 64 is based on the following fact situation.

Acme is a Georgia corporation which has its principal place of business in Alabama. Polly used to live in Alabama and work at Acme's Arkansas plant. However, she was recently terminated from her employment with Acme. She consulted an attorney who advised her that her termination was wrongful under a law recently enacted by Congress. The lawyer also informed Polly that Georgia had the most liberal procedures for prosecuting this type of action. Polly moved to Georgia, where she is now working as a waitress, and commenced an action in the appropriate state court against Acme for wrongful termination under the applicable U.S. law and a similar Georgia statute. Polly seeks $80,000 in damages. Acme filed a petition to remove the case to the U.S. District Court in Georgia.

64. The petition should be:

    (A) Denied, because Polly moved to Georgia only for the purpose of acquiring a litigationally more advantageous forum.
    (B) Denied, because there is a lack of diversity.
    (C) Granted, because one of her actions is a federal claim.
    (D) Granted, because there is no diversity of citizenship (citizenship being determined at the time the cause of action arose).

Question 65 is based on the following fact situation.

Each of twenty persons who are domiciled throughout Texas, Oklahoma and Nebraska, asserted a claim in the amount of $50,000 against XYZ Corp., a Maryland corporation. Their joinder of claims is based upon the assertion that fumes from XYZ's plant in Arkansas caused them minor respiratory problems. XYZ's principal place of business is in Maryland.

65. May the twenty persons sue XYZ Corp. in a U.S. District Court?

    (A) Yes, but *only* if their claim is based upon a federal statute.
    (B) Yes, but *only* if the plaintiffs aggregate their claims in a class action.
    (C) Yes, because diversity of citizenship exists between the entire plaintiff class and XYZ.
    (D) Yes, but *only* if there is diversity of citizenship between the class representative and XYZ.

Question 66 is based on the following fact situation.

P was injured when he attempted to rescue X from a burning car. X and Y had collided at an intersection. P sued Y in the appropriate U.S. District Court, but not X. Y claims that X's conduct was the exclusive cause of the accident which resulted in injury to P, and seeks to join X in the action. Under applicable state law, if X is not named as a defendant and X and Y were joint and several tortfeasors, Y would have no right of contribution from X if a judgment were obtained against Y in the *P v. X* action. P is a citizen of Minnesota, Y is a citizen of Vermont, and X is a citizen of Minnesota.

66. Y's motion should be:

    (A) Granted, because there is a common nucleus of operative facts.
    (B) Granted, because Y's contention that X was responsible for the accident may (at trial) prove to be correct.
    (C) Denied, because X is not an indispensable party.
    (D) Denied, because joinder of X would destroy subject matter jurisdiction.

Question 67 is based on the following fact situation.

Arnold borrowed $76,000 from Bill and signed a promissory note in which he promised to repay that sum, plus interest in six months. Chuck guaranteed the note, promising to pay the sum due to Bill in the event Arnie defaulted. Arnold became delinquent under the note, and Bill sued Arnold. Arnold claimed that he had a usury defense to Bill's claim.

67. Which of the following statements is correct?

    (A) A judgment in favor of Bill is res judicata as to Chuck.
    (B) A judgment in favor of Bill would result in issue preclusion against Chuck as to those issues which had been fully litigated in *Bill v. Arnold.*
    (C) If Arnold won on the issue of usury, Chuck could probably assert collateral estoppel in an action brought by Bill against Chuck on the guaranty.
    (D) None of the above.

Question 68 is based on the following fact situation.

Paul loaned $78,000 to Jim. Ralph guaranteed the loan. Subsequently, Jim became delinquent in his payments. Paul sued Jim in the appropriate U.S. District Court. Paul is a citizen of State X and Jim is a citizen of State Y. Ralph is a citizen of State X.

68. Which of the following statements is correct?

    (A) Ralph is an indispensable party, because Jim could otherwise be liable for the full amount of Paul's judgment.
    (B) The court would probably permit Ralph to intervene on Jim's side, if the former chose to do so.
    (C) Ralph may intervene on Jim's side as of right, since otherwise he could be precluded from raising any issues which were fully and fairly litigated in Paul's action against Jim (if Paul subsequently sued Ralph on the guarantee).
    (D) None of the above.

Question 69 is based on the following fact situation.

Polly, a citizen of Nevada, purchased $7,000 of ABC Corporation securities from her broker, Don, also a citizen of Nevada. However, because ABC was insolvent, the securities were later shown to be worthless. Polly sued Don in the appropriate U.S. District Court for violation of federal securities law.

69. Which of the following claims maybe joined?

    1. *Polly v. Don* for injuries caused when Don's car rear-ended Polly's car following a party they both attended.
    2. *Don v. ABC Corporation,* a Nevada corporation, because, as part of his contract to sell ABC securities, the latter entity warranted its solvency to Don.

    (A) 1
    (B) 2
    (C) 1 and 2
    (D) Neither 1 or 2

Question 70 is based on the following fact situation.

P sues D for trespass at her Los Angeles residence. The action was properly commenced in a U.S. District Court. D defends by claiming that he was in New York at the time when the incident allegedly took place. D intends to call Wanda as a witness to testify that she saw him in New York on the day in question. P believes Wanda is hopelessly nearsighted and could easily have mistaken someone else for D. In order to impeach Wanda's testimony, P sends Wanda a Notice to Appear for Medical Examination before a licensed ophthalmologist selected by P.

70. Which of the following statements is correct?

    (A) W must appear, but D is entitled to a copy of the ophthalmologist's findings.
    (B) W must appear, since her eyesight is in issue.
    (C) W need not appear, because she is not a party to the action.
    (D) W need not appear, because physicians making medical examinations must be selected by the judge.

Question 71 is based on the following fact situation.

Denny, a citizen of Texas, leased an apartment from Polly, a citizen of California, under a one-year rental agreement at $500 per month. The rental agreement states that Denny may sublet the premises to any person who is not of Oriental ancestry. With six months remaining on the lease, Denny sublet the apartment to a Chinese person. Polly sued Denny in the appropriate U.S. District Court for breach of contract, seeking to evict Denny and recover the remaining six months' rent. The complaint stated that Denny violated the terms of the rental agreement, and asserts that the clause concerning subletting does *not* violate the U.S. Constitution. Denny moves to dismiss the case for lack of subject matter jurisdiction.

71. With respect to Denny's motion:

    (A) Denny will win because subject matter jurisdiction based upon a federal claim is lacking.
    (B) Denny will win because subject matter jurisdiction based upon diversity is lacking.
    (C) Both A and B.
    (D) Denny will lose.

Question 72 is based on the following fact situation.

Mel is an investment banker. He handles the accounts of Ms. Wine and Ms. Ball. Mel decided to invest some of their money in a new entrepreneurial enterprise he had just started. Unfortunately, things did not go well. In a period of months, all of Wine's and Ball's money was gone. Ball sued Mel for breach of a fiduciary duty. She recovered a default judgment for the full amount of her claim.

72. Which of the following statements is correct?

    (A) Ball's judgment is res judicata with respect to a subsequent lawsuit by Wine against Mel.
    (B) Assuming the mutuality doctrine is inapplicable, a court may permit Wine to assert collateral estoppel in a subsequent lawsuit by Wine against Mel.
    (C) Ball's judgment should have no effect upon a subsequent lawsuit by Wine against Mel.
    (D) None of the above.

Question 73 is based on the following fact situation.

P sues as the sole representative of a class of persons who had bought limited partnership interests in worthless oil producing property from D. P alleges that all purchasers received identical written sales materials (which contained numerous misrepresentations), and that many members of the class also received verbal "pitches" which were also fraudulent. P commenced an FRCP 23(b)(3) class action based upon diversity subject matter jurisdiction against D in the appropriate U.S. District Court.

73. Which of the following statements is correct?

    (A) If the court refuses to certify the proposed class, P may appeal the decision immediately.
    (B) Assuming the class is certified, P may enter into a settlement agreement with D, so long as notice is given to all members of the class and a majority approve of the compromise.
    (C) Assuming the class is certified, if P prevails in the suit he is not entitled to recover attorney's fees unless a federal statute explicitly provides for such an award.
    (D) None of the above.

Question 74 is based on the following fact situation.

Art and Bob were riding in a car driven by Art, when they were suddenly rear-ended by Oscar. Art is a citizen of Illinois and Oscar is a citizen of Ohio. Art commenced a lawsuit in the appropriate U.S. District Court of Ohio (where the accident had occurred), claiming $80,000 in injuries and damages as a result of the occurrence. Bob (a citizen of Ohio) seeks to intervene. However, his injuries were far less severe than those suffered by Art. Bob has been informed by his attorney that he would probably not be able to recover more than $8,000.

74. Bob's motion to intervene should be:

    (A) Granted, because there is ancillary jurisdiction.
    (B) Granted, because he is an indispensable party.
    (C) Denied, because there is no subject matter jurisdiction over his claim against Oscar.
    (D) Denied, unless Bob in good faith believes that his attorney's calculation of potential damages is incorrect.

Question 75 is based on the following fact situation.

Bill and Joe were riding in a car owned by Ellwood. Bill is a citizen of Georgia and Joe is a citizen of Arkansas. They were involved in an accident in Tennessee with Carl (a citizen of Alabama). Insurco is a Georgia corporation, which has its principal place of business in Alabama. Ellwood is a citizen of Texas. Melvin, a citizen of Alabama, who was visiting his uncle in Tennessee when the accident occurred, was injured while extricating Bill and Joe from their vehicle. Melvin and Carl have threatened to sue Ellwood, contending that he is vicariously liable for the alleged negligence of Joe (who was driving the car). Insurco contends that it is not liable for Joe's driving, but commences an interpleader action against Bill, Joe, Carl, Ellwood and Melvin in the U.S. District Court in Alabama. The policy limit of Ellwood's insurance is $75,000. Carl and Melvin claim personal injuries in excess of that amount.

75. Which of the following statements is correct?

    (A) The action is appropriate under "statutory" interpleader.
    (B) The action is appropriate under "rule" interpleader.
    (C) Under statutory or rule interpleader the U.S. District Court would be obliged to refer to the long-arm statute enacted in Tennessee to determine if personal jurisdiction could be asserted over the defendants.
    (D) Interpleader is inappropriate, since Insurco is contending that it is not liable under the policy.

Questions 76-78 are based on the following fact situation.

Joan visited Dr. Brown. After examining her, he put some drops in her left ear. She then left. However, she continued to have difficulties with her balance. Three weeks after her visit to Dr. Brown, Joan fell and sustained serious injuries. Joan sued Dr. Brown and requested a jury trial. The action was properly commenced in a U.S. District Court. At trial, Joan testified to the foregoing, and then called Dr. Edward to the stand. He testified that, in his opinion, (1) he had examined Joan and found substantial damage to her inner ear, (2) the damage was caused by a fluid containing acid. Joan rested her case. Dr. Brown took the stand and testified that (1) Joan had been suffering from an infection which affected the inner ear, and (2) he had put some drops of perforium (an innocuous, non-acidic substance) into her ear. He further stated on cross-examination that the bottle containing perforium stood in the vicin ity of a bottle containing an acidic substance. He then rested his case. In rebuttal, Joan called Dr. Edward who stated that the injury to Joan's inner ear is totally inconsistent with Dr. Brown's assertion of an infection. All sides then rested.

76. If Joan moves for a directed verdict:

    (A) Her motion should be granted because of the admission of the non-movant, Dr. Brown, that the perforium bottle stood near a bottle containing an acidic substance.
    (B) Her motion should be granted, but not for the reason set forth in (A).
    (C) Her motion should be denied.
    (D) None of the above.

77. Assume that Dr. Brown (rather than Joan) moved for a directed verdict, and that the motion was granted. Joan then appeals. The Court of Appeals should:

    (A) Reverse the judgment and order a new trial.
    (B) Reverse the judgment and direct that judgment be entered for Joan.
    (C) Affirm the judgment.
    (D) None of the above.

78. Assume that neither party moved for a directed verdict. The case goes to the jury which returns a verdict for Joan. Dr. Brown then moves for a J.N.O.V. and, in the alternative, for a new trial. The trial judge grants the motion for a J.N.O.V., but denies the motion for a new trial. Joan then appealed the J.N.O.V granted by the trial court. The Court of Appeals should:

    (A) Reverse the judgment, since a motion for a new trial cannot be joined with a J.N.O.V.
    (B) Affirm the judgment.
    (C) Reverse the judgment, but order a new trial.
    (D) Reverse the judgment and reinstate the verdict for Joan.

Question 79 is based on the following fact situation.

X, a citizen of Kentucky, entered into a contract to sell a car to Z, also a citizen of Kentucky. However, when Z was late in tendering a prepayment, X advised Z that he was no longer bound to complete the transaction. Z unequivocally informed X that the contract was still binding. Prior to the due date for delivery of the auto mobile under the original agreement, X entered into a new transaction with Y, whereby X agreed to sell the vehicle to Y for a higher amount than had been agreed to by Z. Y is a citizen of Ohio. Y was aware of the outstanding contract which X had with Z, but was assured by the former that Z's right in the automobile had been lawfully terminated. X subsequently repudiated his contract with Y, contending that it was entered into under coercive circumstances. Y commenced an action against X in the appropriate U.S. District Court for specific performance and breach of contract. X moved to dismiss upon the ground that Z was an indispensable party.

79. The court will probably:

    (A) Grant the motion, because Z has an interest in the vehicle.
    (B) Grant the motion, because Z entered into an agreement with X for purchase of the car prior to Y.
    (C) Deny the motion, because ancillary jurisdiction will permit the court to exercise subject matter jurisdiction over Z.
    (D) Deny the motion, because a court in equity and good conscience could proceed with the action.

Questions 80-82 are based on the following fact situation.

Paul was a citizen of Colorado. He was an employee of Construction Company, a Colorado Corporation. Paul was killed one day when some scaffolding collapsed. The scaffolding had been provided by a subcontractor for the job, Big Builders (a U.S. corporation). Paul's wife, Mary, as the executrix of his estate, sued Construction Company. She had moved to South Dakota just prior to commencing the lawsuit. The action is brought in the only U.S. District Court in Colorado on the theory that Construction Company had been negligent in failing to inspect the defective scaffolding supplied by Big Builders. Colorado law provides that a general contractor is presumed to have not inspected materials supplied to it by a subcontractor. This presumption is rebuttable. At the time of his death, Paul owed Construction Company $7,000 in advanced wages. The amount claimed by Mary is $1,000,000.

80. Which of the following statements is correct?

    (A) Big Builders may intervene as a matter of right.
    (B) Construction Company can implead Big Builders, if personal jurisdiction and venue requirements are satisfied.
    (C) Construction Company could assert a counterclaim for the advance in wages which it made to Paul.
    (D) None of the above.

81. At the trial, Construction Company, introduced evidence showing that Paul had been warned by his supervisor not to work near the scaffolding until it had been thoroughly checked, since it looked unsafe. However, Paul had disregarded the supervisor's instruction. Mary had then produced a witness who testified that Paul had always objected to working close to scaffolding. If no further evidence was introduced by either side:

    (A) Construction Company's motion for a directed verdict would have to be granted.
    (B) Construction Company's motion for a directed verdict would have to be denied.
    (C) Mary's motion for a directed verdict would have to be granted.
    (D) If the jury brought in a verdict in favor of Construction Company, Mary's motion for a judgment n.o.v. would have to be granted.

82. Assume that (1) each side introduced substantial evidence pertaining to whether Construction Company had adequately inspected the scaffolding, and (2) the case was tried by the judge. Following the trial, the judge entered findings of fact and conclusions of law. The judge found as a fact (1) Construction Company had adequately inspected the scaffolding, and (2) therefore, Mary was entitled to nothing. Based upon the foregoing:

    (A) The judgment must be set aside, because it is clearly erroneous.
    (B) The judgment must be set aside, because it is inconsistent with the applicable presumption.
    (C) The finding of fact must be set aside, because there was substantial evidence which controverted it.
    (D) None of the above.

Question 83 is based on the following fact situation.

Paul was rear-ended by John, a 17-year old. The car that John was driving was owned by Mary. Paul is a citizen of Vermont. John and Mary (who is John's mother) are citizens of Maine. The accident occurred in Vermont. Paul sued Mary and John in the U.S. District Court in Maine pursuant to a Vermont statute which made parents liable for the negligent driving of their minor children. The suit demanded $90,000 in damages.

83. Which of the following statements is correct?

    (A) Mary may assert a cross-claim against John.
    (B) If Mary fails to assert a cross-claim against John, any claim by her against him will be barred.
    (C) Mary may not assert a cross-claim against John.
    (D) Mary may assert a counterclaim against John.

Questions 84-85 are based on the following fact situation.

Albert had written a best selling book called "The Trials and Tribulations of a First-Year Law Student." However, he began to suspect that the publisher, Beacon House, a Virginia Corporation whose principal place of business is in that state, was not giving him an accurate accounting of his royalties. Albert invaded a meeting of the nine-member Board of Directors of Beacon House, where he found Don (a member of the Board of Directors and the President of Beacon House). When Albert verbally accused Don of cheating him by downscaling the number of Albert's books which had actually been sold, Don grabbed Albert by the shoulders and shouted, "Shut up, you idiot!" Albert then punched Don in the face and left. Albert went to the local newspaper (called "The Star") and advised them that he had been cheated out of thousands of dollars by Don. The Star then printed a story reiterating Don's accusations, and warning writers of how easy it is for publishers to deprive them of an accurate accounting of royalties. The story mentioned that Don was the President of Beacon House. Albert is a citizen of Arizona, Don is a citizen of Massachusetts, and The Star is incorporated in New York and has its principal place of business in Arizona.

84. Assume that The Star was sued by Beacon House for defamation in the U.S. District Court in Arizona. The lawsuit alleged damages of $500,000. Which of the following statements is correct?

    (A) The Star cannot successfully implead Albert, because they are citizens of the same state.
    (B) Albert can intervene as of right on the side of The Star.
    (C) The Star may implead Albert on the ground that he is solely liable to Beacon House.
    (D) The Star probably can implead Albert.

85. Assume that (1) Beacon House sued both the Star and Albert in the only U.S. District Court in Arizona for defamation, claiming damages in the amount $100,000, (2) the "mutuality rule" for collateral estoppel has been abandoned in this jurisdiction, and (3) a verdict was returned in favor of Beacon House in the amount of $50,000. Which of the following statements is correct?

    (A) The Star could not file a cross-claim against Albert, because they are citizens of the same state.
    (B) If Albert counterclaimed against Beacon House for an accounting on his royalties, he would not be entitled to a jury trial.
    (C) Don might be able to assert collateral estoppel offensively against The Star in a subsequent action for defamation against that entity.
    (D) Don would be barred from commencing an action against The Star or Albert, since he could have intervened in the present action (*Beacon House* v. *The Star* and *Albert*) without destroying diversity.

Question 86 is based on the following fact situation.

X left a will creating a trust for the benefit of A, B, C and D, with T as trustee. A owns 25% of the trust, B owns 25%, C owns 25%, and D owns 25%. A, B and C are citizens of California; D and the trustee are citizens of Ohio. A, B and C sue T in the U.S. District Court in Ohio, based on diversity, for distribution of the $10 million trust, claiming that the terms of the trust require immediate distri bution of the res. T interprets the provisions of the trust to permit distribution only after three additional years. For tax purposes, D is content to have the trust continue for three more years. T moves to dismiss the action for failure to join D as an indispensable party.

86. The motion should be:

    (A) Denied, because diversity is not defeated as long as any defendant is diverse from any plaintiff, and the amount in controversy exceeds $75,000.
    (B) Denied, because D's interests are more consistent with T's.
    (C) Granted, because there will be a lack of diversity if D is joined as plaintiff.
    (D) Granted, because D is an indispens-able party.

Question 87 is based on the following fact situation.

Plaintiff sued Defendant in a State X court. The Federal Rules of Civil Procedure are followed in State X. Plaintiff seeks to recover for personal injuries suffered as a result of a battery inflicted upon him by Defendant. Defendant simply denied Plaintiff's allegations. Plaintiff demanded trial by jury. Along with the forms for a general verdict, the court submitted written interrogatories to the jury. In answering these interrogatories, the jury found that: Defendant had hit Plaintiff with a vase; that Defendant intended to so hit Plaintiff; that Defendant caused Plaintiff damages as alleged in the complaint. The jury also returned a judgment against Plaintiff. The judge then ordered a new trial. Plaintiff then filed a stipulation of voluntary dismissal, which was also signed by Defendant.

87. Which of the following statements is correct?

    (A) Plaintiff may later bring an action against Defendant on the same facts.
    (B) Where the jury's answers to interroga-tories conflict with a general verdict, the judge must enter a verdict in con-formity with the such answers.
    (C) Where a jury's answers to interroga-tories conflict with a general verdict, the judge must (1) enter the general verdict, or (2) order a new trial.
    (D) None of the above.

Question 88 is based on the following fact situation.

Don, while traveling to a nearby relative's house, is injured by a vehicle which was negligently operated by an Acme employee who was using his car for an Acme business purpose. After initiating an action against Acme (but prior to trial), Don seeks to discover if Acme has insurance.

88. Assuming this jurisdiction follows the FRCP, which of the following are correct re-garding discovery of the insurance policy covering the Acme vehicle?

    (A) If the insurance policy is not admis-sible at trial, the insurance policy is not discoverable.
    (B) Insurance maintained by a party is never discoverable.
    (C) Discovery of an insurance policy may be obtained where the insurer may be liable for all or part of a judgment entered against the insured.
    (D) Insurance is discoverable only where it is relevant to the prima facie issues of the case.

Question 89 is based on the following fact situation.

Andy Attorney is a new associate at a prestigious downtown law firm. He is involved in a major federal securities fraud case in the local U.S. District Court. Andy has noticed and taken many depositions in the case, but is now confronted with the following allegations:

1. Andy's examination of a witness was conducted in a manner designed to embarrass the deponent.
2. Andy failed to attend a deposition which he had scheduled for another party.
3. Although a party who was deposed by Andy was not represented by counsel, Andy nevertheless insisted upon carrying out the deposition.
4. Andy objected to almost every question asked his client at a deposition, and all answers were made subject to Andy's objections.

89. Which of the foregoing assertions could result in sanctions against Andy and his client?

(A) 1 and 2
(B) 2, 3, and 4
(C) 2 and 4
(D) 2 only

Question 90 is based on the following fact situation.

Ripoff Corporation has engaged in price fixing, causing persons who purchased their stereo equipment to have paid $50 per item more than required. Mark Music sues Ripoff in an appropriate U.S. District Court for a federal anti-trust violation as representative of the class of persons who have bought Ripoff stereo equipment within the applicable statute of limitations. The class is certified under FRCP23(b)(3). The following notice is prepared for mailing to all class members (approximately 125,000 persons):

> "You are hereby notified that a class action has been brought in U.S. District Court under Rule 23(b)(3) of the Federal Rules of Civil Procedure by Mr. Mark Music on behalf of all persons who have purchased Ripoff stereo equipment. You may opt out of the class within one month of this notice. If you choose to remain in the action, you may appear through an attorney."

90. Which of the following statements is correct?

(A) If Mark is unable to pay the costs of mailing notice to all 125,000 class members, the court may, in its discretion and for good cause shown, order Ripoff to pay these costs.
(B) If a class member opts out and Ripoff prevails at trial, Ripoff can assert collateral estoppel against such individual in a subsequent lawsuit by the latter.
(C) The notice to class members is not adequate.
(D) None of the above.

Question 91 is based on the following fact situation.

Counselor Carlos Clark has been retained to defend WDM Corporation, an international micro-chip kingpin, in a federal anti-trust action commenced by Plaintiff, a corporation, in the appropriate U.S. District Court. After Clark sought discovery of a large volume of documents from Plaintiff, Plaintiff advised Clark that it objected to Carlos' discovery requests on the following grounds:

1. The documents sought are privileged.
2. The information is factual in nature and relates to the Plaintiff's claims.
3. The documents sought were not calculated to lead to the discovery of admissible evidence.
4. The evidence sought is obtainable from a less expensive source.

91. Which, if any, of the foregoing objections might be valid?

(A) 1, 3, and 4
(B) 1 and 2
(C) 1 and 3
(D) 2 and 4

Question 92 is based on the following fact situation.

P filed an action against D Corporation for material breach of contract and misrepresentation in the sale of a home located in a subdivision. An agent of D allegedly represented to P that the property was in excellent condition and ready for occupancy. Actually, P found that (1) the plumbing was defective, and (2) there were termites in the basement. Prior to filing the action, P's attorney consulted with an economist concerning Ps damages.

92. Which of the following statements is correct?

(A) Discovery of the economist's opinion cannot be obtained because it constitutes work product.
(B) The opinion of an expert is discoverable.
(C) The opinion of an expert is discoverable only if it is solicited or obtained prior to the commencement of litigation.
(D) Discovery of an expert's opinion is privileged.

Question 93 is based on the following fact situation.

Plaintiff sued Defendant in a State X court of general jurisdiction for injuries suffered in an auto accident in State X. Plaintiff is a citizen of State X and Defendant is a citizen of State Y. State X is a comparative negligence state. The jury finds Defendant 80% at fault, and Plaintiff 20% at fault, and rules that Defendant must pay Plaintiff $16,000 for the latter's injuries. Since all of Defendant's assets are in State Y, Plaintiff sued Defendant on State X judgment in a State Y court. State Y is a contributory negligence state.

93. Assuming the State X decision is final, which of the following statements is correct?

(A) Res judicata precludes Plaintiff from suing on the State X judgment in State Y because the two actions involve the same parties and the same occurrence.
(B) Full faith and credit need not be granted to the State X judgment.
(C) The State Y court may hold a trial de novo because that jurisdiction does not recognize comparative negligence.
(D) State Y must grant full faith and credit to the U.S. District Court judgment in State X, if Defendant had a full and fair opportunity to litigate on the merits.

Question 94 is based on the following fact situation.

A sued B, seeking personal injuries and property damage in the amount of $100,000 for B's negligence in causing a collision with a car driven by A. A lost, with the jury expressly finding that B was not negligent. Thereafter, C (a pedestrian walking along the street when he saw the accident) suffered back injuries when he attempted to extricate A from the latter's vehicle. C sued B, claiming B negligently caused the accident with A's car, and was therefore responsible for C's personal injuries. In the latter action, B made a motion to dismiss based upon the decision rendered in A's earlier lawsuit.

94. The court:

(A) May grant B's motion, because it has discretion to determine if it will apply collateral estoppel principles.
(B) Must grant B's motion, because C's action is barred under res judicata principles.
(C) Should deny B's motion, because it may not apply collateral estoppel in the context of the facts presented.
(D) Should deny B's motion, only if the concept of mutuality of estoppel is not applied in this jurisdiction.

Questions 95-97 are based on the following fact situation.

Dodo is a State X partnership composed of Jim Do and Bob Do. They manufacture and lease large ovens which are used in restaurants. Dodo's only plant and business office is in State X. Three months ago, the president of Dominic's (a fashionable eating spot in State Z) made a trip to State X and leased an oven from Dodo. Dominic's is incorporated in State Z, where its restaurant is located. The stock of Dominic's is held by Carl, Fred and Alice. The Do brothers are domiciled in State X. Two weeks ago, Paul (an employee of Dominic's) was hurt when the "door" of the leased oven suddenly fell open upon him. Paul sued both Dodo and Dominic's in the U.S. District Court in State Z. Jim and Bob Do were personally served in State X. Dominic's was served pursuant to a State Z statute which permits notice of the lawsuit to be (1) left with someone of "suitable discretion" at the defendant's home or main business premises, or (2) if no such person is available, posted on the door which is most often used by the occupants of the defendant's home or main business premises. Paul's process server utilized the latter method. The president of Dominic's saw the notice and delivered the summons and service of process to the corporation's attorneys.

95. To determine if subject matter jurisdiction is proper, it would be helpful to know:

1. The domicile of the shareholders of Dominic's.
2. The domicile of Paul.
3. If State Z has a long-arm statute.
4. The extent of Paul's injuries.

(A) 1 and 3
(B) 2 and 4
(C) 3 and 4
(D) 2 and 3

96. With respect to the notice given to Dominic's, which of the following statements is probably the most accurate?

(A) Under these circumstances, it is constitutionally invalid.
(B) It is invalid because it failed to comply with the FRCP.
(C) It is valid because the corporation received actual notice of Paul's action.
(D) It is valid because the FRCP authorizes service of process in accordance with the law of the state in which it is located.

97. In determining if the assertion of personal jurisdiction over Dodo is proper, which of the following factors are pertinent?

    1. The State Z long-arm statute.
    2. Whether Dodo was aware where the leased range would be used.
    3. Whether Dodo presently does any other business in State Z (whether or not that business is unrelated to the lease Dominic's).
    4. The physical health of Jim and Bob Do.

    (A) 1, 2, and 3
    (B) 2, 3, and 4
    (C) 1, 2, and 4
    (D) 1 and 2

Questions 98-100 are based on the following fact situation.

Paul sued his employer, Acme Corporation, in the proper U.S. District Court in State X, claiming that (1) Dan (an Acme supervisor) had defamed him by informing the president of Acme that Dan was an ineffectual employee, and that this statement was within the scope of Dan's employment at Acme, and (2) Acme owed Dan $15,000 in unused vacation pay. As a consequence of both harms, Paul claimed damages in the aggregate amount of $80,000. Acme responded to Paul's complaint by initially making an FRCP 12(b) motion to dismiss Paul's complaint on the grounds that Dan was an indispensable party and that subject matter jurisdiction was lacking since the two claims aggregated by Paul to satisfy the "in excess of $75,000" requirement did not arise out of the same transaction or occurrence. (You may assume that the court could not obtain personal jurisdiction over Dan.) This motion was denied. Acme then filed an answer which admitted Dan's statement, but denied that it was made within the scope of Dan's employment and asserted the affirmative defense of truth. Paul then filed a summary judgment motion, with his personal supporting affidavit, describing facts which demonstrated that he had performed his job competently. Acme failed to respond to Paul's summary judgment motion.

98. Which of the following statements is correct?

    (A) Dan is an indispensable party.
    (B) Paul may not aggregate unrelated claims to meet the jurisdictional amount.
    (C) Dan is probably not an indispensable party.
    (D) Choices (B) and (C), but not (A).

99. Paul's motion for a summary judgment should be:

    (A) Granted, because Acme failed to respond with an affidavit which disputed Dan's assertions.
    (B) Granted, because there is no genuine issue of fact.
    (C) Denied, because the affidavit was made by a party to the action.
    (D) Denied, because material issues of fact remain.

100. Assume for purposes of this question that (1) Paul never made a motion for summary judgment, (2) the jury rendered a general verdict in favor of Acme, and (3) the mutuality rule has been repudiated in this jurisdiction. If Paul now sued Dan (claiming the latter had defamed him), which of the following statements is correct?

    (A) Dan could probably assert res judicata principles to avoid liability.
    (B) Dan could probably assert collateral estoppel principles to avoid liability.
    (C) Dan probably could not assert collateral estoppel principles to avoid liability.
    (D) Choices (A) and (B), but not (C).

1. **(A)** U.S. DISTRICT COURTS ARE COMPETENT TO HEAR CASES INVOLVING A FEDERAL CLAIM (I.E., ONE ARISING UNDER THE CONSTITUTION, A TREATY OR THE LAWS OF THE U.S.). The correct answer is A. Paul's claim is based upon violation of a ***state*** statute. It does ***not*** arise under the U.S. Constitution, a treaty or a federal law. Thus, Denton's motion should be granted. Choice B is incorrect because, while Denton is asserting a ***defense*** based upon the U.S. Constitution, competency based upon a "federal question" is analyzed only from the viewpoint of the claim being asserted by the plaintiff. Choice C is incorrect because no federal claim has been asserted by Paul. Finally, Choice D is incorrect because Paul's claim does not arise under the U.S. Constitution.

2. **(C)** FOR "DIVERSITY" SUBJECT MATTER JURISDICTION TO EXIST, (1) NO PLAINTIFF AND NO DEFENDANT MAY BE CITIZENS OF THE SAME STATE, AND (2) THE AMOUNT IN CONTROVERSY MUST EXCEED $75,000, EXCLUSIVE OF INTEREST AND COSTS. The correct answer is C. Since (1) the plaintiffs are citizens of Florida, and D is a citizen of Michigan and Delaware (a corporation is deemed to be a citizen of the states in which it is incorporated and has its principal place of business), and (2) each plaintiff is claiming damages in excess of $75,000, "diversity" subject matter jurisdiction is satisfied. Choice D is incorrect because D is also a citizen of Michigan. Choice A is incorrect because diversity subject matter jurisdiction is not dependent upon the place of plaintiff's injury. Finally, Choice B is incorrect because a corporation is a citizen of the state in which it is incorporated and has its principal place of business. The fact that D was headquartered in Florida would not deprive the court of "diversity" subject matter jurisdiction.

3. **(B)** CASES BASED UPON "FEDERAL QUESTION" SUBJECT MATTER JURISDICTION MUST BE COMMENCED IN THE JUDICIAL DISTRICT IN WHICH (1) ANY OF THE DEFENDANTS RESIDE, OR (2) WHERE THE CAUSE OF ACTION AROSE. WHEN VENUE IS IMPROPER, A U.S. DISTRICT COURT, MAY, ON ITS OWN MOTION OR ON THE MOTION OF ANY DEFENDANT, TRANSFER THE ACTION TO ANOTHER U.S. DISTRICT COURT IN WHICH THE MATTER COULD HAVE ORIGINALLY BEEN COMMENCED OR DISMISS THE LAWSUIT; 28 U.S.C. 1406(a). The correct answer is B. Since the action could have been commenced in either California (where the defendant resides) or Texas (where the discrimination took place), it may be transferred to the proper federal judicial district in either of those states. Choice D is incorrect because the court may ***not*** retain the action since the (1) defendant does not reside in Nevada, and (2) cause of action did not arise in Nevada. Choice A is incorrect because the action may be transferred to either California or Texas. Finally, Choice C is incorrect because the action may be transferred to any U.S. District Court where the litigation may have originally been commenced.

4. **(C)** A LACK OF SUBJECT MATTER JURISDICTION MAY ORDINARILY BE RAISED AT ANY TIME THROUGHOUT A LEGAL PROCEEDING. IN STATE COURTS, AN OBJECTION TO PERSONAL JURISDICTION IS ORDINARILY DEEMED TO BE WAIVED BY A GENERAL APPEARANCE. The correct answer is C. Since federal courts have ***exclusive*** subject matter jurisdiction with respect to admiralty claims, the State A court was not competent to render a valid judgment (despite being a court of general jurisdiction). Choice B is incorrect because a lack of personal jurisdiction is ordinarily waived by a general appearance. Choice A is incorrect because Derek is likely to prevail only upon the lack of subject matter jurisdiction objection. Finally, Choice D is incorrect

because the State A court was not competent to render a judgment in this matter, even though any possible objection to personal jurisdiction was probably waived by Derek's general appearance.

5. **(B)** WHERE A SUIT IS PROPERLY COMMENCED IN A STATE COURT AND "FEDERAL CLAIM" SUBJECT MATTER JURISDICTION IS SATISFIED, THE ACTION MAY BE REMOVED TO THE U.S. DISTRICT COURT WHICH IS IN THE JUDICIAL DISTRICT THAT ENCOMPASSES THE STATE COURT, IF (1) ALL OF THE DEFENDANTS JOIN IN THE PETITION FOR REMOVAL, AND (2) REMOVAL IS SOUGHT WITHIN 30 DAYS FROM THE TIME THE MOVING PARTY RECEIVED SERVICE OF PROCESS. The correct answer is B. Since the action involves a federal claim, Defendant is entitled to have the litigation removed to the appropriate U.S. District Court. Choice A is incorrect because, where removal is otherwise proper, the fact that the action could not have originally been commenced in the U.S. District Court to which it is removed is irrelevant. Choice C is incorrect because state courts of general jurisdiction are ordinarily competent to hear federal claims. Finally, Choice D is incorrect because citizenship is ***not*** pertinent where removal is based upon a federal claim.

6. **(C)** U.S. DISTRICT COURTS ARE COMPETENT TO HEAR CASES INVOLVING A FEDERAL CLAIM (I.E., ONE ARISING UNDER THE CONSTITUTION, A TREATY OR THE LAWS OF THE U.S.). The correct answer is C. Since Acme is asserting a federal claim against the Steamroller's Union, subject matter jurisdiction exists (even though the amount in controversy does ***not*** exceed $75,000). Choices A and B are true in that (1) there is no diversity, since an unincorporated association is deemed to be a citizen of each state in which ***any*** of its members are domiciled (Acme and Steamroller's are therefore each citizens of Indiana), and (2) the amount in controversy does not exceed $75,000. However, subject matter jurisdiction still exists because a federal claim is involved (i.e., one arising under a U.S. statute). Finally, Choice D is incorrect because a federal, rather than state, claim has been asserted.

7. **(C)** UNDER ***STATUTORY*** INTERPLEADER, A U.S. DISTRICT COURT IS COMPETENT WHERE (1) ***ANY*** TWO OF THE DEFENDANT/CLAIMANTS ARE CITIZENS OF DIFFERENT STATES, AND (2) THE AMOUNT INVOLVED IS $500 OR MORE. IN A STATUTORY INTERPLEADER ACTION, VENUE IS PROPER IN ANY JUDICIAL DISTRICT IN WHICH ANY OF THE CLAIMANTS RESIDE. The correct answer is C. Since venue is proper only in a judicial district in which a defendant/claimant resides, a U.S. District Court would be obliged to either dismiss the action or to transfer it to a U.S. District Court where the lawsuit could have been commenced. The citizenship of the plaintiff/stakeholder is irrelevant for purposes of determining subject matter jurisdiction in a statutory interpleader case. Choice A is incorrect because Sam's citizenship would ***not*** be imputed to Harry. However, even if it were, diversity of citizenship for a statutory interpleader action would still exist because Sam and Jay are citizens of different states (i.e., Texas and New York). Choice B is incorrect because the jurisdictional amount for statutory interpleader cases is only $500 or more. Finally, Choice D is incorrect because Choices A and B are (as discussed above) erroneous.

8. **(C)** A SUMMONS AND COMPLAINT MAY ***NOT*** ORDINARILY BE DELIVERED BY A PERSON WHO IS A PARTY TO THE ACTION; FRCP 4(c)(2)(A). The correct answer is C. Since Pete is the plaintiff and personally delivered the summons and complaint to Doris, service should be quashed. Choice A is incorrect because Big Time did receive ac-

tual notice of the pending lawsuit through the service upon Doris (service upon a corporate president is deemed to constitute notice). Choice B is incorrect because the fact that Doris was not an officer at the time at which the answer was due is irrelevant. Finally, Choice D is incorrect because service of the summons and complaint was made by Pete.

9. **(A)** A PERSON WHO IS ***NOT*** A PARTY SHOULD BE JOINED WHERE FAILURE TO DO SO WILL LEAVE ANY PARTY TO THE ACTION SUBJECT TO A SUBSTANTIAL RISK OF INCURRING MULTIPLE LIABILITY FOR A SINGLE OBLIGATION. IF THE COURT DETERMINES THAT IN EQUITY AND IN GOOD CONSCIENCE THE ACTION SHOULD BE DISMISSED IN THE NON-PARTY'S ABSENCE, HE/SHE IS REGARDED AS BEING INDISPENSABLE. WHERE THE JOINDER OF AN INDISPENSABLE PARTY WILL DESTROY SUBJECT MATTER JURISDICTION, A FEDERAL COURT MUST DISMISS THE ACTION; FRCP 19. The correct answer is A. Where an action is dismissed because of the failure to join an indispensable party, the court's decision is ***not*** deemed to be on the merits. Thus, dismissal of an action upon this ground would have no res judicata effect. Krooke would probably be considered an indispensable party, since failure to join him in the action would expose Bank to multiple liability (i.e., Krooke could subsequently sue Bank for the full amount of the savings account, since the decision in the *Plaintiff v. Bank* action would not be binding upon him). Choice B is incorrect because the fact that dismissal of the action will result (since diversity would be destroyed), is not, in itself, a justification to refuse to join an indispensable party. Choice C is incorrect because the fact that diversity exists between Plaintiff and Bank would not preclude dismissal for lack of subject matter jurisdiction if Krooke were joined (plaintiff and Krooke both being citizens of the same state). Finally, Choice D is incorrect because (in addition to Statement 2 being incorrect) there is no pendent jurisdiction in this instance. The pendent jurisdiction doctrine is applicable only to a situation where a state cause of action is appended to a federal claim which has been asserted in a U.S. District Court. The facts do not indicate that Plaintiff's claim is based upon the Constitution, a treaty, or a federal law.

10. **(C)** THERE MUST BE SUBJECT MATTER JURISDICTION WITH RESPECT TO A CLAIM FILED BY THE PLAINTIFF AGAINST A THIRD-PARTY DEFENDANT (I.E., THE IMPLEADED PARTY). The correct answer is C. Since P and T are both citizens of Idaho, diversity subject matter jurisdiction is lacking. Choice D is incorrect because the fact that diversity exists between P and D is irrelevant with respect to the plaintiff's action against T. Choice A is incorrect because the pendent jurisdiction doctrine is applicable only to situations where the plaintiff is attempting to attach a state cause of action to a federal claim. Here, P is attempting to assert an action against an additional party (rather than seeking to add a state cause of action to a federal claim). Choice B is incorrect because the U.S. Supreme Court has specifically rejected the application of ancillary jurisdiction to this type of situation; *Owen Equipment & Erection Co. v. Kroger*, 437 U.S. 365 (1978).

11. **(B)** UNDER THE DOCTRINE OF PENDENT JURISDICTION, A U.S. DISTRICT COURT MAY, IF A FEDERAL CLAIM EXISTS, PERMIT THE PLAINTIFF TO APPEND ANY STATE CLAIMS ARISING FROM A "COMMON NUCLEUS OF OPERATIVE FACTS" WITH THE FEDERAL CLAIM; *United Mineworkers v. Gibbs*, 383 U.S. 715 (1966). The correct answer is B. Choice A is incorrect because there is no amount in controversy requirement with respect to federal claims; 28 U.S.C. 1331. Choice C is incorrect because the U.S. District

Court would not have subject matter jurisdiction based upon diversity since the amount in controversy, against each defendant, does not exceed $75,000. Finally, Choice D is incorrect because Statement 2 is true.

12. **(A)** FULL FAITH AND CREDIT MUST BE GIVEN TO AN OUT-OF-STATE DEFAULT JUDGMENT IF IT WAS OBTAINED IN A PROCEDURALLY AND CONSTITUTIONALLY VALID MANNER. The correct answer is A. The court in California, even though one of general jurisdiction, was not competent to hear this matter (i.e., the facts stipulate that patent infringement cases are within the exclusive jurisdiction of federal courts). Thus, the California judgment is not procedurally sound and would not be entitled to Full Faith and Credit by a New York court. Choice B is incorrect because service of process within a jurisdiction has traditionally been recognized as a valid means of obtaining personal jurisdiction over an out-of-state defendant. Choice C is incorrect because a defendant who fails to appear in an out-of-state action does not waive his/her right to later collaterally attack the constitutional and procedural aspects of that default judgment. Finally, Choice D is incorrect because Statement 1 is true.

13. **(D)** WHERE (1) NO PLAINTIFF AND NO DEFENDANT ARE CITIZENS OF THE SAME STATE, AND (2) THE AMOUNT IN CONTROVERSY ***EXCEEDS*** $75,000, EXCLUSIVE OF INTEREST AND COSTS, DIVERSITY SUBJECT MATTER JURISDICTION EXISTS. The correct answer is D. The majority view is that the "amount in controversy" requirement is satisfied as long as the benefit or cost to one of the two parties is not, to a "legal certainty," $75,000 or less. Since P has alleged damages only in the total amount of $75,000 (rather than an amount ***in excess*** of $75,000) the amount in controversy requisite is not satisfied.

14. **(A)** IN ALL AVERMENTS OF FRAUD OR MISTAKE, THE CIRCUMSTANCES CONSTITUTING FRAUD OR MISTAKE SHALL BE STATED WITH PARTICULARITY; FRCP 9(b). The correct answer is A. While the FRCP ordinarily requires only "a short and plain statement of the claim showing that the pleader is entitled to relief" (FRCP 8), fraud claims must be stated with specificity. Choice B is incorrect because the assertion of a fraud constitutes an exception to the general rules for pleading in federal court. Choice C is incorrect because the manner of pleading prescribed by the FRCP would be controlling in the event of conflict with an otherwise applicable state rule of pleading; *Hannah v. Plummer*. Finally, Choice D is incorrect because statement 1 is true.

15. **(D)** THE FACT THAT TWO OR MORE PLAINTIFFS ARE CITIZENS OF THE SAME STATE, OR TWO OR MORE DEFENDANTS ARE CITIZENS OF THE SAME STATE, DOES ***NOT*** DESTROY DIVERSITY. The correct answer is D. Choice A is incorrect because "diversity" requires that no plaintiff and no defendant be citizens of the same state. Choice B is incorrect because plaintiffs are not "compelled" to join their actions simply because their claims arise out of the same transaction or series of transactions. Their joinder is permissive. Finally, Choice C is incorrect because D's motion would probably be denied (rather than granted) if the conditions described in that selection are satisfied.

16. **(D)** IN AN FRCP 23(b)(3) CLASS ACTION IN FEDERAL COURT, EACH MEMBER OF THE CLASS MUST SATISFY THE "AMOUNT IN CONTROVERSY" REQUIREMENT WHERE FEDERAL COURT COMPETENCY IS BASED UPON DIVERSITY; *Zahn v. International Paper*

Co., 414 U.S. 291 (1973). The correct answer is D. Choice A is incorrect because the diversity requirement is satisfied by the fact that no plaintiff and no defendant are citizens of the same state. Choice B is incorrect because a federal court is not ***required*** to dismiss the action because the claims of most of the representatives are not in excess of $75,000, exclusive of interest and costs. However, the representatives and members of the class whose claims did not satisfy the "amount in controversy" requisite would have to be deleted from the class. Finally, Choice C is incorrect because the claims of the class representatives cannot be aggregated to satisfy the amount in controversy requirement.

17. **(D)** WHERE A SUIT IS PROPERLY COMMENCED IN A STATE COURT AND FEDERAL DIVERSITY REQUIREMENTS WOULD BE SATISFIED, THE ACTION CAN BE REMOVED TO THE U.S. DISTRICT COURT WHICH IS IN THE JUDICIAL DISTRICT THAT ENCOMPASSES THE STATE COURT, IF: (1) NO DEFENDANT IS A CITIZEN OF THE STATE IN WHICH THE ACTION WAS BROUGHT, (2) ALL OF THE DEFENDANTS JOIN IN THE PETITION FOR REMOVAL, AND (3) REMOVAL IS SOUGHT WITHIN 30 DAYS OF THE TIME THE PARTY SEEKING REMOVAL RECEIVED SERVICE OF PROCESS. The correct answer is D. Statement 1 is incorrect because the *D v. P* action is not removable since the latter is a citizen of the state (New York) in which the action has been commenced. Statement 2 is incorrect because, even if the state court was competent to hear this matter, P (being a citizen of New York) could not remove the action to the applicable U.S. District Court. Finally, Statement 3 is correct because D's action against P does not appear to have arisen "out of the transaction or occurrence" which is the subject of P's lawsuit against D (the latter litigation involving the failure to manufacture and deliver restaurant equipment). Thus, it was not a compulsory counterclaim.

18. **(A)** THE CORRECT ANSWER IS A. STATEMENT 1 IS THE ONLY CORRECT STATEMENT FOR THE FOLLOWING REASONS. UNDER FRCP 14, A DEFENDANT IS PERMITTED TO SERVE A THIRD-PARTY COMPLAINT AND THUS IMPLEAD A PERSON WHO IS "NOT A PARTY TO THE ACTION" IF THAT PERSON "IS OR MAY BE LIABLE" TO THE DEFENDANT/THIRD-PARTY PLAINTIFF "FOR ALL OR PART OF THE PLAINTIFF'S CLAIM AGAINST THE THIRD-PARTY PLAINTIFF." HERE, BAKER DID NOT SEEK THE IMPLEADER ACTION BECAUSE CHANCE "IS OR MAY BE LIABLE" TO ABLE, HE SOUGHT IMPLEADER BASED ONLY UPON CHANCE'S UNPAID BAR BILL AND FAILURE TO PAY FOR A USED CAR WHICH BAKER SOLD TO CHANCE." THUS, STATEMENT 1 IS TRUE. Statement 2 is false. Under 28 U.S.C. 1367, supplemental jurisdiction will extend to all claims that are part of the same "case or controversy" unless specifically excluded by this statute. Only those claims which arise from the same transaction or occurrence are part of the same "case or controversy." Here, Chance can only assert those claims against Baker that arise from the same transaction or occurrence, not ANY claims he has against Baker. The unpaid bar bill might be considered to be part of the same transaction or occurrence, but the failure to pay for the used car almost certainly would not. Also statement 3 is false. As noted above, supplemental jurisdiction applies to impleader actions; thus, there is no requirement for diversity between either the impleaded and impleading parties or the plaintiff and the impleaded party (third-party defendant). However, unless there is an independent ground for subject matter jurisdiction (diversity and amount), the plaintiff may not assert any claims against the third-party defendant. In general, there are two issues to address when a party seeks to add a new party or claim in a federal court action. The first issue is whether the joinder rules allow the addition of the new party or claim.

FRCP 14 governs third-party claims. So the first issue is satisfied if the defendant impleads a person who is "not a party to the action" if that person "is or may be liable" to the defendant/third-party plaintiff "for all or part of the plaintiff's claim against the third-party plaintiff." Thus, the only way Baker can implead Chance is if he claims that Chance "is or may be liable" to Baker for all or part of Able's claims. The second issue is whether the new party or claim is supported by federal subject matter jurisdiction. For impleader actions under FRCP 14, supplemental jurisdiction will extend to all claims that are part of the same "case or controversy" unless specifically excluded by the supplemental jurisdiction statute. In other words, the claims must arise out of the same transaction or occurrence.

19. **(C)** AN AMENDMENT CHANGING THE DEFENDANT RELATES BACK TO THE ORIGINAL COMPLAINT IF (1) IT AROSE OUT OF THE CONDUCT, TRANSACTION OR OCCURRENCE SET FORTH IN THE ORIGINAL PLEADING, (2) IT IS WITHIN THE PERIOD PROVIDED BY LAW FOR COMMENCING THE ACTION AGAINST THE NEW PARTY, (3) THE NEW PARTY RECEIVED SUCH NOTICE OF THE INSTITUTION OF THE ORIGINAL ACTION THAT HE/SHE WOULD NOT BE PREJUDICED IN MAINTAINING HIS/HER DEFENSE, AND (4) THE NEW PARTY KNEW OR SHOULD HAVE KNOWN THAT, BUT FOR A MISTAKE CONCERNING THE IDENTITY OF THE PROPER PARTY, THE ACTION WOULD HAVE BEEN BROUGHT AGAINST HIM/HER; FRCP 15(c). The correct answer is C. Since the statute of limitations has run against Richard, the complaint can no longer be amended to include the latter person. Statements 1 and 2 are untrue because the second element of the four-part test is not satisfied.

20. **(A)** A PARTY ASSERTING A CLAIM AGAINST A SINGLE DEFENDANT MAY JOIN ANY INDEPENDENT CAUSES OF ACTION WHICH HE HAS AGAINST THE LATTER; FRCP 18(a). PERSONS MAY BE JOINED AS DEFENDANTS IF (1) THERE IS ASSERTED AGAINST THEM JOINTLY, SEVERALLY, OR IN THE ALTERNATIVE, ANY RIGHT ARISING OUT OF THE SAME TRANSACTION, OCCURRENCE, OR SERIES OF TRANSACTIONS OR OCCURRENCES, AND (2) ANY QUESTION OF LAW OR FACT COMMON TO ALL DEFENDANTS WILL ARISE IN THE ACTION; FRCP 20(a). A COURT MAY, HOWEVER, ORDER SEPARATE TRIALS OF ANY CLAIM (OR CROSS-CLAIM) TO (1) AVOID PREJUDICE, AND (2) PROMOTE JUDICIAL ECONOMY; FRCP 42(b). The correct answer is A. Subject to FRCP 42(b), Paul could assert an unrelated breach of contract action against Mary. Statement 2 is incorrect because Peter's cross-claim must arise out of the transaction or occurrence for ancillary jurisdiction to apply. Thus, subject matter jurisdiction is lacking with respect to Peter's counterclaim since the "amount in controversy" requirement is not satisfied. Finally, Statement 3 is incorrect because a plaintiff may aggregate personal injury and property claims to satisfy the "in excess of $75,000" requirement necessary for diversity subject matter jurisdiction.

21. **(B)** IN A CLASS ACTION BASED UPON DIVERSITY SUBJECT MATTER JURISDICTION, NO PLAINTIFF AND NO DEFENDANT MAY BE CITIZENS OF THE SAME STATE; BUT ONLY THE CITIZENSHIP OF THE REPRESENTATIVE(S) IS CONSIDERED. IN A DIVERSITY CASE, THE PROPER JUDICIAL DISTRICT FOR VENUE PURPOSES IS WHERE (1) ANY OF THE DEFENDANTS RESIDE, OR (2) THE CLAIM "AROSE." FOR VENUE PURPOSES, UNINCORPORATED ASSOCIATIONS ARE USUALLY DEEMED TO "RESIDE" IN ANY JUDICIAL DISTRICT IN WHICH THEY ARE LICENSED TO DO BUSINESS OR ARE DOING BUSINESS. The correct answer is B. Since the plaintiff and the representative of the defendant class are citizens of the same state (Pennsylvania), diversity does not

exist. Thus, the plaintiff's action would have to be predicated upon a federal claim to avoid dismissal. If, however, plaintiff's claim was based upon a federal statute, no diversity requirements would exist. Choice A is incorrect because while venue in Ohio is proper since that is where the union is doing business, it is ***not*** the only judicial district in which an action could be brought. Since railroad property was destroyed in Pennsylvania, if such activity was the basis of the plaintiff's claim, the action could have been commenced in that state as well. Statement C is incorrect because there is no ***per se*** rule that actions involving unincorporated labor organizations are without the subject matter jurisdiction of federal courts.

22. **(C)** WHERE THERE HAS BEEN A PRIOR, VALID JUDGMENT ON THE MERITS BETWEEN THE PARTIES (OR THEIR PRIVIES) WITH RESPECT TO THE CAUSE OF ACTION BEING ASSERTED IN A SUBSEQUENT LAWSUIT, THE DOCTRINE OF RES JUDICATA IS APPLICABLE TO PRECLUDE THE LATTER ACTION. The correct answer is C. The fact that John had obtained a judgment against Bill would not preclude Matt from subsequently contesting John's claim, since Matt is not in privy with Bill. Choice A is incorrect because Bill could sue Matt for indemnity. Choice B is incorrect because a plaintiff is not required to sue every possible defendant in one action. Additionally, a judgment by John against Matt would ***not*** be inconsistent with John's prior verdict against Bill. Finally, Choice D is incorrect because John's claim against Bill for personal injuries is, in most jurisdictions, barred by res judicata principles because this action arose out of the same trans action pursuant to which John's judgment for property loss was obtained.

23. **(A)** A COMPULSORY COUNTERCLAIM IS ONE WHICH ARISES OUT OF THE TRANS ACTION OR OCCURRENCE THAT IS THE SUBJECT MATTER OF THE OPPOSING PARTY'S CLAIM AND DOES NOT REQUIRE FOR ITS ADJUDICATION THE PRESENCE OF THIRD PARTIES OVER WHOM THE COURT CANNOT ACQUIRE JURISDICTION; FRCP 13(a). THERE IS ANCILLARY JURISDICTION WITH RESPECT TO COMPULSORY COUNTERCLAIMS. The correct answer is A. If Steamroller's counterclaim is deemed to be compulsory (as opposed to merely permissive) in nature, ancillary jurisdiction would apply to avoid an assertion by Acme that subject matter jurisdiction is lacking. Choice B is incorrect because, if Steamroller's claim is merely permissive in nature, there would have to be an independent basis of subject matter jurisdiction for it to be assertable in a federal court. Since there is no diversity and Steamroller's cause of action is not based on a federal statute, the U.S. Constitution or a treaty, the counterclaim could ***not*** be asserted in a U.S. District Court. Choice C is wrong because the fact that a state claim is being asserted is irrelevant to determine if federal subject matter jurisdiction is satisfied. Finally, Choice D is incorrect because Steamroller's counterclaim would be permissible (even though diversity does not exist), if it was viewed as being compulsory in nature.

24. **(B)** A PARTY MAY ORDINARILY OBTAIN DISCOVERY OF DOCUMENTS AND OTHER TANGIBLE ITEMS PREPARED IN ANTICIPATION OF LITIGATION OR FOR TRIAL, (1) BY OR FOR ANOTHER PARTY, OR (2) BY OR FOR THAT OTHER PARTY'S REPRESENTATIVE (INCLUDING HIS/HER ATTORNEY), ONLY UPON A SHOWING THAT (1) THE PARTY SEEKING SUCH DISCOVERY HAS A SUBSTANTIAL NEED FOR THE ITEMS, AND (2) HE/SHE IS UNABLE, WITHOUT UNDUE HARDSHIP, TO OBTAIN THE EQUIVALENT THEREOF BY OTHER MEANS; FRCP 26(b)(3). The correct answer is B. This choice, in effect, restates the applicable provision of the FRCP. Choice A is incorrect because, even

if the report had been prepared by Brown in anticipation of litigation or trial, it would still be discoverable if Paul could show a substantial need for the document and that he was unable to otherwise obtain it (or its equivalent) without undue hardship. Choice C is incorrect because the "work product" privilege extends to tangible items created by another party (not just to items prepared by that party's representative). Finally, Choice D is incorrect because the fact that Manco had obtained the report at the suggestion of counsel would not, by itself, make the item non-discoverable. It could still be obtained if Paul could persuade the court that (1) there was a substantial need for it, and (2) he was otherwise unable to acquire it without undue hardship (i.e., the machine was destroyed and Brown cannot be deposed).

25. **(C)** IN U.S. DISTRICT COURTS, THE JUDGE MAY CONDUCT THE VOIR DIRE EXAMINATION; FRCP 47(a). BIAS OR PREJUDICE OF A POTENTIAL JUROR AGAINST ONE OF THE PARTIES IS USUALLY A PROPER SUBJECT FOR INQUIRY AT THE VOIR DIRE. The correct answer is C. The defendant's question with respect to prejudice against corporations was probably an appropriate inquiry upon voir dire, and therefore the judge's refusal to ask potential members of the jury that question was probably erroneous. Choice B is incorrect because the fact that a party may exercise three challenges does not detract from the court's failure to inquire about a general prejudice against corporations. Choice A is incorrect because any question which goes to a juror's ability to reach a fair and impartial verdict is appropriate at the voir dire (questions in this context need bear no relationship to the factual issues which will be contested at the trial). Finally, Choice D is incorrect because the judge may utilize his/her discretion in determining if questions which counsel requests be asked of prospective jurors are appropriate.

26. **(C)** A PLAINTIFF WHO ACCEPTS A REMITTITUR IN FEDERAL COURT MAY NOT CHALLENGE THE TRIAL COURT'S RULING ON APPEAL. The correct answer is C. By accepting the remittitur, and thereby avoiding the delay and cost of a new trial, the plaintiff is deemed to have relinquished his/her right to appeal the court's order. If Paul was dissatisfied with the remittitur, he could have refused to undertake a second trial and appealed the court's order upon the basis that the judge had abused his/her discretion (i.e., there was no good faith basis for reducing the verdict of $75,000 to $25,000). However, if Paul's appeal were unsuccessful, the default judgment obtained by Manco at the second trial would be binding upon him. Thus, the fact that Paul agreed to the reduction "under protest" is irrelevant. Choice A is incorrect because the Seventh Amendment argument is overcome by the fact that the plaintiff is considered to have agreed to the remittitur (i.e., the plaintiff was free to have rejected the remittitur and to have had the case re-tried by a jury). Choice B is incorrect because, whether the trial court abused its discretion or not in ordering a new trial, Paul waived his right to review the court's order by accepting the decreased sum. Finally, Choice D is incorrect because, where a legal claim is involved, the Seventh Amendment is applicable to damage issues.

27. **(A)** A U.S. DISTRICT COURT IS COMPETENT TO HEAR FEDERAL CLAIMS (I.E., CLAIMS ARISING UNDER THE CONSTITUTION, A TREATY, OR THE LAWS OF THE U.S.); 28 U.S.C. 1331. The correct answer is A. Since the plaintiffs are asserting a right under the U.S. Constitution, "federal claim" subject matter jurisdiction exists (regardless of diversity or the amount in controversy). Choice B is incorrect because the court

would have subject matter jurisdiction whether or not (1) there is diversity of citizenship between the plaintiff's representative and the defendants, and (2) the "amount in controversy" requirement was satisfied. Choice C is incorrect because where a federal claim is involved, there ordinarily is no "amount in controversy" requirement. Finally, Choice D is incorrect because (1) for purposes of a class action, diversity of citizenship is analyzed from the viewpoint of the class representatives, on the one hand, and the opposing party or parties, on the other hand, and (2) even if diversity was lacking, the motion would still be denied because competency in this instance is predicated upon a federal claim.

28. **(C)** THERE ARE FOUR PREREQUISITES TO A CLASS ACTION: (1) THE CLASS MUST BE SO LARGE THAT JOINDER OF ALL MEMBERS IS NOT FEASIBLE, (2) THE CLAIMS OR DEFENSES OF THE REPRESENTATIVES MUST BE TYPICAL OF THE CLASS HE/SHE SEEKS TO REPRESENT, (3) THERE MUST BE COMMON QUESTIONS OF LAW AND FACT TO THE CLASS, AND (4) THE REPRESENTATIVE MUST FAIRLY AND ADEQUATELY REPRESENT THE INTERESTS OF THE CLASS; FRCP 23(a). The correct answer is C. Since there is the possibility that many potential members of the class (all college students in State X) would not be desirous of challenging the flag desecration statute, the defendants' "strongest" argument for denying certification of the class would probably be upon this ground. Choice A is incorrect because the class would, in all probability, be sufficiently numerous (there are ordinarily thousands of college students within each state). Choice B is incorrect because there ordinarily is no amount in controversy requisite with respect to the assertion of a federal claim. Finally, Choice D is incorrect because plaintiffs' claim would probably be characterized as a FRCP 23(b)(2) class action, and notice is expressly mandated only with respect to a FRCP 23(b)(3) action. Additionally, (even if due process considerations mandated reasonable notice) it would probably not be impossible to notify the class because persons matriculating at a college presumably disclose their name and address to the institution. Finally, acceptable notice might be possible through college newspapers.

29. **(B)** IF THE TRIAL COURT REFUSED TO CERTIFY THE CLASS, ITS FINDING IS ***NOT*** A FINAL ORDER, AND THEREFORE AN IMMEDIATE APPEAL MAY NOT BE TAKEN THEREFROM. THE CASE MUST BE TRIED AS A NON-CLASS ACTION, AND ONLY AFTER A JUDGMENT IS RENDERED CAN THE CORRECTNESS OF THE TRIAL COURT'S REFUSAL TO GRANT CERTIFICATION BE REVIEWED. The correct answer is B. This result is required as a consequence of the holding in *Coopers & Lybrand v. Livesay*, 437 U.S. 463 (1978). Choice A is incorrect because the "death knell" doctrine was specifically rejected in the decision cited immediately above. Choice C is incorrect because the opposite is true (the party seeking class certification must try the case on the merits before he/she can appeal the trial judge's refusal to permit the class action). Finally, Choice D is incorrect because the existing parties may litigate the case, even though certification of the class has been refused.

30. **(A)** WHERE A STATE ATTEMPTS TO EXERCISE PERSONAL JURISDICTION OVER AN OUT-OF-STATE DEFENDANT, AND NO TRADITIONAL BASIS OF PERSONAL JURISDICTION EXISTS, THERE (1) MUST BE AN APPROPRIATE LONG-ARM STATUTE WHICH PERMITS SERVICE OF PROCESS, AND (2) THE ASSERTION OF SUCH PERSONAL JURISDICTION MUST BE CONSISTENT WITH DUE PROCESS. The correct answer is A. Since Manco was served outside of State X and has no presence within that forum, (1) service of

process must be within the purview of an applicable long-arm statute, and (2) the assertion of personal jurisdiction must comport with due process. The latter element is arguably satisfied because (1) it was reasonably foreseeable that Manco's machinery would ultimately reach State X (since Roe distributed Manco's products in that state), and (2) the impact of the contact (i.e., the injuries to Arnold and Bates) was significant. Choice B is incorrect because U.S. District Courts ordinarily "borrow" (i.e., apply) the long-arm statute of the jurisdiction in which they are located. Thus, with rare exceptions (i.e., statutory interpleader), U.S. District Courts do not have nationwide service of process. Choice C is incorrect because, even if the "amount in controversy" element is satisfied, that would merely establish the court's competency. Subject matter jurisdiction is irrelevant with respect to determining if the assertion of personal jurisdiction is appropriate. Finally, Choice D is incorrect because, where an action is brought in federal court, service of process may be accomplished in accordance with either the FRCP or the applicable state procedural rules; FRCP 4(c)(C)(i).

31. **(C)** A COMPULSORY COUNTERCLAIM IS ONE WHICH ARISES OUT OF THE TRANS ACTION OR OCCURRENCE THAT IS THE SUBJECT MATTER OF THE OPPOSING PARTY'S CLAIM AND DOES NOT REQUIRE FOR ITS ADJUDICATION THE PRESENCE OF THIRD PARTIES OVER WHOM THE COURT CANNOT ACQUIRE JURISDICTION; FRCP 13(a). THERE IS ANCILLARY JURISDICTION WITH RESPECT TO COMPULSORY COUNTERCLAIMS. The correct answer is C. Storeco's counterclaim against Arnold is totally unrelated to the occurrence upon which the latter is contending that the former is liable. Since the amount involved does not exceed $75,000, the U.S. District Court does not have subject matter jurisdiction over Storeco's counterclaim. Choice D is incorrect because Storeco's counterclaim is permissive (rather than compulsory) in nature. Choice A is incorrect because there is no ancillary jurisdiction with respect to permissive counterclaims. Finally, Choice B is incorrect because the fact that Arnold may have consented to personal jurisdiction in State X by commencing the action does not cure the lack of subject matter jurisdiction with respect to Storeco's counterclaim.

32. **(A)** A CROSS-CLAIM ARISING OUT OF THE TRANSACTION OR OCCURRENCE THAT IS THE SUBJECT MATTER OF (1) THE ORIGINAL ACTION, OR (2) A COUNTERCLAIM THEREIN, MAY BE MADE BY ONE PARTY AGAINST ANOTHER; FRCP 13(g). THERE IS ANCILLARY JURISDICTION WITH RESPECT TO CROSSCLAIMS. The correct answer is A. Since Manco's cross-claim against Storeco is unrelated to the plaintiffs' action, it is not permissible (even though there is an independent basis of subject matter jurisdiction). Choice B is incorrect because ancillary jurisdiction is ordinarily applied with respect to permissible cross-claims. However, in this instance, ancillary jurisdiction would not be necessary because diversity and "amount in controversy" requirements would be satisfied. Choice C is incorrect because Manco's cross-claim is ***not*** permissible, regardless of whether or not it might confuse the jury's determination of the original claim. Finally, Choice D is incorrect because, even though there is "diversity" subject matter jurisdiction between Manco and Storeco, this action is unrelated to the underlying claim it may not be asserted.

33. **(B)** WHERE THE PRECISE ISSUE WAS ACTUALLY LITIGATED IN A PRIOR LAWSUIT BY THE PARTY (OR HIS/HER PRIVY) AGAINST WHOM ISSUE PRECLUSION IS BEING ASSERTED IN A SUBSEQUENT ACTION, AND THAT ISSUE WAS ESSENTIAL TO THE DECI-

SION WHICH WAS RENDERED IN THE EARLIER LAWSUIT, ISSUE PRECLUSION WILL ORDINARILY BE APPLIED. The correct answer is B. Federal courts must ordinarily follow the issue preclusion rules of an earlier, valid state court decision; *Marrese v. American Academy of Orthopaedic Surgeons*, 105 U.S. 1327 (1985). Since mutuality is not required in this jurisdiction, collateral estoppel may be asserted by Bank against Paul. This is because in the latter's action against Doris, it was decided that Carol had made a gift to Doris of the funds in question. This fact (Carol's gift) would also serve as a defense to Paul's action against the Bank for unauthorized withdrawals (if Carol had consented to the transfer, it cannot be said that the disbursement to Doris was unauthorized). Choice A is incorrect because federal courts must give res judicata and collateral estoppel affect to an earlier, valid, state court decision. Choice C is incorrect because Bank and Carol are ***not*** in privity. Finally, Choice D is incorrect because Statement 2 is true.

34. **(C)** A JUDGMENT IN AN FRCP 23(b)(2) CLASS ACTION IS BINDING UPON THE ENTIRE CLASS. The correct answer is C. X would be bound by determination that there was insufficient proof that D had not read the exams; FRCP 23(c)(3). This issue is critical for both injunctive relief and monetary damages. Choice A is incorrect because a judgment rendered by a court which lacked subject matter jurisdiction can be collaterally attacked by a non-party. It therefore would not be entitled to Full Faith and Credit. Choice B is incorrect because diversity did exist (P and D being citizens of different states). Finally, Choice D is incorrect because Statement 3 is true.

35. **(D)** THE ASSERTION OF PERSONAL JURISDICTION PURSUANT TO AN APPLICABLE LONG-ARM STATUTE MUST BE CONSISTENT WITH DUE PROCESS (I.E., THE DEFENDANT MUST HAVE SUCH "MINIMUM CONTACTS" WITH THE FORUM AS TO NOT OFFEND "TRADITIONAL NOTIONS OF FAIR PLAY AND SUBSTANTIAL JUSTICE"); *INTERNATIONAL SHOE CO. v. WASHINGTON*, 326 U.S. 310 (1945). The correct answer is D. None of the statements is correct. Even if State Y had a typical non-resident motorist statute (i.e., one which purported to assert personal jurisdiction over a non-resident who was involved in a motor vehicle accident within the state), such fact alone would not necessarily be an adequate basis for obtaining personal jurisdiction over D. The exercise of such personal jurisdiction must still be consistent with due process. Choice B is incorrect because in the absence of a long-arm statute or a traditional basis for the assertion of personal jurisdiction, a court may not assume personal jurisdiction over an out-of-state defendant. The fact that D recently acquired some property within the state probably would ***not*** constitute an adequate basis to require him to stand trial in the forum (especially since the land was unrelated to the litigation). Finally, Choice C is incorrect because by refusing to appear in the State Y proceeding, D would not have waived his right to object to that state's attempt to assume personal jurisdiction over him (i.e., D would be able to collaterally attack the State Y default judgment).

36. **(D)** PERSONS MAY JOIN IN AN ACTION AS PLAINTIFFS IF (1) THEY ASSERT ANY RIGHT TO RELIEF JOINTLY, SEVERALLY, OR IN THE ALTERNATIVE IN RESPECT OF ANY CLAIM ARISING OUT OF THE SAME TRANSACTION, OCCURRENCE OR SERIES OF TRANS ACTIONS OR OCCURRENCES, AND (2) ANY QUESTION OF LAW OR FACT COMMON TO ALL PLAINTIFFS WILL ARISE IN THE ACTION; FRCP 20(a). The correct answer is D. Choice B is incorrect because there is no subject matter jurisdiction with respect to Q's claim against D, since the amount in controversy is ***not*** in excess of $75,000,

exclusive of interest and costs. Pendent jurisdiction would not be applicable, since that doctrine permits a plaintiff to append a state cause of action to a federal claim (it does not permit a party to append his/her claim to a different plaintiff's federal claim). Choice A is incorrect because joinder of claims would be appropriate, since there is a common issue of fact (i.e., was P's termination from his employment wrongful?). Choice C is incorrect because P's claim for damages to his car is unrelated to dismissal from his job. Thus, no claim-splitting would result from P's failure to assert the damage to his car in the present action (and so res judicata principles would ***not*** be applicable). Of course, if P had not asserted the claim for damage to his car, subject matter jurisdiction based upon diversity would not exist (i.e., P's claim would not exceed $75,000).

37. **(D)** IN AN IMPLEADER ACTION, THE THIRD-PARTY DEFENDANT (THE IMPLEADED PARTY) MAY ASSERT ANY CLAIM AGAINST THE PLAINTIFF WHICH ARISES OUT OF THE TRANSACTION OR OCCURRENCE THAT IS THE SUBJECT MATTER OF THE PLAINTIFF'S CLAIM AGAINST THE THIRD-PARTY PLAINTIFF (THE IMPLEADING PARTY). The correct answer is D. Statement 1 is correct. The U.S. District Court did ***not*** have subject matter jurisdiction in the initial action since P and D were citizens of the same state (State X) and no federal claim appears to have been involved. Statement 2 is correct because it conforms to the operative rule of law found in FRCP 14. Finally, Statement 3 is correct because under res judicata principles (1) P could not split his claim against D (i.e., P was required to bring all causes of action arising out of the accident against D in the original lawsuit), and (2) D was required to file a counterclaim against P in the original lawsuit with respect to any claims arising out of the accident, or thereafter be barred therefrom. It should be mentioned that even though P and D are citizens of the same state, ancillary subject matter jurisdiction would have permitted D to counterclaim against P. In any event, Statement 3 specifically directs the reader to disregard subject matter jurisdiction problems in the initial lawsuit.

38. **(D)** THE CORRECT ANSWER IS D. ACCORDING TO LAWS GOVERNING REMOVAL (SECTIONS 1441, 1446 & 1447 OF THE U.S.C.). WHENEVER A SEPARATE AND INDEPENDENT CLAIM OR CAUSE OF ACTION WITHIN THE JURISDICTION CONFERRED BY SECTION 1331 OF THIS TITLE (FEDERAL QUESTION JURISDICTION), IS JOINED WITH ONE OR MORE OTHERWISE NONREMOVABLE CLAIMS OR CAUSES OF ACTION. IN THIS BREACH OF CONTRACT ACTION FOR $75,000, THE ENTIRE CASE MAY BE REMOVED AND THE DISTRICT COURT MAY DETERMINE ALL ISSUES THEREIN, OR, IN ITS DISCRETION, MAY REMAND ALL MATTERS NOT OTHERWISE WITHIN ITS ORIGINAL JURISDICTION. Here, the Plaintiffs are suing for both breach of contract and copyright violations. They could sue in state court and the Defendants would have the right to remove under 1441(c). Also, note that 1441(b) infers that a Plaintiff can file a claim in a state court in which the Federal courts should have original Jurisdiction. According to Section 1441(b) Any civil action of which the district courts have original jurisdiction founded on a claim or right arising under the Constitution, treaties or laws of the United States shall be removable without regard to the citizenship or residence of the parties.

39. **(C)** IN A STATUTORY INTERPLEADER ACTION (1) ONLY MINIMAL DIVERSITY (I.E., DIVERSITY BETWEEN ANY TWO CLAIMANTS) IS REQUIRED, AND (2) THE OBLIGATION OR PROPERTY INVOLVED MUST EXCEED $500 IN VALUE ONLY; 28 U.S.C. 1335. VENUE

IS PROPER IN ANY JUDICIAL DISTRICT IN WHICH ANY CLAIMANT RESIDES. The correct answer is C. Since venue in a statutory interpleader action is proper where any claimant-defendant resides, Statement 3 is correct. Statement 1 is incorrect (a U.S. District Court is competent to hear this matter) since there is minimal diversity (i.e., there is diversity amongst D and E), and (2) the amount involved exceeds $500. Statement 2 is incorrect because the court would ***not*** be competent to hear E's claim against F (diversity and a claim in excess of $75,000 are lacking). It should be mentioned that E's claim against F is not an impleader action (in which event there would have been ancillary jurisdiction) because E is not asserting an indemnity-type of claim against F. Finally, Choice D is incorrect because Statement 3 is true.

40. **(B)** THE PARTIES IN A FEDERAL CIVIL CASE MAY STIPULATE TO A JURY OF LESS THAN TWELVE PERSONS. UNLESS THE PARTIES OTHERWISE AGREE, THE VERDICT IN A FEDERAL CIVIL TRIAL MUST BE UNANIMOUS; FRCP 48. The correct answer is B. Since one of the jurors voted in favor of Defendant, the ruling was defective. Choice A is incorrect because the parties stipulated to a jury of less than twelve persons. Choice C is incorrect because the fact that a verdict fails to ultimately satisfy the "in excess of $75,000" requirement is irrelevant (the "amount in controversy" requirement is measured only at the time the action is filed). Finally, Choice D is incorrect because any lack of personal jurisdiction over Defendant appears to have been waived when he/she failed to assert this alleged defect in a FRCP 12(b)(2) motion or his/her answer; FRCP 12(h)(1).

41. **(B)** WHERE A SUIT IS PROPERLY COMMENCED IN A STATE COURT AND FEDERAL COMPETENCY REQUIREMENTS WOULD BE SATISFIED BASED UPON DIVERSITY, THE ACTION MAY BE REMOVED TO THE U.S. DISTRICT COURT WHICH IS IN THE JUDICIAL DISTRICT THAT ENCOMPASSES THE STATE COURT, IF (1) NO DEFENDANT IS A CITIZEN IN THE STATE IN WHICH THE LAWSUIT WAS COMMENCED, (2) ALL OF THE DEFENDANTS JOIN IN THE PETITION FOR REMOVAL, AND (3) REMOVAL IS SOUGHT WITHIN 30 DAYS OF THE TIME THAT THE MOVING PARTY RECEIVED SERVICE OF PROCESS. WHERE, IN A DIVERSITY ACTION WHICH HAS BEEN PROPERLY COMMENCED, A MATTER IS TRANSFERRED FROM ONE U.S. DISTRICT COURT TO ANOTHER, THE LAW (INCLUDING THE CONFLICT OF THE LAW RULES) OF THE STATE IN WHICH THE ACTION WAS ORIGINALLY COMMENCED MUST BE APPLIED. The correct answer is B. A forum non conveniens motion would probably be successful since (1) State W has no apparent relationship to the litigation (it is merely a state in which D "resides" by reason of it's doing business there), (2) the accident occurred in State Y, and (3) any witnesses to the action probably reside in State Y. However, the law (including the conflict of law rules) of State W would have to be applied by the federal court in State Y. Statement 1 is incorrect because all of the requisites for removal to a federal court are satisfied. Statement 3 is incorrect because where a joint claim is involved, each plaintiff is deemed to be asserting the entire amount requested. Finally, choice D is incorrect because Statement 2 is true.

42. **(A)** USE FRCP 19(a). The correct answer is A. C should be joined if feasible because he/she has an interest in the subject matter of the action (the trust res) and is so situated that the disposition of the action in his absence may impair his ability, to protect that interest (i.e., a decision in favor of the plaintiffs would result in disbursement of the trust res). If he/she refuses to join the action, he may be made an

involuntary plaintiff; FRCP 19(a). Choice B is incorrect because the court could order a separate trial for the *T v. X* claim; FRCP 20(b). Since a U.S. District Court would have subject matter jurisdiction over this action (based upon ancillary jurisdiction), dismissal would not be required (even though T could ***not*** have initially commenced a diversity action against X in federal court). Choice C is incorrect because a plaintiff in an impleader action may assert an indemnity-type claim against the third-party defendant (i.e., the impleaded party); provided, of course, it arises out of the transaction or occurrence that is the basis of the plaintiff's claim against the third-party plaintiff (i.e., the impleading party). Since diversity and "amount in controversy" requisites would be satisfied in an action by A and B against X, A and B could assert an action against X. Note, however, personal jurisdiction and venue would have to be satisfied for the plaintiffs to maintain this action. Finally, Choice D is incorrect because Statement 1 is true.

43. **(B)** WHERE A SUIT IS PROPERLY COMMENCED IN A STATE COURT AND FEDERAL COMPETENCY REQUIREMENTS WOULD BE SATISFIED BASED UPON DIVERSITY, THE ACTION MAY BE REMOVED TO THE U.S. DISTRICT COURT WHICH IS IN THE JUDICIAL DISTRICT THAT ENCOMPASSES THE STATE COURT, IF (1) NO DEFENDANT IS A CITIZEN IN THE STATE IN WHICH THE LAWSUIT WAS COMMENCED, (2) ALL OF THE DEFENDANTS JOIN IN THE PETITION FOR REMOVAL, AND (3) REMOVAL IS SOUGHT WITHIN 30 DAYS OF THE TIME THAT THE MOVING PARTY RECEIVED SERVICE OF PROCESS. WHERE, IN A DIVERSITY ACTION WHICH HAS BEEN PROPERLY COMMENCED, A MATTER IS TRANSFERRED FROM ONE U.S. DISTRICT COURT TO ANOTHER, THE LAW (INCLUDING THE CONFLICT OF LAW RULES) OF THE STATE IN WHICH THE ACTION WAS ORIGINALLY COMMENCED MUST BE APPLIED. The correct answer is B. A forum non conveniens motion would probably be successful since (1) State W has no apparent relationship to the litigation (it is merely a state in which D "resides" by reason of its doing business there), (2) the accident occurred in State Y, and (3) any witnesses to the action probably reside in State Y. However, the law (including the conflict of law rules) of State W would have to be applied by the federal court in State Y. Statement 1 is incorrect because all of the requisites for removal to a federal court are satisfied. Statement 3 is incorrect because where a joint claim is involved, each plaintiff is deemed to be asserting the entire amount requested. Finally, Choice D is incorrect because Statement 2 is true.

44. **(B)** UNDER THE FRCP, A PLEADING MUST ORDINARILY CONTAIN (1) A STATEMENT OF THE COURT'S COMPETENCY, (2) A SHORT AND PLAIN STATEMENT OF THE CLAIM SHOWING THAT THE PLEADER IS ENTITLED TO RELIEF, AND (3) A DEMAND FOR JUDGMENT OR THE RELIEF TO WHICH THE PLEADER DEEMS HIM/HERSELF ENTITLED; FRCP 8(a). The correct answer is B. Phil's complaint is arguably defective in that he has failed to properly describe the basis upon which he is entitled to relief. Although he has stated that he suffered personal injuries and property damage in the amount of $80,000, he has not indicated why Dowd is liable to him for that amount (i.e., Phil has failed to allege that Dowd improperly drove his car into Phil's vehicle, or even that Dowd was "negligent"). Phil has stated only that there was an accident and Dowd is liable to Phil in the amount of $80,000. Thus, a court would probably grant Dowd's motion, with leave to Phil to amend his pleading. Choice A is incorrect because a complaint will not be dismissed without leave to amend "unless it appears beyond doubt that the plaintiff can prove no set of facts in support of his claim which would entitle him to relief;" *Conley v. Gibson*, 355 U.S. 41 (1957).

Choice D is incorrect because, as described above, the court would probably grant Phil leave to amend his complaint. Thus, even if the applicable statute of limitation had not expired, Dowd's motion would probably be granted (subject to Phil having the opportunity to amend the complaint). Choice C is incorrect because under the FRCP it is ***not*** necessary for a plaintiff to articulate the precise legal theory upon which he/she is seeking relief.

45. **(C)** A PARTY MAY SET FORTH TWO OR MORE CLAIMS ALTERNATIVELY; FRCP 8(e)(2). The correct answer is C. Since the FRCP specifically authorizes separate claims, regardless of consistency, a complaint setting forth two different factual bases for recovery is permissible. In this instance, the inconsistency may be explainable by Phil's inability to recollect the exact circumstances of the accident. Choice B is incorrect because a federal pleading is not subject to a motion for dismissal simply because it contains a legal conclusion. Finally, Choices A and D are incorrect because federal pleadings may contain inconsistent claims or defenses.

46. **(A)** IN THE ABSENCE OF A TRADITIONAL BASIS FOR OBTAINING PERSONAL JURISDICTION, THE ASSERTION OF PERSONAL JURISDICTION OVER AN OUT-OF-STATE CITIZEN MUST (1) CONFORM TO THE APPLICABLE LONG-ARM STATUTE, AND (2) BE CONSISTENT WITH DUE PROCESS (I.E., THE DEFENDANT MUST HAVE SUFFICIENT MINIMUM CONTACTS WITH THE FORUM AS TO NOT OFFEND TRADITIONAL NOTIONS OF FAIR PLAY AND SUBSTANTIAL JUSTICE). The correct answer is A. Since E (1) could not foresee being haled into New York (D had misrepresented to E that his trip would terminate in New Jersey), and (2) apparently has no other contacts with New York, the assertion of personal jurisdiction over E would probably violate due process. Choice B is incorrect because, even if New York had a long-arm statute which purported to give personal jurisdiction over E in these circumstances, the actual application of that statute would still have to satisfy due process. Choice D is incorrect because the fact that New York law might extend liability to E under these circumstances is irrelevant for purposes of determining personal jurisdiction. Finally, Choice C is incorrect because federal courts do ***not*** ordinarily have nationwide personal jurisdiction.

47. **(C)** IN A DIVERSITY CASE THE PROPER JUDICIAL DISTRICT IN WHICH TO COMMENCE AN ACTION IS THE ONE IN WHICH (1) ANY OF THE DEFENDANTS RESIDE, ***OR*** (2) THE CLAIM AROSE. The correct answer is C. Statement 1 is correct because there is diversity subject matter jurisdiction (i.e., P is deemed to be a citizen of States X and Z, while D is a citizen of State Y) and there is alienage jurisdiction with respect to E; U.S Constitution, Article III, Section 2. Additionally, venue is proper because (1) D certainly resides in State Y (where it has its principal place in business), and (2) an alien may be sued in any judicial district; 28 U.S.C. 1391(d). Finally, it is possible that P would be deemed to reside in State Y because it is licensed to do business in that jurisdiction. Statement 2 is correct because a "diversity" action may be removed to the applicable U.S. District Court when (1) no defendant is a citizen of the jurisdiction in which the action was commenced, and (2) all of the defendants join in the petition for removal. Removal may occur even though the action could not originally have been commenced in the U.S. District Court to which the case is removed. Finally, Statement 3 is incorrect because all persons may be joined in one action as defendants if there is asserted against them jointly, severally, or in the alternative, (1) any right to relief arising out of the same transaction, occurrence

or series of transactions or occurrences, and (2) any question of law or fact which is common to all defendants will arise in the action; FRCP 20(a). Since P's action arises out of the fire which occurred at its plant, and there is at least one common issue of fact (i.e., the exact amount of P's damages), joining D and E as defendants is proper.

48. **(D)** UPON TIMELY APPLICATION, A PERSON MAY INTERVENE IN AN ACTION AS OF RIGHT WHEN HE/SHE (1) CLAIMS AN INTEREST RELATING TO THE PROPERTY OR TRANSACTION WHICH IS THE SUBJECT OF THE ACTION, (2) HE/SHE IS SO SITUATED THAT DISPOSITION OF THE ACTION MAY, AS A PRACTICAL MATTER, IMPAIR HIS/HER ABILITY TO PROTECT THAT INTEREST, AND (3) THE APPLICANT'S INTEREST IS NOT ADEQUATELY REPRESENTED BY THE EXISTING PARTIES; FRCP 24(a)(2). The correct answer is D. Statement 1 is incorrect because P is still the real party-in-interest since she is seeking damages in excess of the maximum limit of her insurance policy. Statement 2 is incorrect because there is no diversity between D and E with respect to D's claim against E (both parties being citizens of state Y). Ancillary jurisdiction is not applicable in this instance, since D's action cannot be characterized as an impleader (D is not asserting an indemnity-type of claim against E because D has asserted that E was the ***exclusive*** cause of P's injuries). Statement 3 is incorrect because E cannot intervene into the action as of right. Her interests would not be impaired by a successful judgment by P against D (since D and E are legally unrelated, there would be no collateral estoppel or res judicata effect in the event that P's action against D were successful).

49. **(A)** UNDER THE SEVENTH AMENDMENT, THE RIGHT TO A JURY TRIAL EXISTS AS TO ANY ISSUE WHICH PERTAINS TO A LEGAL REMEDY. The correct answer is A. Since an action for trespass existed in 1791 (when the Seventh Amendment to the U.S. Constitution was ratified), it must be characterized as a "legal" claim. Thus, Delbert would be entitled to a jury trial with respect to all issues pertaining to this action. Choice C is incorrect because the "clean-up doctrine" (pursuant to which a federal court would determine legal issues which were "incidental" to a primarily equitable claim) has been repudiated; *Dairy Queen, Inc. v. Wood*, 369 U.S. 469 (1982). Choice B is incorrect because in a federal court each party is entitled to a jury trial with respect to any legal issue (regardless of the "primary" relief which the plaintiff is seeking). Finally, Choice D is incorrect because trespass did exist in 1791 (when the Seventh Amendment was ratified), and therefore would constitute a "suit at common law."

50. **(A)** IN DIVERSITY CASES, THE PROPER JUDICIAL DISTRICT FOR VENUE PURPOSES IS ONE IN WHICH (1) ANY OF THE DEFENDANTS RESIDE, OR (2) THE CLAIM AROSE. IF VENUE IS IMPROPER, A U.S. DISTRICT COURT MAY DISMISS THE CASE OR TRANSFER THE ACTION TO ANOTHER U.S. DISTRICT COURT IN WHICH THE MATTER COULD HAVE ORIGINALLY BEEN COMMENCED; 28 U.S.C. 1406(a). The correct answer is A. The action was not properly commenced in the U.S. District Court in State Y, since it is not the judicial district in which ***all*** of the plaintiffs reside. However, under the applicable law, the action may be transferred to the U.S. District Court in State Y (where the sole defendant was domiciled). Choice B is incorrect because, where venue is improper, a U.S. District Court may transfer the matter to a different U.S. District Court where the action could have been commenced. Choice C is incorrect because an objection based upon improper service was probably waived when D

failed to assert this defect in his/her initial pleading; FRCP 12(h)(1). Finally, Choice D is incorrect because Statement 1 is true.

51. **(C)** A PARTY MAY GENERALLY DISCOVER ANY MATTER, NOT PRIVILEGED, WHICH IS RELEVANT TO THE ACTION. HOWEVER, DOCUMENTS AND TANGIBLE ITEMS PREPARED IN ANTICIPATION OF LITIGATION OR TRIAL, BY OR FOR (1) ANOTHER PARTY, OR (2) THAT OTHER PARTY'S REPRESENTATIVE (INCLUDING HIS/HER ATTORNEY), ARE DISCOVERABLE ONLY UPON A SHOWING THAT THE PARTY SEEKING DISCOVERY HAS SUBSTANTIAL NEED FOR THE MATERIALS AND WOULD OTHERWISE BE UNABLE TO OBTAIN THE SUBSTANTIAL EQUIVALENT THEREOF WITHOUT UNDUE HARDSHIP; FRCP 26(b)(3). The correct answer is C. Jones' memorandum to the President of E is probably ***not*** within the "work product" privilege because there is no indication that it was ". . . prepared in anticipation of litigation." Rather, it appears to be an internal memorandum by one member of the Board of Directors to the president of his/her corporation. Jones was, in fact, probably attempting to avoid prospective litigation by advising the president of E as to what Withers had said. Choices A and B are incorrect because the work product rule is probably not triggered (Jones' memorandum was probably not made in anticipation of trial or litigation). Finally, Choice D is incorrect because the work product privilege is assertable whether or not the attorney who prepared the document in question is actually representing the party in the current action.

52. **(D)** A PARTY IS ENTITLED TO A SUMMARY JUDGMENT WHERE, AS A CONSEQUENCE OF THERE BEING NO "GENUINE ISSUE OF MATERIAL FACT," HE/SHE IS ENTITLED TO JUDGMENT AS A MATTER OF LAW; FRCP 56. The correct answer is D. Choice A is correct because, even if Builder Corp. had utilized substandard materials in the construction, this fact alone would not prove that E was negligent. E would be negligent only if (1) it failed to utilize reasonable care in overseeing the activities of Builder Corp., and (2) there was a causal relationship between the substandard materials and the building's collapse. Thus, genuine issues of fact would remain even if substandard materials had, in fact, been utilized by Builder Corp. in the construction of the building. Choice B is correct because, for a plaintiff to prevail on a summary judgment motion, he/she must address any affirmative defenses raised by the defendant. Finally, Choice C is incorrect because a summary judgment probably would ***not*** be appropriate based upon Wither's affidavit.

53. **(C)** A PARTY IS ENTITLED TO A SUMMARY JUDGMENT WHERE, AS A CONSEQUENCE OF THERE BEING NO "GENUINE ISSUE OF MATERIAL FACT," HE/SHE IS ENTITLED TO JUDGMENT AS A MATTER OF LAW; FRCP 56. The correct answer is C. Although the facts indicate that a two-year statute of limitation is applicable, negligence actions ordinarily do not begin to run until an injury or damages have been sustained. Thus, E's summary judgment motion was properly denied. Choice A is incorrect because the fact that the building was constructed six years ago would be irrelevant if the statute of limitation did not begin to run until the accident. Choice B is incorrect because one need not respond to a summary judgment motion if it would, by itself, be unsuccessful. Finally, Choice D is incorrect because the fact that E has the burden of proof on this issue is irrelevant in determining whether there is a triable issue of fact. It might be noted that E could have raised the statute of limitation defense through a motion for failure to state a claim upon which relief can be

granted; FRCP 12. However, since E supported its motion with an affidavit, it must be treated as a summary judgment motion.

54. **(B)** DEFAULT JUDGMENTS WHICH ARE CONSTITUTIONALLY OR PROCEDURALLY DEFECTIVE ARE SUBJECT TO COLLATERAL ATTACK. The correct answer is B. Under FRCP 4 (which has been enacted in State X), if no acknowledgment is made to a summons and complaint which are sent by first-class mail, the defendant must be served as otherwise provided in that Rule. Since the State X judgment was procedurally defective (i.e., P failed to conform with the applicable service of process statute), it was subject to collateral attack. Choice A is incorrect because, despite actual receipt of the documents by D, he/she was not served in accordance with applicable law. Choice C is incorrect because, while a default judgment is usually deemed to be "on the merits," the State X judgment is ***not*** entitled to Full Faith and Credit (P having failed to conform to the statute pertaining to service of process). Finally, Choice D is incorrect because (1) Statements (A) and (C) are ***not*** correct, and (2) Statement (B) is true.

55. **(A)** QUASI-IN-REM JURISDICTION WILL ORDINARILY BE TESTED BY THE DUE PROCESS STANDARD APPLICABLE TO PERSONAL JURISDICTION (I.E., THE DEFENDANT MUST HAVE HAD SUFFICIENT MINIMUM CONTACTS WITH THE FORUM AS TO NOT OFFEND TRADITIONAL NOTIONS OF FAIR PLAY AND SUBSTANTIAL JUSTICE); *Shaffer v. Heitner*. The correct answer is A. If D does not have sufficient contacts with Texas as would support personal jurisdiction over him, the attachment should be quashed. Choice B is incorrect because pre-judgment attachments are not, per se, unconstitutional; *Mitchell v. W.T. Grant Co.*, 416 U.S. 600 (1974). Assuming proper due process safeguards exist, a defendant's property can be seized prior to the time a judgment is actually rendered against him/her. Choice C is incorrect because, even if the motion to quash were denied and the boat sold, A could only retain proceeds in an amount equal to his obligation. The balance would have to be remitted to D. Finally, Choice D is incorrect for the reasons described above.

56. **(B)** WHERE A SUIT IS PROPERLY COMMENCED IN A STATE COURT AND FEDERAL SUBJECT MATTER JURISDICTION REQUIREMENTS ARE SATISFIED BASED UPON DIVERSITY, THE ACTION CAN BE REMOVED TO THE U.S. DISTRICT COURT WHICH IS IN THE JUDICIAL DISTRICT THAT ENCOMPASSES THE STATE COURT, IF: (1) NONE OF THE DEFENDANTS IS A CITIZEN OF THE STATE IN WHICH THE LAWSUIT WAS COMMENCED, (2) ALL OF THE DEFENDANTS JOIN IN THE PETITION FOR REMOVAL, AND (3) REMOVAL IS SOUGHT WITHIN 30 DAYS OF THE TIME THE MOVING PARTY RECEIVED SERVICE OF PROCESS. The correct answer is B. Removal would not be possible since C is a citizen of the forum in which the action has been commenced (i.e., a corporation is deemed to be a citizen of the state in which it is incorporated ***and*** the jurisdiction in which it has its principal place of business). Choice A is incorrect because removal cannot occur when ***any*** defendant is a citizen of the state in which the action was commenced. Choice D is incorrect because C would be deemed to be a citizen of Utah. Finally, Choice C is incorrect because removal could not be granted (C being a citizen of the state in which the action has been commenced), even if C joined in the petition.

57. **(B)** IF A FEDERAL CLAIM IS DISMISSED OR DEEMED TO BE INVALID PRIOR TO THE TIME A VERDICT IS RENDERED, A U.S. DISTRICT COURT MAY (PROBABLY) STILL HEAR A

PENDENT (I.E., NON-FEDERAL) CLAIM; *Rosado v. Wyman*, 397 U.S. 397 (1970). The correct answer is B. Even though it has been conclusively established that the federal claim cannot be successfully asserted, the pendent claim can probably still be heard. Choice A is incorrect because, under the above cited case, federal courts probably have discretion in deciding whether or not to dismiss a state claim after a federal claim is found to be wanting. Choice C is incorrect because remand can occur only where the action was commenced in a state court. Finally, Choice D is incorrect because, under pendent jurisdiction principles, a federal court may hear a state claim which derives from the same nucleus of operative facts as the federal claim.

58. **(D)** PERMISSIVE COUNTERCLAIMS MAY BE JOINED ONLY IF THERE IS AN INDEPENDENT, SUBJECT MATTER BASIS FOR SUCH CLAIMS. CLAIMS BY A PLAINTIFF AGAINST A THIRD-PARTY DEFENDANT (THE IMPLEADED PARTY) MUST HAVE AN INDEPENDENT SUBJECT MATTER BASIS; *Owen Equipment Co. v. Kroger*, 437 U.S. 365 (1978). The correct answer is D. if the $1,000 counterclaim by Dumb against Pam is deemed to be permissive in nature (i.e., ***not*** arising out of the transaction or occurrence which is the basis of the plaintiff's claim), ancillary jurisdiction would ***not*** exist. Since Dumb's claim does not satisfy the "amount in controversy" requirement (it is not in excess of $75,000), it could not be joined in this action. Finally, Pam's claim against Insurance Co. could not be joined because both parties are citizens of State B.

59. **(B)** WHERE EVIDENCE IS OBJECTED TO AT TRIAL ON THE GROUNDS THAT IT IS NOT WITHIN THE PLEADINGS, A COURT MAY ALLOW AN AMENDMENT WHEN THE (1) PRESENTATION OF THE MERITS OF THE ACTION WILL BE SUBSERVED THEREBY, AND (2) OBJECTING PARTY FAILS TO SATISFY THE COURT THAT ADMISSION OF SUCH EVIDENCE WOULD PREJUDICE HIM/HER IN MAINTAINING HIS/HER ACTION OR DEFENSE ON THE MERITS; FRCP 15(b). The correct answer is B. Although B had failed to raise anticipatory repudiation as a defense, he could be permitted by the court to amend his pleadings at trial to conform to the evidence which he wishes to introduce. Choice A is incorrect because there is no ***per se*** procedural rule in federal courts that evidence outside of the pleadings is thereafter inadmissible. Choice D is incorrect because the admission of evidence outside of the pleadings is discretionary with the court (in fact, FRCP 15(b) instructs a court to adopt a liberal approach in admitting such evidence). Finally, Choice C is incorrect because amendments to pleadings may be made after trial has commenced.

60. **(C)** A PARTY MAY AMEND HIS/HER PLEADINGS ONCE, AS A MATTER OF RIGHT, AT ANY TIME BEFORE A RESPONSIVE PLEADING HAS BEEN SERVED; FRCP 15(a). The correct answer is C. Since a motion under FRCP 12(b) does not constitute a "responsive" pleading, Paul was entitled to amend his complaint without leave of the court. Choice D is incorrect because affidavits in support of a motion for summary judgment must be based upon ***personal*** knowledge; FRCP 56(e). In this instance, Bill's affidavit is based upon information related to him by Paul (rather than firsthand knowledge). Choice A is incorrect because a complaint in federal court need not articulate the particular legal theory being asserted. Finally, Choice B is incorrect because alternative claims may be asserted, regardless of consistency; FRCP 8(e)(2).

61. **(B)** A CONTRACTUAL PROVISION STIPULATING A PARTICULAR CHOICE OF FORUM IN THE EVENT OF LITIGATION WILL ORDINARILY BE OBSERVED. WHERE A MOTION TO TRANSFER VENUE IS GRANTED, THE LAW OF THE TRANSFERRING STATE WILL BE APPLIED IN THE TRANSFEREE FORUM. The correct answer is B. Statement 2 conforms to the applicable principles of law. Choice A is incorrect because a plaintiff's choice of forum will rarely be disturbed. The fact that litigation in Oregon will be inconvenient to a party's employees would probably ***not*** be sufficient grounds to transfer the action to such party's "home state." Y Corp.'s contention is further diminished by the contractual clause stipulating to litigation in Oregon. Choice C is incorrect because a "choice of forum" contractual provision would not be disregarded simply because it would otherwise be inconsistent with due process to assert personal jurisdiction over a party in that forum. While a court could refuse to exercise jurisdiction where (1) neither party or the cause of the action has a nexus with the forum, or (2) the party asserting the clause had a grossly favorable bargaining position, neither of those situations appear to be applicable in this instance (X is a citizen of Oregon and Y Corp. is a "large" corporation). Finally, Choice D is incorrect because Statement 2 is true.

62. **(B)** IN A CLASS ACTION ASSERTED UNDER FRCP 23(b)(3), THE COURT IS REQUIRED TO GIVE MEMBERS OF THE CLASS THE BEST NOTICE PRACTICABLE UNDER THE CIRCUMSTANCES, INCLUDING INDIVIDUAL NOTICE TO MEMBERS WHO CAN BE IDENTIFIED THROUGH REASONABLE EFFORT; FRCP 23(c)(2). The correct answer is B. Since the names and addresses of purchasers of the Daleon automobile are unavailable (except for the buyers who are located in New Mexico and Delaware), notice by publication in major newspapers throughout the country will probably be adequate. Choice A is incorrect because, for diversity purposes, only the citizenship of the class representative and the other party are analyzed. Choice C is incorrect because notice is mandated by FRCP 23(c)(2), since it states that "the court ***shall*** . . ." require notification to the class. Thus, a court may not dispense with the notice requirement in an FRCP 23(b)(3) class action. Finally, Choice D is incorrect because Statement 2 is true.

63. **(C)** A PARTY MAY ORDINARILY OBTAIN DISCOVERY OF DOCUMENTS AND TANGIBLE ITEMS PREPARED IN ANTICIPATION OF LITIGATION OR TRIAL BY OR FOR (1) ANOTHER PARTY, OR (2) THAT PARTY'S REPRESENTATIVE (INCLUDING HIS/HER ATTORNEYS), ONLY UPON A SHOWING THAT THE PARTY SEEKING DISCOVERY (1) HAS A SUBSTANTIAL NEED FOR THE MATERIALS, AND (2) IS OTHERWISE UNABLE TO OBTAIN THEM (OR THE SUBSTANTIAL EQUIVALENT) WITHOUT UNDUE HARDSHIP; FRCP 26(b)(3). HOWEVER, OPINIONS HELD BY EXPERTS WHICH HAVE BEEN ACQUIRED OR DEVELOPED IN ANTICIPATION OF LITIGATION OR TRIAL ARE ORDINARILY DISCOVERABLE ONLY THROUGH INTERROGATORIES WHICH REQUIRE (1) THE IDENTIFICATION OF AN EXPERT WITNESS WHO WILL BE CALLED AT TRIAL, (2) THE SUBJECT MATTER ABOUT WHICH THE EXPERT IS EXPECTED TO TESTIFY, (3) THE SUBSTANCE OF THE OPINIONS TO WHICH THE EXPERT IS EXPECTED TO TESTIFY, AND (4) A SUMMARY OF THE GROUNDS FOR EACH SUCH OPINION; FRCP 26(b)(4). The correct answer is C. Since the lock was repaired prior to the time that Amusement Co.'s attorney had an opportunity to examine it, the pictures taken by P's boyfriend are probably discoverable (even though they might arguably be characterized as materials prepared in anticipation of litigation by a party, and therefore "work product"). However, opinions held by experts which have been developed in anticipation of trial can

ordinarily be obtained only through interrogatories. Thus, the locksmith's report would ***not*** be discoverable. Since Choice C is the only selection which correctly describes what is discoverable by Amusement Co., it is the correct answer.

64. **(C)** WHERE A SUIT IS PROPERLY COMMENCED IN A STATE COURT AND FEDERAL SUBJECT MATTER JURISDICTION WOULD BE SATISFIED BASED UPON A FEDERAL CLAIM, THE ACTION IS REMOVABLE TO THE U.S. DISTRICT COURT WHICH IS IN THE JUDICIAL DISTRICT THAT ENCOMPASSES THE STATE COURT, IF; (1) ALL OF THE DEFENDANTS JOIN IN THE PETITION FOR REMOVAL, AND (2) REMOVAL IS SOUGHT WITHIN 30 DAYS FROM THE TIME THE MOVING PARTY RECEIVED SERVICE OF PROCESS; 28 U.S.C. 1441(b). The correct answer is C. Since Polly's claim is based upon a federal claim, Acme may remove the case to the appropriate U.S. District Court. Diversity is not pertinent where a federal claim is involved. Choice D is incorrect because there is ***no*** diversity of citizenship, Polly and Acme both being citizens of Georgia. Choice B is incorrect because, while there is a lack of diversity, removal is appropriate since Polly is asserting a substantial federal claim. Finally, Choice A is incorrect because (1) becoming a citizen of a different state for litigational purposes is usually permissible, and (2) in any event, the citizenship of Polly is irrelevant for purposes of removal since she is asserting a federal claim.

65. **(A)** WHERE A CLASS ACTION IS BASED UPON A FEDERAL CLAIM, THERE IS NO DIVERSITY OR "AMOUNT IN CONTROVERSY" REQUIREMENT. The correct answer is A. A class action based upon ***diversity*** subject matter jurisdiction is not possible in this instance because none of the plaintiffs possesses a claim in excess of $75,000. Thus, an action could be commenced in federal court only if the plaintiffs can premise their right to recovery upon a federal statute (or the U.S. Constitution or a treaty). Choice B is incorrect because separate plaintiffs may ***not*** aggregate their claims in a class action to satisfy the "amount in controversy" requirement. Choice C is incorrect because, even though diversity of citizenship exists, where a class action is based upon diversity subject matter jurisdiction, each plaintiff must claim damages in excess of $75,000. Finally, Choice D is incorrect because, even if there is diversity between the class representative and the defendant, the "amount in controversy" requirement is not satisfied.

66. **(C)** A PERSON WHO IS NOT A PARTY SHOULD BE JOINED WHERE FAILURE TO DO SO WILL LEAVE ANY PARTY TO THE ACTION SUBJECT TO A SUBSTANTIAL RISK OF INCURRING MULTIPLE LIABILITY FOR A SINGLE OBLIGATION. IF THE COURT DETERMINES THAT IN EQUITY AND IN GOOD CONSCIENCE THE ACTION SHOULD BE DISMISSED IN THE NON-PARTY'S ABSENCE, HE/SHE IS REGARDED AS BEING INDISPENSABLE. WHERE THE JOINDER OF AN INDISPENSABLE PARTY WILL DESTROY SUBJECT MATTER JURISDICTION, A FEDERAL COURT MUST DISMISS THE ACTION; FRCP 19. The correct answer is C. A plaintiff is never required to join every potential defendant. In this instance, complete relief can be afforded P on the basis of his lawsuit against Y (i.e., P could obtain a judgment for the full amount of his injuries against Y, if (1) Y were negligent, and (2) Y's conduct contributed to P's injuries). Even if X was a joint tortfeasor, Y could not complain of being exposed to multiple liability because he and X (in addition to being jointly liable) would each be severally liable to P for the full amount of the latter's injuries. While Y might lose a right to contribution from X by P's failure to also name X, this fact alone does not make X an indispensable party. A defendant who could be individually liable to the plaintiff has no expecta-

tion that the latter will name every possible party. Choice A is incorrect because "a common nucleus of operative facts" is not the standard to be considered in determining if an unnamed party should be deemed indispensable. Choice B is incorrect because, even if X was wholly or partially responsible for the accident, Y would still not have the right to insist that X be included in the litigation. Finally, Choice D is incorrect because there is no rule which makes a party "non- indispensable" because his/her joinder would destroy diversity.

67. **(C)** WHERE THE PRECISE ISSUE WAS ACTUALLY LITIGATED IN A PRIOR ACTION BY THE PARTY AGAINST WHOM ISSUE PRECLUSION IS ASSERTED, AND THAT ISSUE WAS ESSENTIAL TO THE DECISION RENDERED IN THE PRIOR LAWSUIT, ISSUE PRECLUSION MAY BE PERMITTED. The correct answer is C. If Arnold prevailed, Chuck would probably be able to assert collateral estoppel against Bill. Choice A is incorrect because the action against Chuck (based upon the guarantee) is different than that asserted against Bill (based upon non-payment of the promissory note). Choice B is incorrect because Chuck was not a party to the *Bill vs. Arnold* action. Finally, Choice D is incorrect because Choice C is true.

68. **(D)** UPON TIMELY APPLICATION, A PERSON MAY INTERVENE IN AN ACTION AS OF RIGHT WHEN HE/SHE (1) CLAIMS AN INTEREST RELATING TO THE PROPERTY OR TRANSACTION WHICH IS THE SUBJECT OF THE ACTION, (2) HE/SHE IS SO SITUATED THAT DISPOSITION OF THE ACTION MAY, AS A PRACTICAL MATTER, IMPAIR HIS/HER ABILITY TO PROTECT THAT INTEREST, AND (3) THE APPLICANT'S INTEREST IS NOT ADEQUATELY REPRESENTED BY THE EXISTING PARTIES; FRCP 24(a)(2). The correct answer is D. Choice A is incorrect because Paul could obtain full relief against Jim (i.e., obtain a judgment for the full amount of the loan) and there would be no substantial risk of Jim incurring multiple liability for a single obligation (Jim would be liable only for an amount for which he was severally liable). Choice B is incorrect because, while Ralph has an interest in the action, permitting him to intervene would destroy diversity. It is therefore unlikely that permissive intervention would be permitted in this instance. Finally, Choice C is incorrect because Ralph's ability to protect his interest would not be impaired or impeded by a judgment in the outstanding action. Any judgment against Jim would probably ***not*** have a res judicata or collateral estoppel effect upon Ralph if Paul subsequently sued him under the guarantee.

69. **(B)** A DEFENDANT MAY IMPLEAD ANOTHER PERSON, NOT A PARTY TO THE ACTION, WHO IS OR MAY BE LIABLE TO HIM/HER FOR ALL OR PART OF THE PLAINTIFF'S CLAIM AGAINST THE DEFENDING/IMPLEADING PARTY; FRCP 14(a). AN IMPLEADED PARTY MAY ASSERT AGAINST THE IMPLEADING PARTY ANY COUNTERCLAIMS PERMITTED PURSUANT TO FRCP 13; FRCP 14(a). The correct answer is B. Statement 2 is correct because Don has an indemnity-type of claim against ABC. Since there is ancillary jurisdiction for impleader actions, the former's claim against the latter is proper (even though diversity and "amount in controversy" requisites would otherwise not be satisfied). Statement 1 is not correct. Polly could ***not*** join her action for personal injury against Don, since it does not arise from the same nucleus of operative facts which constitutes the basis of her federal claim against Don. Thus, an action based upon the car accident is not permissible since (1) Polly and Don are both citizens of the same state, and (2) the amount in controversy does not exceed $75,000.

70. **(C)** WHEN THE MENTAL OR PHYSICAL CONDITION OF A ***PARTY*** IS IN CONTROVERSY, THE COURT MAY ORDER THAT PARTY TO SUBMIT TO A PHYSICAL OR MENTAL EXAMINATION BY A PHYSICIAN. SUCH AN ORDER WILL BE MADE ONLY UPON MOTION, FOR GOOD CAUSE SHOWN, AND PRIOR NOTICE TO THE PERSON TO BE EXAMINED AND ALL OTHER PARTIES; FRCP 35. The correct answer is C. Since Wanda is not a party to the action, an eye examination of her by P cannot be ordered. Choice D is incorrect because, while the order requiring the examination must be issued by the court, it is not necessary that the judge actually select the physician (i.e., he/she might approve a physician recommended by one of the parties). Choice A is incorrect because Wanda, not being a party, cannot be ordered to submit to a physical examination. Finally, Choice B is incorrect because, while Wanda's vision is important to the question of whether D's alibi can be sustained, an eye examination cannot be ordered since she is not a party.

71. **(C)** U.S. DISTRICT COURTS ARE COMPETENT TO HEAR CASES INVOLVING A FEDERAL CLAIM (I.E., ONE ARISING UNDER THE CONSTITUTION, A TREATY OR THE LAWS OF THE U.S.). The correct answer is C. There is no "federal question" subject matter jurisdiction because Polly has alluded to a violation of the U.S. Constitution only in the context of anticipating a possible defense which might be raised by Denny. However, a defense based upon the U.S. Constitution or a federal statute cannot serve as the basis for subject matter jurisdiction in a federal court. Additionally, there is no "diversity" subject matter jurisdiction because Polly's claim is only for $3,000 (six months of rent at $500.00 per month). Thus, Choice C represents the only correct selection.

72. **(C)** WHERE THE PRECISE ISSUE WAS ACTUALLY LITIGATED IN A PRIOR ACTION BY THE PARTY AGAINST WHOM ISSUE PRECLUSION IS BEING ASSERTED, AND THAT ISSUE WAS ESSENTIAL TO THE DECISION RENDERED IN THE PRIOR LAWSUIT, ISSUE PRECLUSION MAY BE PERMITTED. The correct answer is C. Since Ball recovered a default judgment against Mel in the initial lawsuit, it would have no collateral estoppel effect (i.e., obviously, the issues were not ***actually*** litigated). Also, since Wine and Ball are not in privy, the initial judgment would have no res judicata effect. Choice A is incorrect because Wine and Ball are not in privy with each other (they are complete strangers to each other). Choice B is incorrect because the issues in Ball's action against Mel were not actually litigated. Finally, Choice D is incorrect because Choice C is true.

73. **(D)** NOTICE OF A PROPOSED SETTLEMENT OF A CLASS ACTION MUST BE APPROVED BY THE COURT; FRCP 23(e). The correct answer is D. Choice A is incorrect because a decision to refuse to certify a class action is ***not*** a final order, and consequently an immediate appeal therefrom may ***not*** be taken; *Coopers & Lybrand v. Livesay*, 437 U.S. 463 (1978). Choice B is incorrect because a class action settlement must be approved by the courts; FRCP 23(e). Finally, Choice C is incorrect because where a class action is successful (or a favorable settlement is arranged), federal courts will often award the class representatives his/her reasonable attorneys' fees. However, if a class action is predicated upon a specific federal statute, attorneys' fees are awarded only if the enactment explicitly permits them to be recovered; *Alyeska Pipeline Service Co. v. Wilderness Society*, 421 U.S. 240 (1975).

74. **(C)** A PERSON MAY INTERVENE INTO AN EXISTING ACTION AS OF RIGHT WHERE: (1) HE/SHE CLAIMS AN INTEREST RELATING TO THE PROPERTY OR TRANSACTION WHICH IS THE SUBJECT MATTER OF THE PENDING LAWSUIT, (2) THE DISPOSITION OF THE ACTION WILL, AS A PRACTICAL MATTER, IMPAIR OR IMPEDE THE INTERVENOR'S ABILITY TO PROTECT HIS/HER INTEREST, ***AND*** (3) THE INTERVENOR IS NOT ADEQUATELY REPRESENTED BY THE EXISTING PARTIES; FRCP 24(a). WHERE THE REQUISITES OF INTERVENTION AS OF RIGHT ARE SATISFIED, ANCILLARY JURISDICTION WILL ORDINARILY BE APPLIED TO THE INTERVENING PARTY (EXCEPT, POSSIBLY, WHERE THE INTERVENOR COULD BE CHARACTERIZED AS AN INDISPENSABLE PARTY). The correct answer is C. Since Bob's interests will not be impaired as a consequence of the present lawsuit (there would be no res judicata or collateral estoppel affect upon him in the event that Oscar were successful), intervention as of right would ***not*** be applicable. Thus, Bob's intervention would only be permissive in nature, and ordinary subject matter requirements must be satisfied. Since Bob and Oscar are citizens of the same state (Ohio), competency based upon diversity would not be satisfied. Choice D is incorrect because, even if Bob in good faith believed that his damages exceeded $75,000, there would still be a lack of diversity. Choice A is incorrect because there is no ancillary jurisdiction in this instance (Bob's intervention being only permissive in nature). Finally, Choice B is incorrect because Bob is ***not*** an indispensable party. Complete relief can be given to Art in Bob's absence and there is no risk that Oscar would be exposed to multiple liability for the same obligation if Bob does not pursue his claim in the existing action; FRCP 19(a). Oscar owes Art a separate and distinct obligation than that owed to Bob.

75. **(A)** STATUTORY INTERPLEADER IS APPROPRIATE WHERE: (1) THERE IS MINIMAL DIVERSITY (I.E., DIVERSITY BETWEEN ***ANY*** TWO DEFENDANT/CLAIMANTS), AND (2) THE OBLIGATION OR PROPERTY INVOLVED EXCEEDS $500 IN VALUE; 28 U.S.C. 1335. THERE IS NATIONWIDE PERSONAL JURISDICTION FOR STATUTORY INTERPLEADER; 28 U.S.C. 2361. FOR RULE INTERPLEADER, THE ORDINARY RULES FOR COMPETENCY AND PERSONAL JURISDICTION APPLY. The correct answer is A. Since there is minimal diversity amongst the claimant/defendants (i.e., they are not all citizens of the same state) and the amount in controversy exceeds $500, a "statutory" interpleader action is appropriate. Venue is proper in any district in which any claimant/defendant resides. There is a federal statute authorizing nationwide personal jurisdiction for statutory interpleader. Choice B is incorrect because "rule" interpleader is not appropriate since diversity does not exist (Insureco is a citizen of the same states as Bill, Carl and Melvin). Choice C is incorrect because under "rule" interpleader there is a nationwide long-arm statute; 28 U.S.C. 2361. Finally, Choice D is incorrect because the party commencing an interpleader action may claim that he/she has no liability, whatsoever, to the claimant/defendants.

76. **(C)** A MOTION FOR A DIRECTED VERDICT SHOULD BE GRANTED WHERE THERE IS NO SUFFICIENT LEGAL BASIS FOR ANY OTHER JUDGMENT. The correct answer is C. Since it is entirely possible that a jury could conclude that Joan's physical problems were the consequence of the infection (rather than the inadvertent application of an acidic substance by Dr. Brown), a directed verdict would ***not*** be appropriate. Choice A is incorrect because the fact that Dr. Brown admitted that the perforium bottle was located near a container holding an acidic substance would not preclude the jury from reasonably concluding that the wrong bottle had ***not*** been used. Choice B is incorrect because it cannot be said that there was no sufficient legal basis for

concluding that Dr. Brown was ***not*** negligent. Finally, Choice D is incorrect because Choice C is true.

77. **(A)** A MOTION FOR A DIRECTED VERDICT SHOULD BE GRANTED WHERE THERE IS NO LEGALLY SUFFICIENT BASIS FOR ANY OTHER JUDGMENT. The correct answer is A. Since a jury could reasonably conclude that Dr. Brown did inadvertently apply an acidic substance to Joan's ear, a directed verdict in favor of the former would be inappropriate. Thus, the trial court's judgment should be reversed and a new trial ordered. If the trial court had withheld its decision upon the motion for a directed verdict until the jury had rendered its decision, it might not have been necessary to order a new trial (i.e., the jury verdict could be in conformity with the directed verdict). For this reason, a determination upon a motion for a directed verdict will ordinarily be withheld until after the jury's verdict has been returned. Choice B is incorrect because, as described in the answer to the preceding question, a jury could reasonably find that Dr. Brown was ***not*** at fault. Choice C is incorrect because a jury could reasonably render a verdict for Joan. Finally, Choice D is incorrect because Choice A is true.

78. **(D)** A MOTION FOR A DIRECTED VERDICT IS A PREREQUISITE FOR A J.N.O.V.; FRCP 50(b). A MOTION FOR A NEW TRIAL MAY BE JOINED WITH A MOTION FOR A J.N.O.V.; FRCP 50(b). The correct answer is D. Since Dr. Brown did not make a motion for a directed verdict at the close of the evidence, a j.n.o.v. cannot be granted. Since the trial court denied the motion for a new trial and Dr. Brown did not appeal this decision, the jury verdict must be reinstated. Choice A is incorrect because a motion for a new trial may be joined with a j.n.o.v. motion. Choice C is incorrect because no appeal was taken by Dr. Brown from the order denying a new trial. Thus, a new trial cannot be ordered. Finally, Choice B is incorrect because, no motion for a directed verdict having been made, a j.n.o.v. cannot be sustained.

79. **(D)** A PERSON WHO IS NOT A PARTY SHOULD BE JOINED WHERE FAILURE TO DO SO WILL LEAVE ANY PARTY TO THE ACTION SUBJECT TO A SUBSTANTIAL RISK OF INCURRING MULTIPLE LIABILITY FOR A SINGLE OBLIGATION. IF THE COURT DETERMINES THAT IN EQUITY AND GOOD CONSCIENCE THE ACTION SHOULD BE DISMISSED IN THE NON-PARTY'S ABSENCE, HE/SHE IS REGARDED AS BEING INDISPENSABLE. WHERE THE JOINDER OF AN INDISPENSABLE PARTY WILL DESTROY SUBJECT MATTER JURISDICTION, A FEDERAL COURT MUST DISMISS THE ACTION; FRCP 19. The correct answer is D. Z is probably ***not*** an indispensable party because (1) any decision in the *Y v. X* lawsuit would not have a collateral estoppel effect upon him, and (2) since Y was aware of Z's interest in the vehicle, Z could still pursue an action against Y in the event that Y was victorious against X. Additionally, X would be subjected to multiple liability for a single obligation. By entering into separate transactions with two different persons for the same item, X accepted the risk that each buyer would have an action against him if the vehicle were not delivered. Choice C is incorrect because ancillary jurisdiction does ***not*** extend to indispensable parties. Choice A is incorrect because, while Z does have an interest in the vehicle, that interest cannot be seriously impaired by the *Y v. X* lawsuit. Finally, Choice B is incorrect because the fact that the X-Z agreement preceded the X-Y agreement is irrelevant for purposes of determining if a person should be deemed to be an indispensable party.

80. **(B)** UPON TIMELY APPLICATION, A PERSON MAY INTERVENE IN AN ACTION AS OF RIGHT WHEN HE/SHE (1) CLAIMS AN INTEREST RELATING TO THE PROPERTY OR TRANSACTION WHICH IS THE SUBJECT OF THE ACTION, (2) HE/SHE IS SO SITUATED THAT DISPOSITION OF THE ACTION MAY, AS A PRACTICAL MATTER, IMPAIR HIS/HER ABILITY TO PROTECT THAT INTEREST, AND (3) THE APPLICANT'S INTEREST IS NOT ADEQUATELY REPRESENTED BY THE EXISTING PARTIES; FRCP 24(a)(2). The correct answer is B. Since Construction Company might have an indemnity-type of claim against Big Builders (arguably, the latter entity is more at fault than the former for providing the defective scaffolding), impleader would be appropriate if personal jurisdiction and venue requisites were satisfied. Subject matter jurisdiction would ***not*** be a consideration because ancillary jurisdiction would extend to the action by Construction Company against Big Builders. Choice A is incorrect because, while Big Builders arguably has an interest in the *Mary v. Construction Company* lawsuit, there appears to be no reason to believe that Construction Company could not effectively contest Mary's claim. Additionally, any judgment obtained by Mary would ***not*** have a collateral estoppel or res judicata effect in a subsequent action by Construction Company against Big Builders. Choice C is incorrect because, Construction Company's counterclaim being permissive in nature, the "amount in controversy" requirement would not be satisfied. Finally, Choice D is incorrect because Choice B is true.

81. **(A)** WHERE THE PARTY AGAINST WHOM A PRESUMPTION OPERATES HAS INTRODUCED PROOF SUFFICIENT FOR THE FACTFINDER TO RESOLVE THE FACTUAL PROPOSITION EMBODIED BY THE PRESUMPTION IN HIS/HER FAVOR, THE PARTY IN WHOSE FAVOR THE PRESUMPTION OPERATED MUST CARRY THE BURDEN OF PROOF WITH RESPECT TO SUCH FACTUAL PROPOSITION; Federal Rules of Evidence 301. The correct answer is A. Since Construction Company has introduced sufficient proof for a factfinder to determine that it had inspected the scaffolding (i.e., the supervisor had told Paul that it looked "unsafe"), Mary had the obligation to produce proof adequate for a factfinder to conclude that Construction Company had not inspected the scaffolding. However, Mary did not do this (her proof indicated only that Paul was apprehensive about working near the scaffolding). Choice B is incorrect because the evidence introduced by Mary does not pertain to Construction Company's alleged failure to inspect the scaffolding. Since Mary (as the plaintiff) would have the burden of proof on this issue, a verdict would have to be directed for Construction Company. Choice D is incorrect because Construction Company has introduced enough evidence to rebut the presumption against it (i.e., for a jury to conclude it had inspected the scaffolding). Finally, Choice C is incorrect because under these circumstances the court would be obliged to direct a verdict in favor of Construction Company.

82. **(D)** WHERE THE PARTY AGAINST WHOM A PRESUMPTION OPERATES HAS INTRODUCED PROOF SUFFICIENT FOR THE FACTFINDER TO RESOLVE THE FACTUAL PROPOSITION EMBODIED BY THE PRESUMPTION IN HIS/HER FAVOR, THE PARTY IN WHOSE FAVOR THE PRESUMPTION OPERATED MUST CARRY THE BURDEN OF PROOF WITH RESPECT TO SUCH FACTUAL PROPOSITION; Federal Rules of Evidence 301. A VERDICT CANNOT BE SET ASIDE IF THERE IS SUBSTANTIAL EVIDENCE TO SUPPORT IT. The correct answer is D. Since Construction Company introduced enough evidence to rebut the presumption (i.e., to cause Mary to introduce evidence sufficient to carry her burden of proof on the issue of whether Construction Company was negligent in its in-

spection of the scaffolding), the court's factual determination and corresponding judgment could ***not*** be set aside. Choice A is incorrect because, since substantial evidence pertaining to the factual proposition embodied by the presumption was introduced by each side, the presumption could be overcome. Thus, the court's judgment should be sustained. Choice B is incorrect because the presumption was rebutted when Construction Company introduced proof sufficient for a jury to infer that it had made a reasonable inspection of the scaffolding. Finally, Choice C is incorrect because a finding of fact may not be set aside whenever there is substantial evidence to support it.

83. **(A)** A CROSS-CLAIM MAY BE ASSERTED AGAINST A CO-PARTY IF THE CAUSE OF ACTION ARISES OUT OF THE TRANSACTION OR OCCURRENCE WHICH IS THE SUBJECT MATTER OF THE ORIGINAL ACTION; FRCP 13(g). The correct answer is A. Since Mary's cross-claim against John for indemnity arises from the accident, it may be asserted in this action. Although Mary and John are both citizens of Maine, there is ancillary jurisdiction with respect to cross-claims. Choice B is incorrect because cross-claims are not compulsory under the FRCP. Thus, an action is not barred if no cross-claim is made in the original lawsuit. Choice C is incorrect because Mary could assert a cross-claim against John under these circumstances. Finally, Choice D is incorrect because Mary's action against John would be a cross-claim, rather than a counterclaim (John is a co -party and has not commenced an action against Mary).

84. **(D)** A DEFENDANT MAY IMPLEAD ANOTHER PERSON, NOT A PARTY TO THE ACTION, WHO IS OR MAY BE LIABLE TO HIM/HER FOR ALL OR PART OF THE PLAINTIFF'S CLAIM AGAINST THE DEFENDING/IMPLEADING PARTY; FRCP 14(a). AN IMPLEADED PARTY MAY ASSERT AGAINST THE IMPLEADING PARTY ANY COUNTERCLAIMS PERMITTED PURSUANT TO FRCP 13; FRCP 14(a). The correct answer is D. The Star would probably have an indemnity-type claim against Albert if the information which the latter supplied to it was incorrect. The fact that The Star and Albert are citizens of the same state would not prevent the lawsuit, since there is ancillary jurisdiction for impleader actions. Choice C is incorrect because an impleader action may be instituted for an indemnity-type of claim. If The Star were asserting that Albert alone was liable to Beacon House, it would ***not*** satisfy this requisite. Choice A is incorrect because there is ancillary jurisdiction with respect to impleader actions. Finally, Choice B is incorrect because (1) any judgment by Beacon House against The Star would not have a collateral estoppel or res judicata effect upon Albert in the event of a subsequent action against the latter, and (2) Albert's interests will probably be adequately represented by The Star. Thus, intervention into the action by Albert would be permissive (rather than "as of right").

85. **(C)** WHERE THE PRECISE ISSUE WAS ACTUALLY LITIGATED IN A PRIOR SUIT BY THE PERSON AGAINST WHOM ISSUE PRECLUSION IS BEING ASSERTED, AND THAT ISSUE WAS ESSENTIAL TO THE DECISION RENDERED IN THAT ACTION, ISSUE PRECLUSION MAY BE PERMITTED. The correct answer is C. Since The Star would have actually litigated the issues pertaining to whether the statements in its article were true or not, a finding that such statements were untrue would presumably be binding upon The Star in a subsequent action against it by Don. A court could, however, refuse to allow Don to assert collateral estoppel if it felt that he had "hung back" by failing to commence litigation until the initial lawsuit was completed. Choice D

is incorrect because one is never required to intervene in an action (even if he/she could have done so as of right). Thus, a party who fails to intervene in an existing action does not forfeit his/her right to assert an action against a party in the initial lawsuit. Choice B is incorrect because, even though an action for an accounting has traditionally been viewed as being equitable in nature, it is now viewed as one for damages; *Dairy Queen v. Wood*, 369 U.S. 469 (1962). Thus, Albert probably would be entitled to a jury trial upon this question. Finally, Choice A is incorrect because there is ancillary subject matter jurisdiction with respect to cross-claims.

86. **(B)** A COURT MAY RE-ALIGN PARTIES TO REFLECT THEIR TRUE INTERESTS IN THE LITIGATION FOR DIVERSITY PURPOSES. The correct answer is B. Although D has an interest in the action (i.e., D wishes the trust to continue) which might be impaired if the plaintiffs are successful (i.e., D would pay a greater amount of taxes), diversity probably would ***not*** be destroyed by D's joinder. This is because D should be aligned with T (rather than made an involuntary plaintiff) since, as a practical matter, his/her interests coincide with those of T (they both desire to maintain the trial). Thus, complete diversity would exist even if D were compelled to join the litigation. Choice A is incorrect because for diversity to be satisfied, no plaintiff and no defendant may be citizens of the same state. Choice D is incorrect because, while D may be an indispensable party, he/she would probably be aligned with T. Thus, diversity would still exist. Finally, Choice C is incorrect because, even if D were aligned with T, diversity would still exist.

87. **(A)** WHERE ANSWERS TO WRITTEN INTERROGATORIES SUBMITTED AND A GENERAL VERDICT RENDERED BY THE JURY ARE INCONSISTENT, THE JUDGE MAY (1) ENTER A VERDICT IN ACCORDANCE WITH THE ANSWERS TO THE INTERROGATORIES, (2) RETURN THE ANSWERS TO THE JURY FOR FURTHER CONSIDERATION AND VERDICT, OR (3) ORDER A NEW TRIAL; FRCP 49(b). A PARTY MAY ORDINARILY DISMISS A LAWSUIT AFTER THE OTHER SIDE HAS FILED AN ANSWER BY FILING A STIPULATION OF DISMISSAL WHICH IS SIGNED BY ALL OF THE PARTIES WHO HAVE APPEARED IN THE ACTION. UNLESS OTHERWISE STATED IN THE NOTICE OF DISMISSAL OR STIPULATION, A DISMISSAL BY CONSENT IS WITHOUT PREJUDICE; FRCP 41(a)(1). The correct answer is A. Since the dismissal was signed by Defendant, it would be deemed to be without prejudice to Plaintiff's right to subsequently initiate a similar action against Defendant. Choice B is incorrect because a court is not obliged to render a judgment in strict conformity with the jury's answers to interrogatories. Choice C is incorrect because (1) the court cannot enter a general verdict which is inconsistent with the jury's answers to interrogatories, and (2) the court may send the interrogatory answers and verdict back to the jury for further consideration. Finally, Choice D is incorrect because Choice A is true.

88. **(C)** A PARTY MAY OBTAIN DISCOVERY OF THE EXISTENCE AND CONTENTS OF AN INSURANCE AGREEMENT UNDER WHICH ANY PERSON OPERATING AN INSURANCE BUSINESS MAY BE LIABLE FOR PART OR ALL OF THE JUDGMENT WHICH COULD BE ENTERED IN THE ACTION; FRCP 26(b)(2). The correct answer is C. The existence of an insurance policy held by another party to the action is always discoverable, even if it is not admissible at trial (FRCP 26). Choice D is incorrect because the existence of insurance by a party will rarely be relevant to the issues of the case. Choice B is incorrect because the existence of an insurance agreement is discover-

able. Finally, Choice A is incorrect because an insurance policy is explicitly made discoverable under the FRCP, regardless of whether it is admissible at trial.

89. **(A)** IF A DEPOSITION IS CONDUCTED IN BAD FAITH OR IN SUCH A MANNER AS TO ANNOY, EMBARRASS OR OPPRESS THE DEPONENT, THE COURT MAY ORDER THE OFFICER CONDUCTING THE EXAMINATION TO CEASE FORTHWITH FROM TAKING THE DEPOSITION OR LIMIT THE SCOPE AND MANNER OF THE DEPOSITION. IN SUCH EVENT, THE COURT MAY ORDER THE PARTY WHO WAS CONDUCTING THE DEPOSITION TO PAY THE ATTORNEYS' FEES OF THE OBJECTING PARTY; FRCP 30(d). IF THE PARTY WHO GAVE NOTICE OF THE TAKING OF A DEPOSITION FAILS TO ATTEND, THE COURT MAY ORDER THE PARTY WHO GAVE THE NOTICE TO PAY SUCH OTHER PARTY THE REASONABLE EXPENSES INCURRED BY HIM, INCLUDING REASONABLE ATTORNEYS' FEES; FRCP 30(g)(1). The correct answer is A. If Andy (1) conducted a deposition in a manner designed to embarrass the deponent, or (2) failed to attend a deposition which he had scheduled for another party, the party objecting to such behavior would be entitled to obtain his/her reasonable expenses associated with the depositions, including attorneys' fees. Allegation 3 would not be a cause for sanctions against Andy. If the deposed person or party can show that he/she was unable (despite the exercise of diligence) to obtain counsel to represent him/her at a deposition, the testimony may be precluded from being used against such party at trial; FRCP 30(b)(2). Finally, Allegation 4 does not justify sanctions; FRCP 30(c).

90. **(C)** IN AN FRCP 23(b)(3) CLASS ACTION, THE NOTICE MUST ADVISE EACH CLASS MEMBER THAT (1) ANY MEMBER MAY OPT OUT OF THE CLASS, (2) ANY MEMBER WHO DOES ***NOT*** OPT OUT OF THE CLASS WILL BE BOUND BY THE FINAL JUDGMENT, AND (3) ANY MEMBER WHO REMAINS IN THE CLASS MAY APPEAR IN THE ACTION THROUGH AN ATTORNEY; FRCP 23(c)(2). The correct answer is C. Since the notice fails to indicate that a final judgment is binding upon all members of the class, it is inadequate. Choice A is incorrect because the plaintiff (rather than the defendant) ***must*** pay the costs of mailings to class members. If he/she fails to do so, the action will be dismissed. Choice B is incorrect because a class action judgment has no negative collateral estoppel effect with respect to individuals who decided to opt out of the class. Finally, Choice D is incorrect because Choice B is true.

91. **(A)** PARTIES MAY OBTAIN DISCOVERY REGARDING ANY MATTER, NOT PRIVILEGED, WHICH IS RELEVANT TO THE SUBJECT MATTER OF THE PENDING ACTION. IT IS NOT A GROUND FOR OBJECTION THAT THE INFORMATION SOUGHT WILL NOT BE ADMISSIBLE AT TRIAL, IF SUCH INFORMATION IS REASONABLY CALCULATED TO LEAD TO THE DISCOVERY OF ADMISSIBLE EVIDENCE; FRCP 26(b)(1). The correct answer is A. If information sought is (1) privileged, or (2) not reasonably calculated to lead to admissible evidence, it need not be disclosed. Thus, Statements 1 and 3 embody valid objections. Statement 2 is incorrect because factual information relating to the claims of a party is discoverable. Finally, Statement 4 is not a valid objection because, while the fact that evidence might be obtained from a less expensive source may be considered by a court in determining whether or not to limit discovery, this type of limitation upon the ordinary rights of discovery can be successfully asserted only if embodied in a court order; FRCP 26(b)(1).

92. **(B)** DISCOVERY OF OPINIONS HELD BY EXPERTS AND DEVELOPED IN ANTICIPATION OF LITIGATION MAY BE OBTAINED THROUGH INTERROGATORIES; FRCP 26(b)(4)(A). The

correct answer is B. The opinion of P's expert is discoverable through interrogatories, even though this information was developed for purposes of trial. Choice A is incorrect because, even though the economist's opinion would otherwise constitute work product, an exception to this rule exists with respect to opinions to be rendered by an expert witness at trial. Choice D is incorrect because no privilege appears to be applicable to the economist's opinion. Finally, Choice C is incorrect because the fact that an expert's opinion was formed prior to the time litigation was actually commenced would not preclude such information from being discovered.

93. **(D)** UNDER ARTICLE 4, SECTION 1 OF THE U.S. CONSTITUTION, EACH STATE MUST ORDINARILY GIVE THE JUDGMENTS OF OTHER STATES THE SAME EFFECT (I.E., FULL FAITH AND CREDIT) WHICH THE EARLIER JUDGMENT WOULD HAVE IN THE STATE IN WHICH IT WAS RENDERED. The correct answer is D. The State Y court would be obliged under Full Faith and Credit principles to recognize the decision rendered in the State X court. Choice A is incorrect because, while the earlier judgment would prevent Defendant from ***re-litigating*** the claim, Plaintiff is seeking only to enforce the prior judgment. Choice B is incorrect because the State Y court cannot constitutionally disregard the State X judgment. Finally, Choice C is incorrect because the State Y court must give effect to the earlier judgment, even though it was based upon a doctrine which is not adhered to in State Y.

94. **(C)** WHERE THE PRECISE ISSUE WAS ACTUALLY LITIGATED IN A PRIOR ACTION BY THE PERSON AGAINST WHOM ISSUE PRECLUSION IS BEING ASSERTED, AND THAT ISSUE WAS ESSENTIAL TO THE DECISION RENDERED IN THAT LAWSUIT, ISSUE PRECLUSION MAY BE PERMITTED. The correct answer is C. Since C was not in privy with A in any way, the judgment rendered against A could not preclude C from re-litigating the question of B's negligence. The application of collateral estoppel in these circumstances would violate C's due process rights. Choice A is incorrect because the application of collateral estoppel principles would violate C's due process rights. Choice B is incorrect because (i) a different action is involved (C's rights of recovery, rather than A's), and (ii) A and C are not in privy. Finally, Choice D is incorrect because collateral estoppel may not be constitutionally applied, whether or not the mutuality rule has been repudiated in this state.

95. **(B)** FOR PURPOSES OF DIVERSITY, A PARTNERSHIP IS DEEMED TO BE A CITIZEN OF THE STATES IN WHICH EACH ONE OF ITS PARTNERS IS DOMICILED. The correct answer is B. It would be helpful to know where Paul is domiciled to determine if that state is the same one in which (1) either of Dodo's partners is domiciled (State X), or (2) Dominic's is a citizen for diversity purposes (State Z). Thus, Factor 2 is important since, if Paul were a citizen of either State X or State Z, diversity subject matter jurisdiction would not exist. It would also be helpful to know the extent of Paul's injuries to determine if the "in excess of $75,000" requirement is satisfied. Factor 2 is unimportant because the citizenship of a corporation is determined by its states of incorporation and principal place of business. The place of domicile of its shareholders is irrelevant for diversity purposes. Finally, Factor 4 is important for purposes of personal jurisdiction, but is unrelated to determining the court's competency.

96. **(A)** UNDER FRCP 4, NOTICE WITH RESPECT TO ACTIONS COMMENCED IN A U.S. DISTRICT COURT MUST BE ACCOMPLISHED IN ACCORDANCE WITH THE FRCP ***OR*** THE APPLICABLE LOCAL LAW. HOWEVER, AS A MATTER OF DUE PROCESS, NOTICE MUST ALWAYS BE REASONABLY CALCULATED UNDER THE CIRCUMSTANCES TO APPRISE THE DEFENDANT OF THE OUTSTANDING ACTION. The correct answer is A. There is little doubt that a procedure which permits notification by posting in a situation where personal service could probably be effectuated would be unconstitutional; *Schroeder v. City of New York*, 371 U.S. 208 (1962), *Walker v. City of Hutchinson*, 352 U.S. 112 (1956). Since the names of the officers or directors of Dominic's could presumably be ascertained from the State Z corporate records, the State Z notice statute would be unconstitutional as applied to these circumstances. Choice C is incorrect because actual receipt of notice by a defendant does not cure a statutorily invalid statute; *Wuchter v. Pizzutti*, 276 U.S. 13 (1928). Choice C is incorrect because notice in a federal court proceeding may be given in accordance with the applicable state service of process statute (provided, of course, it is valid). Finally, Choice D is incorrect because (while factually true) the state notice statute must be constitutional as applied to the existing circumstances.

97. **(A)** UNLESS A TRADITIONAL BASIS OF PERSONAL JURISDICTION EXISTS, PERSONAL JURISDICTION MAY NOT BE TAKEN OVER AN OUT-OF-STATE DEFENDANT UNLESS IT IS STATUTORILY AND CONSTITUTIONALLY PERMISSIBLE. The correct answer is A. Since Dodo's is not physically present in State Z (i.e., it has no personnel in the jurisdiction), the existence of a long-arm statute which empowered State Z courts to assert personal jurisdiction over a defendant in circumstances such as these would be a very significant inquiry. Thus, Statement 1 is pertinent. Statement 2 is pertinent because Dodoawareness that the oven would be utilized in State Z would certainly make it more likely that it should have reasonably foreseen being haled into court in that state; *World-Wide Volkswagen Corp. v. Woodson*, 444 U.S. 286 (1980). Statement 3 is pertinent because the greater the volume of business done by Dodo in State Z, the less likely it would be that "traditional notions of fair play and substantial justice" would be "offended" by making the defendant stand trial in that state; *International Shoe Co. v. Washington*, 326 U.S. 310 (1945). Finally, the physical health of the parties involved in litigation has never been cited as a relevant factor in the determination of whether personal jurisdiction exists or not (it could presumably be considered in the context of a forum non conveniens motion).

98. **(C)** A PERSON WHO IS NOT A PARTY SHOULD BE JOINED WHERE FAILURE TO DO SO WILL LEAVE ANY PARTY TO THE ACTION SUBJECT TO A SUBSTANTIAL RISK OF INCURRING MULTIPLE LIABILITY FOR A SINGLE OBLIGATION. IF THE COURT DETERMINES THAT IN EQUITY AND IN GOOD CONSCIENCE THE ACTION SHOULD BE DISMISSED IN THE NON-PARTY'S ABSENCE, HE/SHE IS REGARDED AS BEING INDISPENSABLE. WHERE THE JOINDER OF AN INDISPENSABLE PARTY WILL DESTROY SUBJECT MATTER JURISDICTION, A FEDERAL COURT MUST DISMISS THE ACTION; FRCP 19. The correct answer is C. Paul can obtain complete relief (a judgment for the full amount of his damages) without the necessity of joining Dan. Additionally, Acme will not be exposed to multiple liability for the same obligation since (i) Paul can only obtain one recovery for his injuries, and (ii) where the potential defendants are joint tortfeasors, none of them is prejudiced by a plaintiff's decision to refrain from suing every person who could possibly be liable (i.e., the risk that a particular defendant could

have to bear the entire amount of the plaintiff's recovery always exists in joint tortfeasor situations). Choice B is incorrect because a plaintiff in a U.S. District Court suing a single defendant may aggregate totally unrelated claims to meet the jurisdictional amount. It is only where plaintiff asserts actions against more than one defendant that the plaintiff must show that at least one of his/her claims (1) arise from a common transaction or occurrence, and (2) possess a common question of law or fact. Choice A is incorrect because (as explained above) Dan is ***not*** an indispensable party. Finally, Choice D is incorrect because Choice B is ***not*** true.

99. **(D)** A PARTY IS ENTITLED TO A SUMMARY JUDGMENT WHERE, AS A CONSEQUENCE OF THERE BEING NO "GENUINE ISSUE OF MATERIAL FACT," HE/SHE IS ENTITLED TO JUDGMENT AS A MATTER OF LAW; FRCP 56. The correct answer is D. Even though Acme neglected to respond to Paul's affidavit, Paul would only be entitled to a partial summary judgment (i.e., with respect to the issue of his job competency). His affidavit does not address the issues of (1) was Dan's statement about Paul within the scope of Dan's employment, and (2) was Paul entitled to recover for the unused vacation pay? Choice C is incorrect because the affidavit necessary to support a summary judgment motion may be made by the moving party, personally. Choice A is incorrect because, while factually accurate, it would only entitle Paul to a summary judgment with respect to the issue of his competency. Finally, Choice B is incorrect because (as explained above) genuine issues of fact still exist.

100. **(C)** WHERE THE PRECISE ISSUE WAS ACTUALLY LITIGATED IN A PRIOR LAWSUIT BY THE PARTY (OR HIS/HER PRIVY) AGAINST WHOM ISSUE PRECLUSION IS BEING ASSERTED IN A SUBSEQUENT ACTION, AND THAT ISSUE WAS ESSENTIAL TO THE DECISION WHICH WAS RENDERED IN THE EARLIER LAWSUIT, ISSUE PRECLUSION WILL ORDINARILY BE APPLIED. The correct answer is C. Neither issue (whether Dan's statement was true, and whether it was within the scope of Dan's employment), independently, was essential to the judgment. Acme would have been victorious if it had prevailed on either of the issues. It should be noted that some states apply offensive collateral estoppel where a specific factual finding was made on an issue (even if that issue was not essential to the judgment). However, since a general verdict was rendered in this instance, this view could not be applied. Choice B is incorrect because (as explained immediately above) collateral estoppel principles are not applicable. Finally, Choice A is incorrect because (i) a different cause of action is involved (*Paul v. Dan*), and (ii) Dan would probably ***not*** be deemed to be in privy with Acme.

RULES OF CIVIL PROCEDURE FOR THE UNITED STATES DISTRICT COURTS

I. SCOPE OF RULES—ONE FORM OF ACTION

Rule 1. SCOPE AND PURPOSE OF RULES

These rules govern the procedure in the United States district courts in all suits of a civil nature whether cognizable as cases at law or in equity or in admiralty, with the exceptions stated in Rule 81. They shall be construed and administered to secure the just, speedy, and inexpensive determination of every action.

As amended 1949, 1966, 1993.

Rule 2. ONE FORM OF ACTION

There shall be one form of action to be known as "civil action."

II. COMMENCEMENT OF ACTION; SERVICE OF PROCESS, PLEADINGS, MOTIONS, AND ORDERS

Rule 3. COMMENCEMENT OF ACTION

A civil action is commenced by filing a complaint with the court.

Rule 4. SUMMONS

(a) Form. The summons shall be signed by the clerk, bear the seal of the court, identify the court and the parties, be directed to the defendant, and state the name and address of the plaintiff's attorney or, if unrepresented, of the plaintiff. It shall also state the time within which the defendant must appear and defend, and notify the defendant that failure to do so will result in a judgment by default against the defendant for the relief demanded in the complaint. The court may allow a summons to be amended.

(b) Issuance. Upon or after filing the complaint, the plaintiff may present a summons to the clerk for signature and seal. If the summons is in proper form, the clerk shall sign, seal, and issue it to the plaintiff for service on the defendant. A summons, or a copy of the summons if addressed to multiple defendants, shall be issued for each defendant to be served.

(c) Service with Complaint; by Whom Made.

(1) A summons shall be served together with a copy of the complaint. The plaintiff is responsible for service of a summons and complaint within the time allowed under subdivision (m) and shall furnish the person effecting service with the necessary copies of the summons and complaint.

(2) Service may be effected by any person who is not a party and who is at least 18 years of age. At the request of the plaintiff, however, the court may direct that service be effected by a United States marshal, deputy United States marshal, or other person or officer specially appointed by the court for that purpose. Such an appointment must be made when the plaintiff is authorized to proceed in forma pauperis pursuant to 28 U.S.C. § 1915 or is authorized to proceed as a seaman under 28 U.S.C. § 1916.

(d) Waiver of Service; Duty to Save Costs of Service; Request to Waive.

(1) A defendant who waives service of a summons does not thereby waive any objection to the venue or to the jurisdiction of the court over the person of the defendant.

(2) An individual, corporation, or association that is subject to service under subdivision (e), (f), or (h) and that receives notice of an action in the manner provided in this paragraph has a duty to avoid unnecessary costs of serving the summons. To avoid costs, the plaintiff may notify such a defendant of the commencement of the action and request that the defendant waive service of a summons. The notice and request

(A) shall be in writing and shall be addressed directly to the defendant, if an individual, or else to an officer or managing or general agent (or other agent authorized by appointment or law to receive service of process) of a defendant subject to service under subdivision (h);

(B) shall be dispatched through first-class mail or other reliable means;

(C) shall be accompanied by a copy of the complaint and shall identify the court in which it has been filed;

(D) shall inform the defendant, by means of a text prescribed in an official form promulgated pursuant to Rule 84, of the consequences of compliance and of a failure to comply with the request;

(E) shall set forth the date on which the request is sent;

(F) shall allow the defendant a reasonable time to return the waiver, which shall be at least 30 days from the date on which the request is sent, or 60 days from that date if the defendant is addressed outside any judicial district of the United States; and

(G) shall provide the defendant with an extra copy of the notice and request, as well as a prepaid means of compliance in writing.

If a defendant located within the United States fails to comply with a request for waiver made by a plaintiff located within the United States, the court shall impose the costs subsequently incurred in effecting service on the defendant unless good cause for the failure be shown.

(3) A defendant that, before being served with process, timely returns a waiver so requested is not required to serve an answer to the complaint until 60 days after the date on which the request for waiver of service was sent, or 90 days after that date if the defendant was addressed outside any judicial district of the United States.

(4) When the plaintiff files a waiver of service with the court, the action shall proceed, except as provided in paragraph (3), as if a summons and complaint had been served at the time of filing the waiver, and no proof of service shall be required.

(5) The costs to be imposed on a defendant under paragraph (2) for failure to comply with a request to waive service of a summons shall include the costs subsequently incurred in effecting service under subdivision (e), (f), or (h), together with the costs, including a reasonable attorney's fee, of any motion required to collect the costs of service.

(e) Service upon Individuals Within a Judicial District of the United States. Unless otherwise provided by federal law, service upon an individual from whom a waiver has not been obtained and filed, other than an infant or an incompetent person, may be effected in any judicial district of the United States:

(1) pursuant to the law of the state in which the district court is located, or in which service is effected, for the service of a summons upon the defendant in an action brought in the courts of general jurisdiction of the State; or

(2) by delivering a copy of the summons and of the complaint to the individual personally or by leaving copies thereof at the individual's dwelling house or usual place of abode with some person of suitable age and discretion then residing therein or by delivering a copy of the summons and of the complaint to an agent authorized by appointment or by law to receive service of process.

(f) Service upon Individuals in a Foreign Country. Unless otherwise provided by federal law, service upon an individual from whom a waiver has not been obtained and filed, other than an infant or an incompetent person, may be effected in a place not within any judicial district of the United States:

(1) by any internationally agreed means reasonably calculated to give notice, such as those means authorized by the Hague Convention on the Service Abroad of Judicial and Extrajudicial Documents; or

(2) if there is no internationally agreed means of service or the applicable international agreement allows other means of service, provided that service is reasonably calculated to give notice:

(A) in the manner prescribed by the law of the foreign country for service in that country in an action in any of its courts of general jurisdiction; or

(B) as directed by the foreign authority in response to a letter rogatory or letter of request; or

(C) unless prohibited by the law of the foreign, country, by

(i) delivery to the individual personally of a copy of the summons and the complaint; or

(ii) any form of mail requiring a signed receipt, to be addressed and dispatched by the clerk of the court to the party to be served; or

(3) by other means not prohibited by international agreement as may be directed by the court.

(g) Service upon Infants and Incompetent Persons. Service upon an infant or an incompetent person in a judicial district of the United States shall be effected in the manner prescribed by the law of the state in which the service is made for the service of summons or other like process upon any such defendant in an action brought in the courts of general jurisdiction of that state. Service upon an infant or an incompetent person in a place not within any judicial district of the United States shall be effected in the manner prescribed by paragraph (2)(A) or (2)(B) of subdivision (f) or by such means as the court may direct.

(h) Service upon Corporations and Associations. Unless otherwise provided by federal law, service upon a domestic or foreign corporation or upon a partnership or other unincorporated association that is subject to suit under a common name, and from which a waiver of service has not been obtained and filed, shall be effected:

(1) in a judicial district of the United States in the manner prescribed for individuals by subdivision (e)(1), or by delivering a copy of the summons and of the complaint to an officer, a managing or general agent, or to any other agent authorized by appointment or by law to receive service of process and, if the agent is one authorized by statute to receive service and the statute so requires, by also mailing a copy to the defendant, or

(2) in a place not within any judicial district of the United States in any manner prescribed for individuals by subdivision (f) except personal delivery as provided in paragraph (2)(C)(i) thereof

(i) Service upon the United States, and Its Agencies, Corporations, or Officers.

(1) Service upon the United States shall be effected

(A) by delivering a copy of the summons and of the complaint to the United States attorney for the district in which the action is brought or to an assistant United States attorney or clerical employee designated by the United States attorney in a writing filed with the clerk of the court or by sending a copy of the summons and of the complaint by registered or certified mail addressed to the civil process clerk at the office of the United States attorney and

(B) by also sending a copy of the summons and of the complaint by registered or certified mail to the Attorney General of the United States at Washington, District of Columbia, and

(C) in any action attacking the validity of an order of an officer or agency of the United States not made a party, by also sending a copy of the summons and of the complaint by registered or certified mail to the officer or agency.

(2) Service upon an officer, agency, or corporation of the United States shall be effected by serving the United States in the manner prescribed by paragraph (1) of this subdivision and by also sending a copy of the summons and of the complaint by registered or certified mail to the officer, agency, or corporation.

(3) The court shall allow a reasonable time for service of process under this subdivision for the purpose of curing the failure to serve multiple officers, agencies, or corporations of the United States if the plaintiff has effected service on either the United States attorney or the Attorney General of the United States.

(j) Service upon Foreign, State, or Local Governments.

(1) Service upon a foreign state or a political subdivision, agency, or instrumentality thereof shall be effected pursuant to 28 U.S.C. § 1608.

(2) Service upon a state, municipal corporation, or other governmental organization subject to suit shall be effected by delivering a copy of the summons and of the complaint to its chief executive officer or by serving the summons and complaint in the manner prescribed by the law of that state for the service of summons or other like process upon any such defendant.

(k) Territorial Limits of Effective Service.

(1) Service of a summons or filing a waiver of service is effective to establish jurisdiction over the person of a defendant

(A) who could be subjected to the jurisdiction of a court of general jurisdiction in the state in which the district court is located, or

(B) who is a party joined under Rule 14 or Rule 19 and is served at a place within a judicial district of the United States and not more than 100 miles from the place from which the summons issues, or

(C) who is subject to the federal interpleader jurisdiction under 28 U.S.C. § 1335, or

(D) when authorized by a statute of the United States.

(2) If the exercise of jurisdiction is consistent with the Constitution and laws of the United States, serving a summons or filing a waiver of service is also effective, with respect to claims arising under federal law, to establish personal jurisdiction over the person of any defendant who is not subject to the jurisdiction of the courts of general jurisdiction of any state.

(l) Proof of Service. If service is not waived, the person effecting service shall make proof thereof to the court. If service is made by a person other than a United States marshal or deputy United States marshal, the person shall make affidavit thereof. Proof of service in a place not within any judicial district of the United States shall, if effected under paragraph (1) of subdivision (f), be made pursuant to the applicable treaty or convention, and shall, if effected under paragraph (2) or (3) thereof, include a receipt signed by the addressee or other evidence of delivery to the addressee satisfactory to the court. Failure to make proof of service does not affect the validity of the service. The court may allow proof of service to be amended.

(m) Time Limit for Service. If service of the summons and complaint is not made upon a defendant within 120 days after the filing of the complaint, the court, upon motion or on its own initiative after notice to the plaintiff, shall dismiss the action without prejudice as to that defendant or direct that service be effected within a specified time; provided that if the plaintiff shows good cause for the failure, the court shall extend the time for service for an appropriate period. This subdivision does not apply to service in a foreign country pursuant to subdivision (f) or (j)(1).

(n) Seizure of Property; Service of Summons Not Feasible.

(1) If a statute of the United States so provides, the court may assert jurisdiction over property. Notice to claimants of the property shall then be sent in the manner provided by the statute or by service of a summons under this rule.

(2) Upon a showing that personal jurisdiction over a defendant cannot, in the district where the action is brought, be obtained with reasonable efforts by service of summons in any manner authorized by this rule, the court may assert jurisdiction over any of the defendant's assets found within the district by seizing the assets under the circumstances and in the manner provided by the law of the state in which the district court is located.

As amended 1963, 1966, 1980, 1983, 1987, 1993.

Rule 4.1.
SERVICE OF OTHER PROCESS

(a) Generally. Process other than a summons as provided in Rule 4 or subpoena as provided in Rule 45 shall be served by a United States marshal, a deputy United States marshal, or a person specially appointed for that purpose, who shall make proof of service as provided in Rule 4(l). The process may be served anywhere within the territorial limits of the state in which the district court is located, and, when authorized by a statute of the United States, beyond the territorial limits of that state.

(b) Enforcement of Orders: Commitment for Civil Contempt. An order of civil commitment of a person held to be in contempt of a decree or injunction issued to enforce the laws of the United States may be served and enforced in any district. Other orders in civil contempt proceedings shall be served in the state in which the court issuing the order to be enforced is located or elsewhere within the United States if not more than 100 miles from the place at which the order to be enforced was issued.

Added 1993.

Rule 5.
SERVICE AND FILING OF PLEADINGS AND OTHER PAPERS

(a) Service: When Required. Except as otherwise provided in these rules, every order required by its terms to be served, every pleading subsequent to the original complaint unless the court otherwise orders because of numerous defendants, every paper relating to discovery required to be served upon a party unless the court otherwise orders, every written motion other than one which may be heard ex parte, and every written notice, appearance, demand, offer of judgment, designation of record on appeal, and similar paper shall be served upon each of the parties. No service need be made on parties in default for failure to appear except that pleadings asserting new or additional claims for relief against them shall be served upon them in the manner provided for service of summons in Rule 4.

In an action begun by seizure of property, in which no person need be or is named as defendant, any service required to be made prior to the filing of an answer, claim, or appearance shall be made upon the person having custody or possession of the property at the time of its seizure.

(b) Same: How Made. Whenever under these rules service is required or permitted to be made upon a party represented by an attorney the service shall be made upon the attorney unless service upon the party is ordered by the court. Service upon the attorney or upon a party shall be made by delivering a copy to the attorney or party or by mailing it to the attorney or party at the attorney's or party's last known address or, if no address is known, by leaving it with the clerk of the court. Delivery of a copy within this rule means: handing it to the attorney or to the party; or leaving it at the attorney's or party's office with a clerk or other person in charge thereof; or, if there is no one in charge, leaving it in a conspicuous place therein; or, if the office is closed or the person to be served has no office, leaving it at the person's dwelling house or usual place of abode with some person of suitable age and discretion then residing therein. Service by mail is complete upon mailing.

(c) Same: Numerous Defendants. In any action in which there are unusually large numbers of defendants, the court, upon motion or of its own initiative, may order that service of the pleadings of the defendants and replies thereto need not be made as between the defendants and that any cross-claim, counterclaim, or matter constituting an avoidance or affirmative defense contained therein shall be deemed to be denied or avoided by all other parties and that the filing of any such pleading and service thereof upon the plaintiff constitutes due notice of it to the parties. A copy of every such order shall be served upon the parties in such manner and form as the court directs.

(d) Filing; Certificate of Service. All papers after the complaint required to be served upon a party, together with a certificate of service, shall be filed with the court within a reasonable time after service, but the court may on motion of a party or on its own initiative order that depositions upon oral examination and interrogatories, requests for documents, requests for admission, and answers and responses thereto not be filed unless on order of the court or for use in the proceeding.

(e) Filing with the Court Defined. The filing of papers with the court as required by these rules shall be made by filing them with the clerk of the court, except that the judge may permit the papers to be filed with the judge, in which event the judge shall note thereon the filing date and forthwith transmit them to the office of the clerk. A court may, by local rule, permit papers to be filed by facsimile or other electronic means if such means are authorized by and consistent with standards established by the Judicial Conference of the United States. The clerk shall not refuse to accept for filing any paper presented for that purpose solely because it is not presented in proper form as required by these rules or any local rules or practices.

As amended 1963, 1970, 1980, 1987, 1991, 1993.

Rule 6.
TIME

(a) Computation. In computing any period of time prescribed or allowed by these rules, by the local rules of any district court, by order of court, or by any applicable statute, the day of the act, event, or default from which the designated period of time begins to run shall not be included. The last day of the period so computed shall be included, unless it is a Saturday, a Sunday, or a legal holiday, or, when the act to be done is the filing of a paper in court, a day on which weather or other conditions have made the office of the clerk of the district court inaccessible, in which event the period runs until the end of the next day which is not one of the aforementioned days. When the period of time prescribed or allowed is less than 11 days, intermediate Saturdays, Sundays, and legal holidays shall be excluded in the computation. As used in this rule and in Rule 77(c), "legal holiday" includes New Year's Day, Birthday of Martin Luther King, Jr., Washington's Birthday, Memorial Day, Independence Day, Labor Day, Columbus Day, Veterans Day, Thanksgiving Day, Christmas Day, and any other day appointed as a holiday by the President or the Congress of the United States, or by the state in which the district court is held.

(b) Enlargement. When by these rules or by a notice given thereunder or by order of court an act is required or allowed to be done at or within a specified time, the court for cause shown may at any time in its discretion (1) with or without motion or notice order the period enlarged if request therefor is made before the expiration of the period originally prescribed or as extended by a previous order, or (2) upon motion made after the expiration of the specified period permit the act to be done where the failure to act was the result of excusable neglect; but it may not extend the time for taking any action under Rules 50(b) and (c)(2), 52(b), 59(b), (d) and (e), 60(b), and 74(a), except to the extent and under the conditions stated in them.

(c) Unaffected by Expiration of Term. Rescinded Feb. 28, 1966, eff. July 1, 1966.

(d) For Motions—Affidavits. A written motion, other than one which may be heard ex parte, and notice of the hearing thereof shall be served not later than 5 days before the time specified for the hearing, unless a different period is fixed by these rules or by order of the court. Such an order may for cause shown be made on ex parte application. When a motion is supported by affidavit, the affidavit shall be served with the motion; and, except as otherwise provided in Rule 59(c), opposing affidavits may be served not later than 1 day before the hearing, unless the court permits them to be served at some other time.

(e) Additional Time After Service by Mail. Whenever a party has the right or is required to do some act or take some proceedings within a prescribed period after the service of a notice or other paper upon the party and the notice or paper is served upon the party by mail, 3 days shall be added to the prescribed period.

As amended 1948, 1963, 1966, 1968, 1971, 1983, 1985, 1987.

III. PLEADINGS AND MOTIONS

Rule 7.
PLEADINGS ALLOWED; FORM OF MOTIONS

(a) Pleadings. There shall be a complaint and an answer; a reply to a counterclaim denominated as such; an answer to a crossclaim, if the answer contains a cross-claim; a third-party complaint, if a person who was not an original party is summoned under the provisions of Rule 14; and a third-party answer, if a third-party complaint is served. No other pleading shall be allowed, except that the court may order a reply to an answer or a third-party answer.

(b) Motions and Other Papers.

(1) An application to the court for an order shall be by motion which, unless made during a hearing or trial, shall be made in writing, shall state with particularity the grounds therefor,

and shall set forth the relief or order sought. The requirement of writing is fulfilled if the motion is stated in a written notice of the hearing of the motion.

(2) The rules applicable to captions and other matters of form of pleadings apply to all motions and other papers provided for by these rules.

(3) All motions shall be signed in accordance with Rule 11.

(c) Demurrers, Pleas, etc., Abolished. Demurrers, pleas, and exceptions for insufficiency of a pleading shall not be used.

As amended 1948, 1963, 1983.

Rule 8.
GENERAL RULES OF PLEADING

(a) Claims for Relief. A pleading which sets forth a claim for relief, whether an original claim, counterclaim, cross-claim, or third-party claim, shall contain (1) a short and plain statement of the grounds upon which the court's jurisdiction depends, unless the court already has jurisdiction and the claim needs no new grounds of jurisdiction to support it, (2) a short and plain statement of the claim showing that the pleader is entitled to relief, and (3) a demand for judgment for the relief the pleader seeks. Relief in the alternative or of several different types may be demanded.

(b) Defenses; Form of Denials. A party shall state in short and plain terms the party's defenses to each claim asserted and shall admit or deny the averments upon which the adverse party relies. If a party is without knowledge or information sufficient to form a belief as to the truth of an averment, the party shall so state and this has the effect of a denial. Denials shall fairly meet the substance of the averments denied. When a pleader intends in good faith to deny only a part or a qualification of an averment, the pleader shall specify so much of it as is true and material and shall deny only the remainder. Unless the pleader intends in good faith to controvert all the averments of the preceding pleading, the pleader may make denials as specific denials of designated averments or paragraphs or may generally deny all the averments except such designated averments or paragraphs as the pleader expressly admits; but, when the pleader does so intend to controvert all its averments, including averments of the grounds upon which the court's jurisdiction depends, the pleader may do so by general denial subject to the obligations set forth in Rule 11.

(c) Affirmative Defenses. In pleading to a preceding pleading, a party shall set forth affirmatively accord and satisfaction, arbitration and award, assumption of risk, contributory negligence, discharge in bankruptcy, duress, estoppel, failure of consideration, fraud, illegality, injury by fellow servant, laches, license, payment, release, res judicata, statute of frauds, statute of limitations, waiver, and any other matter constituting an avoidance or affirmative defense. When a party has mistakenly designated a defense as a counterclaim or a counterclaim as a defense, the court on terms, if justice so requires, shall treat the pleading as if there had been a proper designation.

(d) Effect of Failure to Deny. Averments in a pleading to which a responsive pleading is required, other than those as to the amount of damage, are admitted when not denied in the responsive pleading. Averments in a pleading to which no responsive pleading is required or permitted shall be taken as denied or avoided.

(e) Pleading to Be Concise and Direct; Consistency.

(1) Each averment of a pleading shall be simple, concise, and direct. No technical forms of pleading or motions are required.

(2) A party may set forth two or more statements of a claim or defense alternately or hypothetically, either in one count or defense or in separate counts or defenses. When two or more statements are made in the alternative and one of them if made independently would be sufficient, the pleading is not made insufficient by the insufficiency of one or more of the alternative statements. A party may also state as many separate claims or defenses as the party has regardless of consistency and whether based on legal, equitable, or maritime grounds. All statements shall be made subject to the obligations set forth in Rule 11.

(f) Construction of Pleadings. All pleadings shall be so construed as to do substantial justice.

As amended 1966, 1987.

Rule 9.
PLEADING SPECIAL MATTERS

(a) Capacity. It is not necessary to aver the capacity of a party to sue or be sued or the authority of a party to sue or be sued in a representative capacity or the legal existence of an organized association of persons that is made a party, except to the extent required to show the jurisdiction of the court. When a party desires to raise an issue as to the legal existence of any party or the capacity of any party to sue or be sued or the authority of a party to sue or be sued in a representative capacity, the party desiring to raise the issue shall do so by specific negative averment, which shall include such supporting particulars as are peculiarly within the pleader's knowledge.

(b) Fraud, Mistake, Condition of the Mind. In all averments of fraud or mistake, the circumstances constituting fraud or mistake shall be stated with particularity. Malice, intent, knowledge, and other condition of mind of a person may be averred generally.

(c) Conditions Precedent. In pleading the performance or occurrence of conditions precedent, it is sufficient to aver generally that all conditions precedent have been performed or have occurred. A denial of performance or occurrence shall be made specifically and with particularity.

(d) Official Document or Act. In pleading an official document or official act it is sufficient to aver that the document was issued or the act done in compliance with law.

(e) Judgment. In pleading a judgment or decision of a domestic or foreign court, judicial or quasi-judicial tribunal, or of a board or officer, it is sufficient to aver the judgment or decision without setting forth matter showing jurisdiction to render it.

(f) Time and Place. For the purpose of testing the sufficiency of a pleading, averments of time and place are material and shall be considered like all other averments of material matter.

(g) Special Damage. When items of special damage are claimed, they shall be specifically stated.

(h) Admiralty and Maritime Claims. A pleading or count setting forth a claim for relief within the admiralty and maritime jurisdiction that is also within the jurisdiction of the district court on some other ground may contain a statement identifying the claim as an admiralty or maritime claim for the purposes of Rules 14(c), 38(e), 82, and the Supplemental Rules for Certain Admiralty and Maritime Claims. If the claim is cognizable only in admiralty, it is an admiralty or maritime claim for those purposes whether so identified or not. The amendment of a pleading to add or withdraw an identifying statement is governed by the principles of Rule 15. The reference in Title 28, U.S.C., § 1292(a)(3), to admiralty cases shall be construed to mean admiralty and maritime claims within the meaning of this subdivision (h).

As amended 1966, 1968, 1970, 1987.

Rule 10.
FORM OF PLEADINGS

(a) Caption; Names of Parties. Every pleading shall contain a caption setting forth the name of the court, the title of the action, the file number, and a designation as in Rule 7(a). In the complaint the title of the action shall include the names of all the parties, but in other pleadings it is sufficient to state the name of the first party on each side with an appropriate indication of other parties.

(b) Paragraphs; Separate Statements. All averments of claim or defense shall be made in numbered paragraphs, the contents of each of which shall be limited as far as practicable to a statement of a single set of circumstances; and a paragraph may be referred to by number in all succeeding pleadings. Each claim founded upon a separate transaction or occurrence and each defense other than denials shall be stated in a separate count or defense whenever a separation facilitates the clear presentation of the matters set forth.

(c) Adoption by Reference; Exhibits. Statements in a pleading may be adopted by reference in a different part of the same pleading or in another pleading or in any motion. A copy of any written instrument which is an exhibit to a pleading is a part thereof for all purposes.

Rule 11.
SIGNING OF PLEADINGS, MOTIONS, AND OTHER PAPERS; REPRESENTATIONS TO COURT; SANCTIONS

(a) Signature. Every pleading, written motion, and other paper shall be signed by at least one attorney of record in the attorney's individual name, or, if the party is not represented by an attorney, shall be signed by the party. Each paper shall state the signer's address and telephone number, if any. Except when otherwise specifically provided by rule or statute, pleadings need not be verified or accompanied by affidavit. An unsigned paper shall be stricken unless omission of the signature is corrected promptly after being called to the attention of the attorney or party.

(b) Representations to Court. By presenting to the court (whether by signing, filing, submitting, or later advocating) a pleading, written motion, or other paper, an attorney or unrepresented party is certifying that to the best of the person's knowledge, information, and belief, formed after an inquiry reasonable under the circumstances,

(1) it is not being presented for any improper purpose, such as to harass or to cause unnecessary delay or needless increase in the cost of litigation;

(2) the claims, defenses, and other legal contentions therein are warranted by existing law or by a nonfrivolous argument for the extension, modification, or reversal of existing law or the establishment of new law;

(3) the allegations and other factual contentions have evidentiary support or, if specifically so identified, are likely to have evidentiary support after a reasonable opportunity for further investigation or discovery; and

(4) the denials of factual contentions are warranted on the evidence or, if specifically so identified, are reasonably based on a lack of information or belief.

(c) Sanctions. If, after notice and a reasonable opportunity to respond, the court determines that subdivision (b) has been violated, the court may, subject to the conditions stated below, impose an appropriate sanction upon the attorneys, law firms, or parties that have violated subdivision (b) or are responsible for the violation.

(1) *How Initiated.*

(A) *By Motion.* A motion for sanctions under this rule shall be made separately from other motions or requests and shall describe the specific conduct alleged to violate subdivision (b). It shall be served as provided in Rule 5, but shall not be filed with or presented to the court unless, within 21 days after service of the motion (or such other period as the court may prescribe), the challenged paper, claim, defense, contention, allegation, or denial is not withdrawn or appropriately corrected. If warranted, the court may award to the party prevailing on the motion the reasonable expenses and attorney's fees incurred in presenting or opposing the motion. Absent exceptional circumstances, a law firm shall be held jointly responsible for violations committed by its partners, associates, and employees.

(B) *On Court's Initiative.* On its own initiative, the court may enter an order describing the specific conduct that appears to violate subdivision (b) and directing an attorney, law firm, or party to show cause why it has not violated subdivision (b) with respect thereto.

(2) *Nature of Sanction; Limitations.* A sanction imposed for violation of this rule shall be limited to what is sufficient to deter repe tition of such conduct or comparable conduct by others similarly situated. Subject to the limitations in subparagraphs (A) and (B), the sanction may consist of, or include, directives of a nonmonetary nature, an order to pay a penalty into court, or, if imposed on motion and warranted for effective deterrence, an order directing payment to the movant of some or all of the reasonable attorneys' fees and other expenses incurred as a direct result of the violation.

(A) Monetary sanctions may not be awarded against a represented party for a violation of subdivision (b)(2).

(B) Monetary sanctions may not be awarded on the court's initiative unless the court issues its order to show cause before a voluntary dismissal or settlement of the claims made by or against the party which is, or whose attorneys are, to be sanctioned.

(3) *Order.* When imposing sanctions, the court shall describe the conduct determined to constitute a violation of this rule and explain the basis for the sanction imposed.

(d) Inapplicability to Discovery. Subdivisions (a) through (c) of this rule do not apply to disclosures and discovery requests, responses, objections, and motions that are subject to the provisions of Rules 26 through 37.

As amended 1983, 1987, 1993.

Rule 12.
DEFENSES AND OBJECTIONS—WHEN AND HOW PRESENTED—BY PLEADING OR MOTION—MOTION FOR JUDGMENT ON THE PLEADINGS

(a) When Presented.

(1) Unless a different time is prescribed in a statute of the United States, a defendant shall serve an answer

(A) within 20 days after being served with the summons and complaint, or

(B) if service of the summons has been timely waived on request under Rule 4(d), within 60 days after the date when the request for waiver was sent, or within 90 days after that date if the defendant was addressed outside any judicial district of the United States.

(2) A party served with a pleading stating a cross-claim against that party shall serve an answer thereto within 20 days after being served. The plaintiff shall serve a reply to a counterclaim in the answer within 20 days after service of the answer, or, if a reply is ordered by the court, within 20 days after service of the order, unless the order otherwise directs.

(3) The United States or an officer or agency thereof shall serve an answer to the complaint or to a cross-claim, or a reply to a counterclaim, within 60 days after the service upon the United States attorney of the pleading in which the claim is asserted.

(4) Unless a different time is fixed by court order, the service of a motion permitted under this rule alters these periods of time as follows:

(A) if the court denies the motion or postpones its disposition until the trial on the merits, the responsive pleading shall be served within 10 days after notice of the court's action; or

(B) if the court grants a motion for a more definite statement, the responsive pleading shall be served within 10 days after the service of the more definite statement.

(b) How Presented. Every defense, in law or fact, to a claim for relief in any pleading, whether a claim, counterclaim, cross-claim, or third-party claim, shall be asserted in the responsive pleading thereto if one is required, except that the following defenses may at the option of the pleader be made by, motion: (1) lack of jurisdiction over the subject matter, (2) lack of jurisdiction over the person, (3) improper venue, (4) insufficiency of process, (5) insufficiency of service of process, (6) failure to state a claim upon which relief can be granted, (7) failure to join a party under Rule 19. A motion making any of these defenses shall be made before pleading if a further pleading is permitted. No defense or objection is waived by being joined with one or more other defenses or objections in a responsive pleading or motion. If a pleading sets forth a claim for relief to which the adverse party is not required to serve a responsive pleading, the adverse party may assert at the trial any defense in law or fact to that claim for relief. If, on a motion asserting the defense numbered (6) to dismiss for failure of the pleading to state a claim upon which relief can be granted, matters outside the pleading are presented to and not excluded by the court, the motion shall be treated as one for summary judgment and disposed of as provided in Rule 56, and all parties shall be given reasonable opportunity to present all material made pertinent to such a motion by Rule 56.

(c) Motion for Judgment on the Pleadings. After the pleadings are closed but within such time as not to delay the trial, any party may move for judgment on the pleadings. If, on a motion for judgment on the pleadings, matters outside the pleadings are presented to and not excluded by the court, the motion shall be treated as one for summary judgment and disposed of as provided in Rule 56, and all parties shall be given reasonable opportunity to present all material made pertinent to such a motion by Rule 56.

(d) Preliminary Hearings. The defenses specifically enumerated (1)–(7) in subdivision (b) of this rule, whether made in a pleading or by motion, and the motion for judgment mentioned in subdivision (c) of this rule shall be heard and determined before trial on application of any party, unless the court orders that the hearing and determination thereof be deferred until the trial.

(e) Motion for More Definite Statement. If a pleading to which a responsive pleading is permitted is so vague or ambiguous that a party cannot reasonably be required to frame a responsive pleading, the party may move for a more definite statement before interposing a responsive pleading. The motion shall point out the defects complained of and the details desired. If the motion is granted and the order of the court is not obeyed within 10 days after notice of the order or within such other time as the court may fix, the court may strike the pleading to which the motion was directed or make such order as it deems just.

(f) Motion to Strike. Upon motion made by a party before responding to a pleading or, if no responsive pleading is permitted by these rules, upon motion made by a party within 20 days after the service of the pleading upon the party or upon the court's own initiative at any time, the court may order stricken from any pleading any insufficient defense or any redundant, immaterial, impertinent, or scandalous matter.

(g) Consolidation of Defenses in Motion. A party who makes a motion under this rule may join with it any other motions herein provided for and then available to the party. If a party makes a motion under this rule but omits therefrom any defense or objection then available to the party which this rule permits to be raised by motion, the party shall not thereafter make a motion based on the defense or objection so omitted, except a motion as provided in subdivision (h)(2) hereof on any of the grounds there stated.

(h) Waiver or Preservation of Certain Defenses.

(1) A defense of lack of jurisdiction over the person, improper venue, insufficiency of process, or insufficiency of service of process is waived (A) if omitted from a motion in the circumstances described in subdivision (g), or (B) if it is neither made by motion under this rule nor included in a responsive pleading or an amendment thereof permitted by Rule 15(a) to be made as a matter of course.

(2) A defense of failure to state a claim upon which relief can be granted, a defense of failure to join a party indispensable under Rule 19, and an objection of failure to state a legal defense to a claim may be made in any pleading permitted or ordered under Rule 7(a), or by motion for judgment on the pleadings, or at the trial on the merits.

(3) Whenever it appears by suggestion of the parties or otherwise that the court lacks jurisdiction of the subject matter, the court shall dismiss the action.

As amended 1948, 1963, 1966, 1987, 1993.

Rule 13.
COUNTERCLAIM AND CROSS-CLAIM

(a) Compulsory Counterclaims. A pleading shall state as a counterclaim any claim which at the time of serving the pleading the pleader has against any opposing party, if it arises out of the trans action or occurrence that is the subject matter of the opposing party's claim and does not require for its adjudication the presence of third parties of whom the court cannot acquire jurisdiction. But the pleader need not state the claim if (1) at the time the action was commenced the claim was the subject of another pending action, or (2) the opposing party brought suit upon the claim by attachment or other process by which the court did not acquire jurisdiction to render a personal judgment on that claim, and the pleader is not stating any counterclaim under this Rule 13.

(b) Permissive Counterclaims. A pleading may state as a counterclaim any claim against an opposing party not arising out of the transaction or occurrence that is the subject matter of the opposing party's claim.

(c) Counterclaim Exceeding Opposing Claim. A counterclaim may or may not diminish or defeat the recovery sought by the opposing party. It may claim relief exceeding in amount or different in kind from that sought in the pleading of the opposing party.

(d) Counterclaim Against the United States. These rules shall not be construed to enlarge beyond the limits now fixed by law the right to assert counterclaims or to claim credits against the United States or an officer or agency thereof

(e) Counterclaim Maturing or Acquired After Pleading. A claim which either matured or was acquired by the pleader after serving a pleading may, with the permission of the court, be presented as a counterclaim by supplemental pleading.

(f) Omitted Counterclaim. When a pleader fails to set up a counterclaim through oversight, inadvertence, or excusable neglect, or when justice requires, the pleader may by leave of court set up the counterclaim by amendment.

(g) Cross-Claim Against Co-party. A pleading may state as a cross-claim any claim by one party against a co-party arising out of the transaction or occurrence that is the subject matter either of the original action or of a counterclaim therein or relating to any property that is the subject matter of the original action. Such cross-claim may include a claim that the party against whom it is asserted is or may be liable to the cross-claimant for all or part of a claim asserted in the action against the cross-claimant.

(h) Joinder of Additional Parties. Persons other than those made parties to the original action may be made parties to a counterclaim or cross-claim in accordance with the provisions of Rules 19 and 20.

(i) Separate Trials; Separate Judgments. If the court orders separate trials as provided in Rule 42(b), judgment on a counterclaim or cross-claim may be rendered in accordance with the terms of Rule 54(b) when the court has jurisdiction so to do, even if the claims of the opposing party have been dismissed or otherwise disposed of.

As amended 1948, 1963, 1966, 1987.

Rule 14.
THIRD-PARTY PRACTICE

(a) When Defendant May Bring in Third Party. At any time after commencement of the action a defending party, as a third-party plaintiff, may cause a summons and complaint to be served upon a person not a party to the action who is or may be liable to the third-party plaintiff for all or part of the plaintiff's claim against the third-party plaintiff. The third-party plaintiff need not obtain leave to make the service if the third-party plaintiff files the third-party complaint not later than 10 days after serving the original answer. Otherwise the third-party plaintiff must obtain leave on motion upon notice to all parties to the action. The person served with the summons and third-party complaint, hereinafter called the third-party defendant, shall make any defenses to the third-party plaintiffclaim as provided in Rule 12 and any counterclaims against the third-party plaintiff and cross-claims against other third-party defendants as provided in Rule 13. The third-party defendant may assert against the plaintiff any defenses which the third-party plaintiff has to the plaintiff's claim. The third-party defendant may also assert any claim against the plaintiff arising out of the transaction or occurrence that is the subject matter of the plaintiff's claim against the third-party plaintiff. The plaintiff may assert any claim against the third-party defendant arising out of the transaction or occurrence that is the subject matter of the plaintiff's claim against the third-party plaintiff, and the third-party defendant thereupon shall assert any defenses as provided in Rule 12 and any counterclaims and cross-claims as provided in Rule 13. Any party may move to strike the third-party claim, or for its severance or separate trial. A third-party defendant may proceed under this rule against any person not a party to the action who is or may be liable to the third-party defendant for all or part of the claim made in the action against the third-party defendant. The third-party complaint, if within the admiralty and maritime jurisdiction, may be in rem against a vessel, cargo, or other property subject to admiralty or maritime process in rem, in which case references in this rule to the summons include the warrant of arrest, and references to the third-party plaintiff or defendant include, where appropriate, the claimant of the property arrested.

(b) When Plaintiff May Bring in Third Party. When a counterclaim is asserted against a plaintiff, the plaintiff may cause a third party to be brought in under circumstances which under this rule would entitle a defendant to do so.

(c) Admiralty and Maritime Claims. When a plaintiff asserts an admiralty or maritime claim within the meaning of Rule 9(h), the defendant or claimant, as a third-party plaintiff, may bring in a third-party defendant who may be wholly or partly liable, either to the plaintiff or to the third-party plaintiff, by way of remedy over, contribution, or otherwise on account of the same transaction, occurrence, or series of transactions or occurrences. In such a case the third-party plaintiff may also demand judgment against the third-party defendant in favor of the plaintiff, in which event the third-party defendant shall make any defenses to the claim of the plaintiff as well as to that of the third-party plaintiff in the manner provided in Rule 12 and the action shall proceed as if the plaintiff had commenced it against the third-party defendant as well as the third-party plaintiff.

As amended 1948, 1963, 1966, 1987.

Rule 15.
AMENDED AND SUPPLEMENTAL PLEADINGS

(a) Amendments. A party may amend the party's pleading once as a matter of course at any time before a responsive pleading is served or, if the pleading is one to which no responsive pleading is permitted and the action has not been placed upon the trial calendar, the party may so amend it at any time within 20 days after it is served. Otherwise a party may amend the party's pleading only by leave of court or by written consent of the adverse party; and leave shall be freely given when justice so requires. A party shall plead in response to an amended pleading within the time remaining for response to the original pleading or within 10 days after service of the amended pleading, whichever period may be the longer, unless the court otherwise orders.

(b) Amendments to Conform to the Evidence. When issues not raised by the pleadings are tried by express or implied consent of the parties, they shall be treated in all respects as, if they had been raised in the pleadings. Such amendment of the pleadings as may be necessary to cause them to conform to the evidence and to raise these issues may be made upon motion of any party at any time, even after judgment; but failure so to amend does not affect the result of the trial of these issues. If evidence is objected to at the trial on the ground that it is not within the issues made by the pleadings, the court may allow the pleadings to be amended and shall do so freely when the presentation of the merits of the action will be subserved thereby and the objecting party fails to satisfy the court that the admission of such evidence would prejudice the party in maintaining the party's action or defense upon the merits. The court may grant a continuance to enable the objecting party to meet such evidence.

(c) Relation Back of Amendments. An amendment of a pleading relates back to the date of the original pleading when

(1) relation back is permitted by the law that provides the statute of limitations applicable to the action, or

(2) the claim or defense asserted in the amended pleading arose out of the conduct, transaction, or occurrence set forth or attempted to be set forth in the original pleading, or

(3) the amendment changes the party or the naming of the party against whom a claim is asserted if the foregoing provision (2) is satisfied and, within the period provided by Rule 4(m) for service of the summons and complaint, the party to be brought in by amendment (A) has received such notice of the institution of the action that the party will not be prejudiced in maintaining a defense on the merits, and (B) knew or should have known that, but for a mistake concerning the identity of the proper party, the action would have been brought against the party.

The delivery or mailing of process to the United States Attorney, or United States Attorney's designee, or the Attorney General of the United States, or an agency or officer who would have been a proper defendant if named, satisfies the requirement of subparagraphs (A) and (B) of this paragraph (3) with respect to the United States or any agency or officer thereof to be brought into the action as a defendant.

(d) Supplemental Pleadings. Upon motion of a party the court may, upon reasonable notice and upon such terms as are just, permit the party to serve a supplemental pleading setting forth transactions or occurrences or events which have happened since the date of the pleading sought to be supplemented. Permission may be granted even though the original pleading is defective in its statement of a claim for relief or defense. If the court deems it advisable that the adverse party plead to the supplemental pleading, it shall so order, specifying the time therefor.

As amended 1963, 1966, 1987, 1991, 1993.

Rule 16.
PRETRIAL CONFERENCES; SCHEDULING; MANAGEMENT

(a) Pretrial Conferences; Objectives. In any action, the court may in its discretion direct the attorneys for the parties and any unrepresented parties to appear before it for a conference or conferences before trial for such purposes as

(1) expediting the disposition of the action;

(2) establishing early and continuing control so that the case will not be protracted because of lack of management;

(3) discouraging wasteful pretrial activities;

(4) improving the quality of the trial through more thorough preparation, and;

(5) facilitating the settlement of the case.

(b) Scheduling and Planning. Except in categories of actions exempted by district court rule as inappropriate, the district judge, or a magistrate judge when authorized by district court rule, shall, after receiving the report from the parties under Rule 26(f) or after consulting with the attorneys for the parties and any unrepresented parties by a scheduling conference, telephone, mail, or other suitable means, enter a scheduling order that limits the time

(1) to join other parties and to amend the pleadings;

(2) to file motions; and

(3) to complete discovery.

The scheduling order also may include

(4) modifications of the times for disclosures under Rules 26(a) and 26(e)(1) and of the extent of discovery to be permitted;

(5) the date or dates for conferences before trial, a final pretrial conference, and trial; and

(6) any other matters appropriate in the circumstances of the case.

The order shall issue as soon as practicable but in any event within 90 days after the appearance of a defendant and within 120 days after the complaint has been served on a defendant. A schedule shall not be modified except upon a showing of good cause and by leave of the district judge or, when authorized by local rule, by a magistrate judge.

(c) Subjects for Consideration at Pretrial Conferences. At any conference under this rule consideration may be given, and the court may take appropriate action, with respect to

(1) the formulation and simplification of the issues, including the elimination of frivolous claims or defenses;

(2) the necessity or desirability of amendments to the pleadings;

(3) the possibility of obtaining admissions of fact and of documents which will avoid unnecessary proof, stipulations regarding the authenticity of documents, and advance rulings from the court on the admissibility of evidence;

(4) the avoidance of unnecessary proof and of cumulative evidence, and limitations or restrictions on the use of testimony under Rule 702 of the Federal Rules of Evidence;

(5) the appropriateness and timing of summary adjudication under Rule 56;

(6) the control and scheduling of discovery, including orders affecting disclosures and discovery pursuant to Rule 26 and Rules 29 through 37;

(7) the identification of witnesses and documents, the need and schedule for filing and exchanging pretrial briefs, and the date or dates for further conferences and for trial;

(8) the advisability of referring matters to a magistrate judge or master;

(9) settlement and the use of special procedures to assist in resolving the dispute when authorized by statute or local rule;

(10) the form and substance of the pretrial order;

(11) the disposition of pending motions;

(12) the need for adopting special procedures for managing potentially difficult or protracted actions that may involve complex issues, multiple parties, difficult legal questions, or unusual proof problems;

(13) an order for a separate trial pursuant to Rule 42(b) with respect to a claim, counterclaim, cross-claim, or third-party claim, or with respect to any particular issue in the case;

(14) an order directing a party or parties to present evidence early in the trial with respect to a manageable issue that could, on the evidence, be the basis for a judgment as a matter of law under Rule 50(a) or a judgment on partial findings under Rule 52(c);

(15) an order establishing a reasonable limit on the time allowed for presenting evidence; and

(16) such other matters as may facilitate the just, speedy, and inexpensive disposition of the action.

At least one of the attorneys for each party participating in any conference before trial shall have authority to enter into stipulations and to make admissions regarding all matters that the participants may reasonably anticipate may be discussed. If appropriate, the court may require that a party or its representative be present or reasonably available by telephone in order to consider possible settlement of the dispute.

(d) Final Pretrial Conference. Any final pretrial conference shall be held as close to the time of trial as reasonable under the circumstances. The participants at any such conference shall formulate a plan for trial, including a program for facilitating the admission of evidence. The conference shall be attended by at least one of the attorneys who will conduct the trial for each of the parties and by any unrepresented parties.

(e) Pretrial Orders. After any conference held pursuant to this rule, an order shall be entered reciting the action taken. This order shall control the subsequent course of the action unless modified by a subsequent order. The order following a final pretrial conference shall be modified only to prevent manifest injustice.

(f) Sanctions. If a party or party's attorney fails to obey a scheduling or pretrial order, or if no appearance is made on behalf of a party at a scheduling or pretrial conference, or if a party or party's attorney is substantially unprepared to participate in the conference, or if a party or party's attorney fails to participate in good faith, the judge, upon motion or the judge's own initiative, may make such orders with regard thereto as are just, and among others any of the orders provided in Rule 37(b)(2)(B), (C), (D). In lieu of or in addition to any other sanction, the judge shall require the party or the attorney representing the party or both to pay the reasonable expenses incurred because of any noncompliance with this rule, including attorney's fees, unless the judge finds that the noncompliance was substantially justified or that other circumstances make an award of expenses unjust.

As amended 1983, 1987, 1993.

IV. PARTIES

Rule 17.
PARTIES PLAINTIFF AND DEFENDANT; CAPACITY

(a) Real Party in Interest. Every action shall be prosecuted in the name of the real party in interest. An executor, administrator, guardian, bailee, trustee of an express trust, a party with whom or in whose name a contract has been made for the benefit of another, or a party authorized by statute may sue in that person's own name without joining the party for whose benefit the action is brought; and when a statute of the United States so provides, an action for the use or benefit of another shall be brought in the name of the United States. No action shall be dismissed on the ground that it is not prosecuted in the name of the real party in interest until a reasonable time has been allowed after objection for ratification of commencement of the action by, or joinder or substitution of, the real party in interest; and such ratification, joinder, or substitution shall have the same effect as if the action had been commenced in the name of the real party in interest.

(b) Capacity to Sue or Be Sued. The capacity of an individual, other than one acting in a representative capacity, to sue or be sued shall be determined by the law of the individual's domicile. The capacity of a corporation to sue or be sued shall be determined by the law under which it was organized. In all other cases capacity to sue or be sued shall be determined by the law of the state in which the district court is held, except (1) that a partnership or other unincorporated association, which has no such capacity by the law of such state, may sue or be sued in its common name for the purpose of enforcing for or against it a substantive right existing under the Constitution or laws of the United States, and (2) that the capacity of a receiver appointed by a court of the United States to sue or be sued in a court of the United States is governed by Title 28, U.S.C. §§ 754 and 959(a).

(c) Infants or Incompetent Persons. Whenever an infant or incompetent person has a representative, such as a general guardian, committee, conservator, or other like fiduciary, the representative may sue or defend on behalf of the infant or incompetent person. An infant or incompetent person who does not have a duly appointed representative may sue by a next friend or by a guardian ad litem. The court shall appoint a guardian ad litem for an infant or incompetent person not otherwise represented in an action or shall make such other order as it deems proper for the protection of the infant or incompetent person.

As amended 1948, 1949, 1966, 1987, 1988.

Rule 18.
JOINDER OF CLAIMS AND REMEDIES

(a) Joinder of Claims. A party asserting a claim to relief as an original claim, counterclaim, cross-claim, or third-party claim, may join, either as independent or as alternate claims, as many claims, legal, equitable, or maritime, as the party has against an opposing party.

(b) Joinder of Remedies; Fraudulent Conveyances. Whenever a claim is one heretofore cognizable only after another claim has been prosecuted to a conclusion, the two claims may be joined in a single action; but the court shall grant relief in that action only in accordance with the relative substantive rights of the parties. In particular, a plaintiff may state a claim for money and a claim to have set aside a conveyance fraudulent as to that plaintiff, without first having obtained a judgment establishing the claim for money.

As amended 1966, 1987.

Rule 19.
JOINDER OF PERSONS NEEDED FOR JUST ADJUDICATION

(a) Persons to Be Joined if Feasible. A person who is subject to service of process and whose joinder will not deprive the court of jurisdiction over the subject matter of the action shall be joined as a party in the action if (1) in the person's absence complete relief cannot be accorded among those already parties, or (2) the person claims an interest relating to the subject of the action and is so situated that the disposition of the action in the person's absence may (i) as a practical matter impair or impede the person's ability to protect that interest or (ii) leave any of the persons already parties subject to a substantial risk of incurring double, multiple, or otherwise inconsistent obligations by reason of the claimed interest. If the person has not been so joined, the court shall order that the person be made a party. If the person should join as a plaintiff but refuses to do so, the person may be made a defendant, or, in a proper case, an involuntary plaintiff. If the joined party objects to venue and joinder of that party would render the venue of the action improper, that party shall be dismissed from the action.

(b) Determination by Court Whenever Joinder Not Feasible. If a person as described in subdivision (a)(1)–(2) hereof cannot be made a party, the court shall determine whether in equity and good conscience the action should proceed among the parties before it, or should be dismissed, the absent person being thus regarded as indispensable. The factors to be considered by the court include: first, to what extent a judgment rendered in the person's absence might be prejudicial to the person or those already parties; second, the extent to which, by protective provisions in the judgment, by the shaping of relief, or other measures, the prejudice can be lessened or avoided; third, whether a judgment rendered in the person's absence will be adequate; fourth, whether the plaintiff will have an adequate remedy if the action is dismissed for nonjoinder.

(c) Pleading Reasons for Nonjoinder. A pleading asserting a claim for relief shall state the names, if known to the pleader, of any persons as described in subdivision (a)(1)–(2) hereof who are not joined, and the reasons why they are not joined.

(d) Exception of Class Actions. This rule is subject to the provisions of Rule 23.

As amended 1966, 1987.

Rule 20.
PERMISSIVE JOINDER OF PARTIES

(a) Permissive Joinder. All persons may join in one action as plaintiffs if they assert any right to relief jointly, severally, or in the alternative in respect of or arising out of the same transaction, occurrence, or series of transactions or occurrences and if any question of law or fact common to all these persons will arise in the action. All persons (and any vessel, cargo or other property subject to admiralty process in rem) may be joined in one action as defendants if there is asserted against them jointly, severally, or in the alternative, any right to relief in respect of or arising out of the same transaction, occurrence, or series of transactions or occurrences and if any question of law or fact common to all defendants will arise in the action. A plaintiff or defendant need not be interested in obtaining or defending against all the relief demanded. Judgment may be given for one or more of the plaintiffs according to their respective rights to relief, and against one or more defendants according to their respective liabilities.

(b) Separate Trials. The court may make such orders as will prevent a party from being embarrassed, delayed, or put to expense by the inclusion of a party against whom the party asserts no claim and who asserts no claim against the party, and may order separate trials or make other orders to prevent delay or prejudice.

As amended 1966, 1987.

Rule 21.
MISJOINDER AND NON-JOINDER OF PARTIES

Misjoinder of parties is not ground for dismissal of an action. Parties may be dropped or added by order of the court on motion of any party or of its own initiative at any stage of the action and on such terms as are just. Any claim against a party may be severed and proceeded with separately.

Rule 22.
INTERPLEADER

(1) Persons having claims against the plaintiff may be joined as defendants and required to interplead when their claims are such that the plaintiff is or may be exposed to double or multiple liability. It is not ground for objection to the joinder that the claims of the several claimants or the titles on which their claims depend do not have a common origin or are not identical but are adverse to and independent of one another, or that the plaintiff avers that the plaintiff is not liable in whole or in part to any or all of the claimants. A defendant exposed to similar liability may obtain such interpleader by way of cross-claim or counterclaim. The provisions of this rule supplement and do not in any way limit the joinder of parties permitted in Rule 20.

(2) The remedy herein provided is in addition to and in no way supersedes or limits the remedy provided by Title 28, U.S.C. §§ 1335, 1397, and 2361. Actions under those provisions shall be conducted in accordance with these rules.

As amended 1949, 1987.

Rule 23.
CLASS ACTIONS

(a) Prerequisites to a Class Action. One or more members of a class may sue or be sued as representative parties on behalf of all only if (1) the class is so numerous that joinder of all members is impracticable, (2) there are questions of law or fact common to the class, (3) the claims or defenses of the representative parties are typical of the claims or defenses of the class, and (4) the representative parties will fairly and adequately protect the interests of the class.

(b) Class Actions Maintainable. An action may be maintained as a class action if the prerequisites of subdivision (a) are satisfied, and in addition:

(1) the prosecution of separate actions by or against individual members of the class would create a risk of

(A) inconsistent or varying adjudications with respect to individual members of the class which would establish incompatible standards of conduct for the party opposing the class, or

(B) adjudications with respect to individual members of the class which would as a practical matter be dispositive of the interests of the other members not parties to the adjudications or substantially impair or impede their ability to protect their interests; or

(2) the party opposing the class has acted or refused to act on grounds generally applicable to the class, thereby making appropriate final injunctive relief or corresponding declaratory relief with respect to the class as a whole; or

(3) the court finds that the questions of law or fact common to the members of the class predominate over any questions affecting only individual members, and that a class action is superior to other available methods for the fair and efficient adjudication of the controversy. The matters pertinent to the findings include: (A) the interest of members of the class in individually controlling the prosecution or defense of separate actions; (B) the extent and nature of any litigation concerning the controversy already commenced by or against members of the class; (C) the desirability or undesirability of concentrating the litigation of the claims in the particular forum; (D) the difficulties likely to be encountered in the management of a class action.

(c) Determination by Order Whether Class Action to Be Maintained; Notice; Judgment; Actions Conducted Partially as Class Actions.

(1) As soon as practicable after the commencement of an action brought as a class action, the court shall determine by order whether it is to be so maintained. An order under this subdivision may be conditional, and may be altered or amended before the decision on the merits.

(2) In any class action maintained under subdivision (b)(3), the court shall direct to the members of the class the best notice practicable under the circumstances, including individual notice to all members who can be identified through reasonable effort. The notice shall advise each member that (A) the court will exclude the member from the class if the member so requests by a specified date; (B) the judgment, whether favorable or not, will include all members who do not request exclusion; and (C) any member who does not request exclusion may, if the member desires, enter an appearance through counsel.

(3) The judgment in an action maintained as a class action under subdivision (b)(1) or (b)(2), whether or not favorable to the class, shall include and describe those whom the court finds to be members of the class. The judgment in an action maintained as a class action under subdivision (b)(3), whether or not favorable to the class, shall include and specify or describe those to whom the notice provided in subdivision (c)(2) was directed, and who have not requested exclusion, and whom the court finds to be members of the class.

(4) When appropriate (A) an action may be brought or maintained as a class action with respect to particular issues, or (B) a class may be divided into subclasses and each subclass treated as a class, and the provisions of this rule shall then be construed and applied accordingly.

(d) Orders in Conduct of Actions. In the conduct of actions to which this rule applies, the court may make appropriate orders: (1) determining the course of proceedings or prescribing measures to prevent undue repetition or complication in the presentation of evidence or argument; (2) requiring, for the protection of the members of the class or otherwise for the fair conduct of the action, that notice be given in such manner as the court may direct to some or all of the members of any step in the action, or of the proposed extent of the judgment, or of the opportunity of members to signify whether they consider the representation fair and adequate, to intervene and present claims or defenses, or otherwise to come into the action; (3) im posing conditions on the representative parties or on intervenors; (4) requiring that the pleadings be amended to eliminate therefrom allegations as to representation of absent persons, and that the action proceed accordingly; (5) dealing with similar procedural matters. The orders may be combined with an order under Rule 16, and may be altered or amended as may be desirable from time to time.

(e) Dismissal or Compromise. A class action shall not be dismissed or compromised without the approval of the court, and notice of the proposed dismissal or compromise shall be given to all members of the class in such manner as the court directs.

As amended 1966, 1987.

Rule 23.1.
DERIVATIVE ACTIONS BY SHAREHOLDERS

In a derivative action brought by one or more shareholders or members to enforce a right of a corporation or of an unincorporated association, the corporation or association having failed to enforce a right which may properly be asserted by it, the complaint shall be verified and shall allege (1) that the plaintiff was a shareholder or member at the time of the transaction of which the plaintiff complains or that the plaintiff's share or membership thereafter devolved on the plaintiff by operation of law, and (2) that the action is not a collusive one to confer jurisdiction on a court of the United States which it would not otherwise have. The complaint shall also allege with particularity the efforts, if any, made by the plaintiff to obtain the action the plaintiff desires from the directors or comparable authority and, if necessary, from the shareholders or members, and the reasons for the plaintiff's failure to obtain the action or for not making the effort. The derivative action may not be maintained if it appears that the plaintiff does not fairly and adequately represent the interests of the shareholders or members similarly situated in enforcing the right of the corporation or association. The action shall not be dismissed or compromised without the approval of the court, and notice of the proposed dismissal or compromise shall be given to shareholders or members in such manner as the court directs.

Added 1966; as amended 1987.

Rule 23.2.
ACTIONS RELATING TO UNINCORPORATED ASSOCIATIONS

An action brought by or against the members of an unincor porated association as a class by naming certain members as rep resentative parties may be maintained only if it appears that the representative parties will fairly and adequately protect the interests of the association and its members. In the conduct of the action the court may make appropriate orders corresponding with those described in Rule 23(d), and the procedure for dismissal or compromise of the action shall correspond with that provided in Rule 23(e).

Added 1966.

Rule 24.
INTERVENTION

(a) Intervention of Right. Upon timely application anyone shall be permitted to intervene in an action: (1) when a statute of the United States confers an unconditional right to intervene; or (2) when the applicant claims an interest relating to the property or transaction which is the subject of the action and the applicant is so situated that the disposition of the action may as a practical matter impair or impede the applicant's ability to protect that interest, unless the applicant's interest is adequately represented by existing parties.

(b) Permissive Intervention. Upon timely application anyone may be permitted to intervene in an action: (1) when a statute of the United States confers a conditional right to intervene; or (2) when an applicant's claim or defense and the main action have a question of law or fact in common. When a party to an action relies for ground of claim or defense upon any statute or executive order administered by a federal or state governmental officer or agency or upon any regulation, order, requirement or agreement issued or made pursuant to the statute or executive order, the officer or agency upon timely application may be permitted to intervene in the action. In exercising its discretion the court shall consider whether the intervention will unduly delay or prejudice the adjudication of the rights of the original parties.

(c) Procedure. A person desiring to intervene shall serve a motion to intervene upon the parties as provided in Rule 5. The motion shall state the grounds therefor and shall be accompanied by a pleading setting forth the claim or defense for which intervention is sought. The same procedure shall be followed when a statute of the United States gives a right to intervene. When the constitutionality of an act of Congress affecting the public interest is drawn in question in any action to which the United States or an officer, agency, or employee thereof is not a party, the court shall notify the Attorney General of the United States as provided in Title 28, U.S.C. § 2403. When the constitutionality of any statute of a State affecting the public interest is drawn in question in any action in which that State or any agency, officer, or employee thereof is not a party, the court shall notify the attorney general of the State as provided in Title 28, U.S.C. § 2403. A party challenging the constitutionality of legislation should call the attention of the court to its consequential duty, but failure to do so is not a waiver of any constitutional right otherwise timely asserted.

As amended 1948, 1949, 1963, 1966, 1987, 1991.

Rule 25.
SUBSTITUTION OF PARTIES

(a) Death.

(1) If a party dies and the claim is not thereby extinguished, the court may order substitution of the proper parties. The motion for substitution may be made by any party or by the successors or representatives of the deceased party and, together with the notice of hearing, shall be served on the parties as provided in Rule 5 and upon persons not parties in the manner provided in Rule 4 for the service of a summons, and may be served in any judicial district. Unless the motion for substitution is made not later than 90 days after the death is suggested upon the record by service of a statement of the fact of the death as provided herein for the service of the motion, the action shall be dismissed as to the deceased party.

(2) In the event of the death of one or more of the plaintiffs or of one or more of the defendants in an action in which the right sought to be enforced survives only to the surviving plaintiffs or only against the surviving defendants, the action does not abate. The death shall be suggested upon the record and the action shall proceed in favor of or against the surviving parties.

(b) Incompetency. If a party becomes incompetent, the court upon motion served as provided in subdivision (a) of this rule may allow the action to be continued by or against the party's representative.

(c) Transfer of Interest. In case of any transfer of interest, the action may be continued by or against the original party, unless the court upon motion directs the person to whom the interest is transferred to be substituted in the action or joined with the original party. Service of the motion shall be made as provided in subdivision (a) of this rule.

(d) Public Officers; Death or Separation from Office.

(1) When a public officer is a party to an action in an official capacity and during its pendency dies, resigns, or otherwise ceases to hold office, the action does not abate and the officer's successor is automatically substituted as a party. Proceedings following the substitution shall be in the name of the substituted party, but any misnomer not affecting the substantial rights of the parties shall be disregarded. An order of substitution may be entered at any time, but the omission to enter such an order shall not affect the substitution.

(2) A public officer who sues or is sued in an official capacity may be described as a party by the officer's official title rather than by name; but the court may require the officer's name to be added.

As amended 1949, 1961, 1963, 1987.

V. DEPOSITIONS AND DISCOVERY

Rule 26.
GENERAL PROVISIONS GOVERNING DISCOVERY; DUTY OF DISCLOSURE

(a) Required Disclosures; Methods to Discover Additional Matter.

(1) *Initial Disclosures.* Except to the extent otherwise stipulated or directed by order or local rule, a party shall, without awaiting a discovery request, provide to other parties:

(A) the name and, if known, the address and telephone number of each individual likely to have discoverable information relevant to disputed facts alleged with particularity in the pleadings, identifying the subjects of the information;

(B) a copy of, or a description by category and location of, all documents, data compilations, and tangible things in the possession, custody, or control of the party that are relevant to disputed facts alleged with particularity in the pleadings;

(C) a computation of any category of damages claimed by the disclosing party, making available for inspection and copying as under Rule 34 the documents or other evidentiary material, not privileged or protected from disclosure, on which such computation is based, including materials bearing on the nature and extent of injuries suffered; and

(D) for inspection and copying as under Rule 34 any insurance agreement under which any person carrying on an insurance business may be liable to satisfy part or all of a judgment which may be entered in the action or to indemnify or reimburse for payments made to satisfy the judgment.

Unless otherwise stipulated or directed by the court, these disclosures shall be made at or within 10 days after the meeting of the parties under subdivision (f). A party shall make its initial disclosures based on the information then reasonably available to it and is not excused from making its disclosures because it has not fully completed its investigation of the case or because it challenges the sufficiency of another party's disclosures or because another party has not made its disclosures.

(2) *Disclosure of Expert Testimony.*

(A) The addition to the disclosures required by paragraph (1), a party shall disclose to other parties the identity of any person who may be used at trial to present evidence under Rules 702, 703, or 705 of the Federal Rules of Evidence.

(B) Except as otherwise stipulated or directed by the court, this disclosure shall, with respect to a witness who is retained or specially employed to provide expert testimony in the case or whose duties as an employee of the party regularly involve giving expert testimony, be accompanied by a written report prepared and signed by the witness. The report shall contain a complete statement of all opinions to be expressed and the basis and reasons therefor; the data or other information considered by the witness in forming the opinions; any exhibits to be used as a summary of or support for the opinions; the qualifications of the witness, including a list of all publications authored by the witness within the preceding ten years; the compensation to be paid for the study and testimony; and a listing of any other cases in which the witness has testified as an expert at trial or by deposition within the preceding four years.

(C) These disclosures shall be made at the times and in the sequence directed by the court. In the absence of other directions from the court or stipulation by the parties, the disclosures shall be made at least 90 days before the trial date or the date the case is to be ready for trial or, if the evidence is intended solely to contradict or rebut evidence on the same subject matter identified by another party under paragraph (2)(B), within 30 days after the disclosure made by the other party. The parties shall supplement these disclosures when required under subdivision (e)(1).

(3) *Pretrial Disclosures.* In addition to the disclosures required in the preceding paragraphs, a party shall provide to other parties the following information regarding the evidence that it may present at trial other than solely for impeachment purposes:

(A) the name and, if not previously provided, the address and telephone number of each witness, separately identifying those whom the party expects to present and those whom the party may call if the need arises;

(B) the designation of those witnesses whose testimony is expected to be presented by means of a deposition and, if not taken stenographically, a transcript of the pertinent portions of the deposition testimony; and

(C) an appropriate identification of each document or other exhibit, including summaries of other evidence, separately identifying those which the party expects to offer and those which the party may offer if the need arises.

Unless otherwise directed by the court, these disclosures shall be made at least 30 days before trial. Within 14 days thereafter, unless a different time is specified by the court, a party may serve and file a list disclosing (i) any objections to the use under Rule 32(a) of a deposition designated by another party under subparagraph (B) and (ii) any objection, together with the grounds therefor, that may be made to the admissibility of materials identified under subparagraph (C). Objections not so disclosed, other than objections under Rules 402 and 403 of the Federal Rules of Evidence, shall be deemed waived unless excused by the court for good cause shown.

(4) *Form of Disclosures; Filing.* Unless otherwise directed by order or local rule, all disclosures under paragraphs (1) through (3) shall be made in writing, signed, served, and promptly filed with the court.

(5) *Methods to Discover Additional Matter.* Parties may obtain discovery by one or more of the following methods: depositions upon oral examination or written questions; written interrogatories; production of documents or things or permission to enter upon land or other property under Rule 34 or 45(a)(1)(C), for inspection and other purposes; physical and mental examinations; and requests for admission.

(b) Discovery Scope and Limits. Unless otherwise limited by order of the court in accordance with these rules, the scope of discovery is as follows:

(1) *In General.* Parties may obtain discovery regarding any matter, not privileged, which is relevant to the subject matter involved in the pending action, whether it relates to the claim or defense of the party seeking discovery or to the claim or defense of any other party, including the existence, description, nature, custody, condition, and location of any books, documents, or other tangible things and the identity and location of persons having knowledge of any discoverable matter. The information sought need not be admissible at the trial if the information sought appears reasonably calculated to lead to the discovery of admissible evidence.

(2) *Limitations.* By order or by local rule, the court may alter the limits in these rules on the number of depositions and interrogatories and may also limit the length of depositions under Rule 30 and the number of requests under Rule 36. The frequency or extent of use of the discovery methods otherwise permitted under these rules and by any local rule shall be limited by the court if it determines that: (i) the discovery sought is unreasonably cumulative or duplicative, or is obtainable from some other source that is more convenient, less burdensome, or less expensive; (ii) the party seeking discovery has had ample opportunity by discovery in the action to obtain the information sought; or (iii) the burden or expense of the proposed discovery outweighs its likely benefit, taking into account the needs of the case, the amount in controversy, the parties' resources, the importance of the issues at stake in the litigation, and the importance of the proposed discovery in resolving the issues. The court may act upon its own initiative after reasonable notice or pursuant to a motion under subdivision (c).

(3) *Trial Preparation: Materials.* Subject to the provisions of subdivision (b)(4) of this rule, a party may obtain discovery of documents and tangible things otherwise discoverable under subdivision (b)(1) of this rule and prepared in anticipation of litigation or for trial by or for another party or by or for that other party's representative (including the other party's attorney, consultant, surety, indemnitor, insurer, or agent) only upon a showing that the party seeking discovery has substantial need of the materials in the preparation of the party's case and that the party is unable without undue hardship to obtain the substantial equivalent

of the materials by other means. In ordering discovery of such materials when the required showing has been made, the court shall protect against disclosure of the mental impressions, conclusions, opinions, or legal theories of an attorney or other representative of a party concerning the litigation.

A party may obtain without the required showing a statement concerning the action or its subject matter previously made by that party. Upon request, a person not a party may obtain without the required showing a statement concerning the action or its subject matter previously made by that person. If the request is refused, the person may move for a court order. The provisions of Rule 37(a)(4) apply to the award of expenses incurred in relation to the motion. For purposes of this paragraph, a statement previously made is (A) a written statement signed or otherwise adopted or approved by the person making it, or (B) a stenographic, mechanical, electrical, or other recording, or a transcription thereof, which is a substantially verbatim recital of an oral statement by the person making it and contemporaneously recorded.

(4) *Trial Preparation: Experts.*

(A) A party may depose any person who has been identified as an expert whose opinions may be presented at trial. If a report from the expert is required under subdivision (a)(2)(B), the deposition shall not be conducted until after the report is provided.

(B) A party may, through interrogatories or by deposition, discover facts known or opinions held by an expert who has been retained or specially employed by another party in anticipation of litigation or preparation for trial and who is not expected to be called as a witness at trial only as provided in Rule 35(b) or upon a showing of exceptional circumstances under which it is impracticable for the party seeking discovery to obtain facts or opinions on the same subject by other means.

(C) Unless manifest injustice would result, (i) the court shall require that the party seeking discovery pay the expert a reasonable fee for time spent in responding to discovery under this subdivision; and (ii) with respect to discovery obtained under subdivision (b)(4)(B) of this rule the court shall require the party seeking discovery to pay the other party a fair portion of the fees and expenses reasonably incurred by the latter party in obtaining facts and opinions from the expert.

(5) *Claims of Privilege or Protection of Trial Preparation Materials.* When a party withholds information otherwise discoverable under these rules by claiming that it is privileged or subject to protection as trial preparation material, the party shall make the claim expressly and shall describe the nature of the documents, communications, or things not produced or disclosed in a manner that, without revealing information itself privileged or protected, will enable other parties to assess the applicability of the privilege or protection.

(c) Protective Orders. Upon motion by a party or by the person from whom discovery is sought, accompanied by a certification that the movant has in good faith conferred or attempted to confer with other affected parties in an effort to resolve the dispute without court action, and for good cause shown, the court in which the action is pending or alternatively, on matters relating to a deposition, the court in the district where the deposition is to be taken may make any order which justice requires to protect a party or person from annoyance, embarrassment, oppression, or undue burden or expense, including one or more of the following:

(1) that the disclosure or discovery not be had;

(2) that the disclosure or discovery may be had only on specified terms and conditions, including a designation of the time or place;

(3) that the discovery may be had only by a method of discovery other than that selected by the party seeking discovery;

(4) that certain matters not be inquired into, or that the scope of the disclosure or discovery be limited to certain matters;

(5) that discovery be conducted with no one present except persons designated by the court;

(6) that a deposition, after being sealed, be opened only by order of the court;

(7) that a trade secret or other confidential research, development, or commercial information not be revealed or be revealed only in a designated way; and

(8) that the parties simultaneously file specified documents or information enclosed in sealed envelopes to be opened as directed by the court.

If the motion for a protective order is denied in whole or in part, the court may, on such terms and conditions as are just, order that any party or other person provide or permit discovery. The provisions of Rule 37(a)(4) apply to the award of expenses incurred in relation to the motion.

(d) Timing and Sequence of Discovery. Except when authorized under these rules or by local rule, order, or agreement of the parties, a party may not seek discovery from any source before the parties have met and conferred as required by subdivision (f). Unless the court upon motion, for the convenience of parties and witnesses and in the interests of justice, orders otherwise, methods of discovery may be used in any sequence, and the fact that a party is conducting discovery, whether by deposition or otherwise, shall not operate to delay any other party's discovery.

(e) Supplementation of Disclosures and Responses. A party who has made a disclosure under subdivision (a) or responded to a request for discovery with a disclosure or response is under a duty to supplement or correct the disclosure or response to include information thereafter acquired if ordered by the court or in the following circumstances:

(1) A party is under a duty to supplement at appropriate intervals its disclosures under subdivision (a) if the party learns that in some material respect the information disclosed is incomplete or incorrect and if the additional or corrective information has not otherwise been made known to the other parties during the discovery process or in writing. With respect to testimony of an expert from whom a report is required under subdivision (a)(2)(B) the duty extends both to information contained in the report and to information provided through a deposition of the expert, and any additions or other changes to this information shall be disclosed by the time the party's disclosures under Rule 26(a)(3) are due.

(2) A party is under a duty seasonably to amend a prior response to an interrogatory, request for production, or request for admission if the party learns that the response is in

some material respect incomplete or incorrect and if the additional or corrective information has not otherwise been made known to the other parties during the discovery process or in writing.

(f) Meeting of Parties; Planning for Discovery. Except in actions exempted by local rule or when otherwise ordered, the parties shall, as soon as practicable and in any event at least 14 days before a scheduling conference is held or a scheduling order is due under Rule 16(b), meet to discuss the nature and basis of their claims and defenses and the possibilities for a prompt settlement or resolution of the case, to make or arrange for the disclosures required by subdivision (a)(1), and to develop a proposed discovery plan. The plan shall indicate the parties' views and proposals concerning:

(1) what changes should be made in the timing, form, or requirement for disclosures under subdivision (a) or local rule, including a statement as to when disclosures under subdivision (a)(1) were made or will be made;

(2) the subjects on which discovery may be needed, when discovery should be completed, and whether discovery should be conducted in phases or be limited to or focused upon particular issues;

(3) what changes should be made in the limitations on discovery imposed under these rules or by local rule, and what other limitations should be imposed; and

(4) any other orders that should be entered by the court under subdivision (c) or under Rule 16(b) and (c).

The attorneys of record and all unrepresented parties that have appeared in the case are jointly responsible for arranging and being present or represented at the meeting, for attempting in good faith to agree on the proposed discovery plan, and for submitting to the court within 10 days after the meeting a written report outlining the plan.

(g) Signing of Disclosures, Discovery Requests, Responses, and Objections.

(1) Every disclosure made pursuant to subdivision (a)(1) or subdivision (a)(3) shall be signed by at least one attorney of record in the attorney's individual name, whose address shall be stated. An unrepresented party shall sign the disclosure and state the party's address. The signature of the attorney or party constitutes a certification that to the best of the signer's knowledge, information, and belief, formed after a reasonable inquiry, the disclosure is complete and correct as of the time it is made.

(2) Every discovery request, response, or objection made by a party represented by an attorney shall be signed by at least one attorney of record in the attorney's individual name, whose address shall be stated. An unrepresented party shall sign the request, response, or objection and state the party's address. The signature of the attorney or party constitutes a certification that to the best of the signer's knowledge, information, and belief, formed after a reasonable inquiry, the request, response, or objection is:

(A) consistent with these rules and warranted by existing law or a good faith argument for the extension, modification, or reversal of existing law;

(B) not interposed for any improper purpose, such as to harass or to cause unnecessary delay or needless increase in the cost of litigation; and

(C) not unreasonable or unduly burdensome or expensive, given the needs of the case, the discovery already had in the case, the amount in controversy, and the importance of the issues at stake in the litigation.

If a request, response, or objection is not signed, it shall be stricken unless it is signed promptly after the omission is called to the attention of the party making the request, response, or objection, and a party shall not be obligated to take any action with respect to it until it is signed.

(3) If without substantial justification a certification is made in violation of the rule, the court, upon motion or upon its own initiative, shall impose upon the person who made the certification, the party on whose behalf the disclosure, request, response, or objection is made, or both, an appropriate sanction, which may include an order to pay the amount of the reasonable expenses incurred because of the violation, including a reasonable attorney's fee.

As amended 1948, 1963, 1966, 1970, 1980, 1983, 1987, 1993.

Rule 27.
DEPOSITIONS BEFORE ACTION OR PENDING APPEAL

(a) Before Action.

(1) *Petition.* A person who desires to perpetuate testimony regarding any matter that may be cognizable in any court of the United States may file a verified petition in the United States district court in the district of the residence of any expected adverse party. The petition shall be entitled in the name of the petitioner and shall show: 1, that the petitioner expects to be a party to an action cognizable in a court of the United States but is presently unable to bring it or cause it to be brought, 2, the subject matter of the expected action and the petitioner's interest therein, 3, the facts which the petitioner desires to establish by the proposed testimony and the reasons for desiring to perpetuate it, 4, the names or a description of the persons the petitioner expects will be adverse parties and their addresses so far as known, and 5, the names and addresses of the persons to be examined and the substance of the testimony which the petitioner expects to elicit from each, and shall ask for an order authorizing the petitioner to take the depositions of the persons to be examined named in the petition, for the purpose of perpetuating their testimony.

(2) *Notice and Service.* The petitioner shall thereafter serve a notice upon each person named in the petition as an expected adverse party, together with a copy of the petition, stating that the petitioner will apply to the court, at a time and place named therein, for the order described in the petition. At least 20 days before the date of hearing the notice shall be served either within or without the district or state in the manner provided in Rule 4(d) for service of summons; but if such service cannot with due diligence be made upon any expected adverse party named in the petition, the court may make such order as is just for service by publication or otherwise, and shall appoint, for persons not served in the manner provided in Rule 4(d), an attorney who shall represent them, and, in case they are not otherwise represented, shall cross-examine the deponent. If any expected adverse party is a minor or incompetent the provisions of Rule 17(c) apply.

(3) *Order and Examination.* If the court is satisfied that the perpetuation of the testimony may prevent a failure or delay of justice, it shall make an order designating or describing the persons whose depositions may be taken and specifying the subject matter of the examination and whether the depositions shall be taken upon oral examination or written interrogatories. The depositions may then be taken in accordance with these rules; and the court may make orders of the character provided for by Rules 34 and 35. For the purpose of applying these rules to depositions for perpetuating testimony, each reference therein to the court in which the action is pending shall be deemed to refer to the court in which the petition for such deposition was filed.

(4) *Use of Deposition.* If a deposition to perpetuate testimony is taken under these rules or if, although not so taken, it would be admissible in evidence in the courts of the state in which it is taken, it may be used in any action involving the same subject matter subsequently brought in a United States district court, in accordance with the provisions of Rule 32(a).

(b) Pending Appeal. If an appeal has been taken from a judgment of a district court or before the taking of an appeal if the time therefor has not expired, the district court in which the judgment was rendered may allow the taking of the depositions of witnesses to perpetuate their testimony for use in the event of further proceedings in the district court. In such case the party who desires to perpetuate the testimony may make a motion in the district court for leave to take the depositions, upon the same notice and service thereof as if the action was pending in the district court. The motion shall show (1) the names and addresses of persons to be examined and the substance of the testimony which the party expects to elicit from each; (2) the reasons for perpetuating their testimony. If the court finds that the perpetuation of the testimony is proper to avoid a failure or delay of justice, it may make an order allowing the depositions to be taken and may make orders of the character provided for by Rules 34 and 35, and thereupon the depositions may be taken and used in the same manner and under the same conditions as are prescribed in these rules for depositions taken in actions pending in the district court.

(c) Perpetuation by Action. This rule does not limit the power of a court to entertain an action to perpetuate testimony.

As amended 1948, 1949, 1971, 1987.

Rule 28.
PERSONS BEFORE WHOM DEPOSITIONS MAY BE TAKEN

(a) Within the United States. Within the United States or within a territory or insular possession subject to the jurisdiction of the United States, depositions shall be taken before an officer authorized to administer oaths by the laws of the United States or of the place where the examination is held, or before a person appointed by the court in which the action is pending. A person so appointed has power to administer oaths and take testimony. The term officer as used in Rules 30, 31 and 32 includes a person appointed by the court or designated by the parties under Rule 29.

(b) In Foreign Countries. Depositions may be taken in a foreign country (1) pursuant to any applicable treaty or convention, or (2) pursuant to a letter of request (whether or not captioned a letter rogatory), or (3) on notice before a person authorized to administer oaths in the place where the examination is held, either by the law thereof or by the law of the United States, or (4) before a person commissioned by the court, and a person so commissioned shall have the power by virtue of the commission to administer any necessary oath and take testimony. A commission or a letter of request shall be issued on application and notice and on terms that are just and appropriate. It is not requisite to the issuance of a commission or a letter of request that the taking of the deposition in any other manner is impracticable or inconvenient; and both a commission and a letter of request may be issued in proper cases. A notice or commission may designate the person before whom the deposition is to be taken either by name or descriptive title. A letter of request may be addressed "To the Appropriate Authority in [here name the country]." When a letter of request or any other device is used pursuant to any applicable treaty or convention, it shall be captioned in the form prescribed by that treaty or convention. Evidence obtained in response to a letter of request need not be excluded merely because it is not a verbatim transcript, because the testimony was not taken under oath, or because of any similar departure from the requirements for depositions taken within the United States under these rules.

(c) Disqualification for Interest. No deposition shall be taken before a person who is a relative or employee or attorney or counsel of any of the parties, or is a relative or employee of such attorney or counsel, or is financially interested in the action.

As amended 1948, 1963, 1980, 1987, 1993.

Rule 29.
STIPULATIONS REGARDING DISCOVERY PROCEDURE

Unless otherwise directed by the court, the parties may by written stipulation (1) provide that depositions may be taken before any person, at any time or place, upon any notice, and in any manner and when so taken may be used like other depositions, and (2) modify other procedures governing or limitations placed upon discovery, except that stipulations extending the time provided in Rules 33, 34, and 36 for responses to discovery may, if they would interfere with any time set for completion of discovery, for hearing of a motion, or for trial, be made only with the approval of the court.

As amended 1970, 1993.

Rule 30.
DEPOSITIONS UPON ORAL EXAMINATION

(a) When Depositions May Be Taken; When Leave Required.

(1) A party may take the testimony of any person, including a party, by deposition upon oral examination without leave of court except as provided in paragraph (2). The attendance of witnesses may be compelled by subpoena as provided in Rule 45.

(2) A party must obtain leave of court, which shall be granted to the extent consistent with the principles stated in Rule 26(b)(2), if the person to be examined is confined in prison or if, without the written stipulation of the parties,

(A) a proposed deposition would result in more than ten depositions being taken under this rule or Rule 31 by the plaintiffs, or by the defendants, or by third-party defendants;

(B) the person to be examined already has been deposed in the case; or

(C) a party seeks to take a deposition before the time specified in Rule 26(d) unless the notice contains a certification, with supporting facts, that the person to be examined is expected to leave the United States and be unavailable for examination in this country unless deposed before that time.

(b) Notice of Examination: General Requirements; Method of Recording; Production of Documents and Things; Deposition of Organization; Deposition by Telephone.

(1) A party desiring to take the deposition of any person upon oral examination shall give reasonable notice in writing to every other party to the action. The notice shall state the time and place for taking the deposition and the name and address of each person to be examined, if known, and, if the name is not known, a general description sufficient to identify the person or the particular class or group to which the person belongs. If a subpoena duces tecum is to be served on the person to be examined, the designation of the materials to be produced as set forth in the subpoena shall be attached to, or included in, the notice.

(2) The party taking the deposition shall state in the notice the method by which the testimony shall be recorded. Unless the court orders otherwise, it may be recorded by sound, sound-and-visual, or stenographic means, and the party taking the deposition shall bear the cost of the recording. Any party may arrange for a transcription to be made from the recording of a deposition taken by nonstenographic means.

(3) With prior notice to the deponent and other parties, any party may designate another method to record the deponent's testimony in addition to the method specified by the person taking the deposition. The additional record or transcript shall be made at that party's expense unless the court otherwise orders.

(4) Unless otherwise agreed by the parties, a deposition shall be conducted before an officer appointed or designated under Rule 28 and shall begin with a statement on the record by the officer that includes (A) the officer's name and business address; (B) the date, time, and place of the deposition; (C) the name of the deponent; (D) the administration of the oath or affirmation to the deponent; and (E) an identification of all persons present. If the deposition is recorded other than stenographically, the officer shall repeat items (A) through (C) at the beginning of each unit of recorded tape or other recording medium. The appearance or demeanor of deponents or attorneys shall not be distorted through camera or sound-recording techniques. At the end of the deposition, the officer shall state on the record that the deposition is complete and shall set forth any stipulations made by counsel concerning the custody of the transcript or recording and the exhibits, or concerning other pertinent matters.

(5) The notice to a party deponent may be accompanied by a request made in compliance with Rule 34 for the production of documents and tangible things at the taking of the deposition. The procedure of Rule 34 shall apply to the request.

(6) A party may in the party's notice and in a subpoena name as the deponent a public or private corporation or a partnership or association or governmental agency and describe with reasonable particularity the matters on which examination is requested. In that event, the organization so named shall designate one or more officers, directors, or managing agents, or other persons who consent to testify on its behalf, and may set forth, for each person designated, the matters on which the person will testify. A subpoena shall advise a non-party organization of its duty to make such a designation. The persons so designated shall testify

as to matters known or reasonably available to the organization. This subdivision (b)(6) does not preclude taking a deposition by any other procedure authorized in these rules.

(7) The parties may stipulate in writing or the court may upon motion order that a deposition be taken by telephone or other remote electronic means. For the purposes of this rule and Rules 28(a), 37(a)(1), and 37(b)(1), a deposition taken by such means is taken in the district and at the place where the deponent is to answer questions.

(c) Examination and Cross-Examination; Record of Examination; Oath; Objections. Examination and cross-examination of witnesses may proceed as permitted at the trial under the provisions of the Federal Rules of Evidence except Rules 103 and 615. The officer before whom the deposition is to be taken shall put the witness on oath or affirmation and shall personally, or by someone acting under the officer's direction and in the officer's presence, record the testimony of the witness. The testimony shall be taken stenographically or recorded by any other method authorized by subdivision (b)(2) of this rule. All objections made at the time of the examination to the qualifications of the officer taking the deposition, to the manner of taking it, to the evidence presented, to the conduct of any party, or to any other aspect of the proceedings shall be noted by the officer upon the record of the deposition; but the examination shall proceed, with the testimony being taken subject to the objections. In lieu of participating in the oral examination, parties may serve written questions in a sealed envelope on the party taking the deposition and the party taking the deposition shall transmit them to the officer, who shall propound them to the witness and record the answers verbatim.

(d) Schedule and Duration; Motion to Terminate or Limit Examination.

(1) Any objection to evidence during a deposition shall be stated concisely and in a non-argumentative and non-suggestive manner. A party may instruct a deponent not to answer only when necessary to preserve a privilege, to enforce a limitation on evidence directed by the court, or to present a motion under paragraph (3).

(2) By order or local rule, the court may limit the time permitted for the conduct of a deposition, but shall allow additional time consistent with Rule 26(b)(2) if needed for a fair examination of the deponent or if the deponent or another party impedes or delays the examination. If the court finds such an impediment, delay, or other conduct that has frustrated the fair examination of the deponent, it may impose upon the persons responsible an appropriate sanction, including the reasonable costs and attorney's fees incurred by any parties as a result thereof.

(3) At any time during a deposition, on motion of a party or of the deponent and upon a showing that the examination is being conducted in bad faith or in such manner as unreasonably to annoy, embarrass, or oppress the deponent or party, the court in which the action is pending or the court in the district where the deposition is being taken may order the officer conducting the examination to cease forthwith from taking the deposition, or may limit the scope and manner of the taking of the deposition as provided in Rule 26(c). If the order made terminates the examination, it shall be resumed thereafter only upon the order of the court in which the action is pending. Upon demand of the objecting party or deponent, the taking of the deposition shall be suspended for the time necessary to make a motion for an order. The provisions of Rule 37(a)(4) apply to the award of expenses incurred in relation to the motion.

(e) Review by Witness; Changes; Signing. If requested by the deponent or a party before completion of the deposition, the deponent shall have 30 days after being notified by the officer that the transcript or recording is available in which to review the transcript or recording and, if there are changes in form or substance, to sign a statement reciting such changes and the reasons given by the deponent for making them. The officer shall indicate in the certificate prescribed by subdivision (f)(1) whether any review was requested and, if so, shall append any changes made by the deponent during the period allowed.

(f) Certification and Filing by Officer; Exhibits; Copies; Notice of Filing.

(1) The officer shall certify that the witness was duly sworn by the officer and that the deposition is a true record of the testimony given by the witness. This certificate shall be in writing and accompany the record of the deposition. Unless otherwise ordered by the court, the officer shall securely seal the deposition in an envelope or package indorsed with the title of the action and marked "Deposition of [here insert name of witness]" and shall promptly file it with the court in which the action is pending or send it to the attorney who arranged for the transcript or recording, who shall store it under conditions that will protect it against loss, destruction, tampering, or deterioration. Documents and things produced for inspection during the examination of the witness, shall, upon the request of a party be marked for identification and annexed to the deposition and may be inspected and copied by any party, except that if the person producing the materials desires to retain them the person may (A) offer copies to be marked for identification and annexed to the deposition and to serve thereafter as originals if the person affords to all parties fair opportunity to verify the copies by comparison with the originals, or (B) offer the originals to be marked for identification, after giving to each party an opportunity to inspect and copy them, in which event the materials may then be used in the same manner as if annexed to the deposition. Any party may move for an order that the original be annexed to and returned with the deposition to the court, pending final disposition of the case.

(2) Unless otherwise ordered by the court or agreed by the parties, the officer shall retain stenographic notes of any deposition taken stenographically or a copy of the recording of any deposition taken by another method. Upon payment of reasonable charges therefor, the officer shall furnish a copy of the transcript or other recording of the deposition to any party or to the deponent.

(3) The party taking the deposition shall give prompt notice of its filing to all other parties.

(g) Failure to Attend or to Serve Subpoena; Expenses.

(1) If the party giving the notice of the taking of a deposition fails to attend and proceed therewith and another party attends in person or by attorney pursuant to the notice, the court may order the party giving the notice to pay to such other party the reasonable expenses incurred by that party and that party's attorney in attending, including reasonable attorney's fees.

(2) If the party giving the notice of the taking of a deposition of a witness fails to serve a subpoena upon the witness and the witness because of such failure does not attend, and if another party attends in person or by attorney because that party expects the deposition of that witness to be taken, the court may order the party giving the notice to pay to such other

party the reasonable expenses incurred by that party and that party's attorney in attending, including reasonable attorney's fees.

As amended 1963, 1970, 1971, 1975, 1980, 1987, 1993.

Rule 31.
DEPOSITIONS UPON WRITTEN QUESTIONS

(a) Serving Questions; Notice.

(1) A party may take the testimony of any person, including a party, by deposition upon written questions without leave of court except as provided in paragraph (2). The attendance of witnesses may be compelled by the use of subpoena as provided in Rule 45.

(2) A party must obtain leave of court, which shall be granted to the extent consistent with the principles stated in Rule 26(b)(2), if the person to be examined is confined in prison or if, without the written stipulation of the parties,

(A) a proposed deposition would result in more than ten depositions being taken under this rule or Rule 30 by the plaintiffs, or by the defendants, or by third-party defendants;

(B) the person to be examined has already been deposed in the case; or

(C) a party seeks to take a deposition before the time specified in Rule 26(d).

(3) A party desiring to take a deposition upon written questions shall serve them upon every other party with a notice stating (1) the name and address of the person who is to answer them, if known, and if the name is not known, a general description sufficient to identify the person or the particular class or group to which the person belongs, and (2) the name or descriptive title and address of the officer before whom the deposition is to be taken. A deposition upon written questions may be taken of a public or private corporation or a partnership or association or governmental agency in accordance with the provisions of Rule 30(b)(6).

(4) Within 14 days after the notice and written questions are served, a party may serve cross questions upon all other parties. Within 7 days after being served with cross questions, a party may serve redirect questions upon all other parties. Within 7 days after being served with redirect questions, a party may serve recross questions upon all other parties. The court may for cause shown enlarge or shorten the time.

(b) Officer to Take Responses and Prepare Record. A copy of the notice and copies of all questions served shall be delivered by the party taking the deposition to the officer designated in the notice, who shall proceed promptly, in the manner provided by Rule 30(c), (e), and (f), to take the testimony of the witness in response to the questions and to prepare, certify, and file or mail the deposition, attaching thereto the copy of the notice and the questions received by the officer.

(c) Notice of Filing. When the deposition is filed the party taking it shall promptly give notice thereof to all other parties.

As amended 1970, 1987, 1993.

Rule 32.
USE OF DEPOSITIONS IN COURT PROCEEDINGS

(a) Use of Depositions. At the trial or upon the hearing of a motion or an interlocutory proceeding, any part or all of a deposition, so far as admissible under the rules of evidence applied as though the witness were then present and testifying, may be used against any party who was present or represented at the taking of the deposition or who had reasonable notice thereof, in accordance with any of the following provisions:

(1) Any deposition may be used by any party for the purpose of contradicting or impeaching the testimony of deponent as a witness, or for any other purpose permitted by the Federal Rules of Evidence.

(2) The deposition of a party or of anyone who at the time of taking the deposition was an officer, director, or managing agent, or a person designated under Rule 30(b)(6) or 31(a) to testify on behalf of a public or private corporation, partnership or association or governmental agency which is a party may be used by an adverse party for any purpose.

(3) The deposition of a witness, whether or not a party, may be used by any party for any purpose if the court finds:

(A) that the witness is dead; or

(B) that the witness is at a greater distance than 100 miles from the place of trial or hearing, or is out of the United States, unless it appears that the absence of the witness was procured by the party offering the deposition; or

(C) that the witness is unable to attend or testify because of age, illness, infirmity, or imprisonment; or

(D) that the party offering the deposition has been unable to procure the attendance of the witness by subpoena; or

(E) upon application and notice, that such exceptional circumstances exist as to make it desirable, in the interest of justice and with due regard to the importance of presenting the testimony of witnesses orally in open court, to allow the deposition to be used.

A deposition taken without leave of court pursuant to a notice under Rule 30(a)(2)(C) shall not be used against a party who demonstrates that, when served with the notice, it was unable through the exercise of diligence to obtain counsel to represent it at the taking of the deposition; nor shall a deposition be used against a party who, having received less than 11 days notice of a deposition, has promptly upon receiving such notice filed a motion for a protective order under Rule 26(c)(2) requesting that the deposition not be held or be held at a different time or place and such motion is pending at the time the deposition is held.

(4) If only part of a deposition is offered in evidence by a party, an adverse party may require the offeror to introduce any other part which ought in fairness to be considered with the part introduced, and any party may introduce any other parts.

Substitution of parties pursuant to Rule 25 does not affect the right to use depositions previously taken; and, when an action has been brought in any court of the United States or of any State and another action involving the same subject matter is afterward brought between the same parties or their representatives or successors in interest, all depositions lawfully taken and duly filed in the former action may be used in the latter as if originally taken therefor. A deposition previously taken may also be used as permitted by the Federal Rules of Evidence.

(b) Objections to Admissibility. Subject to the provisions of Rule 28(b) and subdivision (d)(3) of this rule, objection may be made at the trial or hearing to receiving in evidence any deposition or part thereof for any reason which would require the exclusion of the evidence if the witness were then present and testifying.

(c) Form of Presentation. Except as otherwise directed by the court, a party offering deposition testimony pursuant to this rule may offer it in stenographic or nonstenographic form, but, if in nonstenographic form, the party shall also provide the court with a transcript of the portions so offered. On request of any party in a case tried before a jury, deposition testimony offered other than for impeachment purposes shall be presented in nonstenographic form, if available, unless the court for good cause orders otherwise.

(d) Effect of Errors and Irregularities in Depositions.

(1) *As to Notice.* All errors and irregularities in the notice for taking a deposition are waived unless written objection is promptly served upon the party giving the notice.

(2) *As to Disqualification of Officer.* Objection to taking a deposition because of disqualification of the officer before whom it is to be taken is waived unless made before the taking of the deposition begins or as soon thereafter as the disqualification becomes known or could be discovered with reasonable diligence.

(3) *As to Taking of Deposition.*

(A) Objections to the competency of a witness or to the competency, relevancy, or materiality of testimony are not waived by failure to make them before or during the taking of the deposition, unless the ground of the objection is one which might have been obviated or removed if presented at that time.

(B) Errors and irregularities occurring at the oral examination in the manner of taking the deposition, in the form of the questions or answers, in the oath or affirmation, or in the conduct of parties, and errors of any kind which might be obviated, removed, or cured if promptly presented, are waived unless seasonable objection thereto is made at the taking of the deposition.

(C) Objections to the form of written questions submitted under Rule 31 are waived unless served in writing upon the party propounding them within the time allowed for serving the succeeding cross or other questions and within 5 days after service of the last questions authorized.

(4) *As to Completion and Return of Deposition.* Errors and irregularities in the manner in which the testimony is transcribed or the deposition is prepared, signed, certified, sealed, indorsed, transmitted, filed, or otherwise dealt with by the officer under Rules 30 and 31 are waived unless a motion to suppress the deposition or some part thereof is made with reasonable promptness after such defect is, or with due diligence might have been, ascertained.

As amended 1970, 1975, 1980, 1987, 1993.

Rule 33.
INTERROGATORIES TO PARTIES

(a) Availability. Without leave of court or written stipulation, any party may serve upon any other party written interrogatories, not exceeding 25 in number including all discrete subparts, to be answered by the party served or, if the party served is a public or private corporation or a partnership or association or governmental agency, by any officer or agent, who shall furnish such information as is available to the party. Leave to serve additional interrogatories shall be granted to the extent consistent with the principles of Rule 26(b)(2). Without leave of court or written stipulation, interrogatories may not be served before the time specified in Rule 26(d).

(b) Answers and Objections.

(1) Each interrogatory shall be answered separately and fully in writing under oath, unless it is objected to, in which event the objecting party shall state the reasons for objection and shall answer to the extent the interrogatory is not objectionable.

(2) The answers are to be signed by the person making them, and the objections signed by the attorney making them.

(3) The party upon whom the interrogatories have been served shall serve a copy of the answers, and objections if any, within 30 days after the service of the interrogatories. A shorter or longer time may be directed by the court or, in the absence of such an order, agreed to in writing by the parties subject to Rule 29.

(4) All grounds for an objection to an interrogatory shall be stated with specificity. Any ground not stated in a timely objection is waived unless the party's failure to object is excused by the court for good cause shown.

(5) The party submitting the interrogatories may move for an order under Rule 37(a) with respect to any objection to or other failure to answer an interrogatory.

(c) Scope; Use at Trial. Interrogatories may relate to any matters which can be inquired into under Rule 26(b)(1), and the answers may be used to the extent permitted by the rules of evidence.

An interrogatory otherwise proper is not necessarily objectionable merely because an answer to the interrogatory involves an opinion or contention that relates to fact or the application of law to fact, but the court may order that such an interrogatory need not be answered until after designated discovery has been completed or until a pre-trial conference or other later time.

(d) Option to Produce Business Records. Where the answer to an interrogatory may be derived or ascertained from the business records of the party upon whom the interrogatory has been served or from an examination, audit or inspection of such business records, including a compilation, abstract or summary thereof and the burden of deriving or ascertaining the answer is substantially the same for the party serving the interrogatory as for the party served, it is a sufficient answer to such interrogatory to specify the records from which the answer may be derived or ascertained and to afford to the party serving the interrogatory reasonable opportunity to examine, audit or inspect such records and to make copies, compilations, abstracts or summaries. A specification shall be in sufficient detail to permit the interrogating party to locate and to identify, as readily as can the party served, the records from which the answer may be ascertained.

As amended 1948, 1970, 1980, 1993.

Rule 34.
PRODUCTION OF DOCUMENTS AND THINGS AND ENTRY UPON LAND FOR INSPECTION AND OTHER PURPOSES

(a) Scope. Any party may serve on any other party a request (1) to produce and permit the party making the request, or someone acting on the requestor's behalf, to inspect and copy, any designated documents (including writings, drawings, graphs, charts, photo graphs, phono-records, and other data compilations from which information can be obtained, translated, if necessary, by the respondent through detection devices into reasonably usable form), or to inspect and copy, test, or sample any tangible things which constitute or contain matters within the scope of Rule 26(b) and which are in the possession, custody or control of the party upon whom the request is served; or (2) to permit entry upon designated land or other property in the possession or control of the party upon whom the request is served for the purpose of inspection and measuring, surveying, photographing, testing, or sampling the property or any designated object or operation thereon, within the scope of Rule 26(b).

(b) Procedure. The request shall set forth, either by individual item or by category, the items to be inspected, and describe each with reasonable particularity. The request shall specify a reasonable time, place, and manner of making the inspection and performing the related acts. Without leave of court or written stipulation, a request may not be served before the time specified in Rule 26(d).

The party upon whom the request is served shall serve a written response within 30 days after the service of the request. A shorter or longer time may be directed by the court or, in the absence of such an order, agreed to in writing by the parties, subject to Rule 29. The response shall state, with respect to each item or category, that inspection and related activities will be permitted as requested, unless the request is objected to, in which event the reasons for objection shall be stated. If objection is made to part of an item or category, the part shall be specified and inspection permitted of the remaining parts. The party submitting the request may move for an order under Rule 37(a) with respect to any objection to or other failure to respond to the request or any part thereof, or any failure to permit inspection as requested.

A party who produces documents for inspection shall produce them as they are kept in the usual course of business or shall organize and label them to correspond with the categories in the request.

(c) Persons Not Parties. A person not a party to the action may be compelled to produce documents and things or to submit to an inspection as provided in Rule 45.

As amended 1948, 1970, 1980, 1987, 1991, 1993.

Rule 35.
PHYSICAL AND MENTAL EXAMINATION OF PERSONS

(a) Order for Examination. When the mental or physical condition (including the blood group) of a party, or of a person in the custody or under the legal control of a party, is in controversy, the court in which the action is pending may order the party to submit to a physical or mental examination by a suitably licensed or certified examiner or to produce for examination the person in the party's custody or legal control. The order may be made only on motion for good cause shown and upon notice to the person to be examined and to all parties and shall specify the time, place, manner, conditions, and scope of the examination and the person or persons by whom it is to be made.

(b) Report of Examiner.

(1) If requested by the party against whom an order is made under Rule 35(a) or the person examined, the party causing the examination to be made shall deliver to the requesting party a copy of the detailed written report of the examiner setting out the examiner's findings, including results of all tests made, diagnoses and conclusions, together with like reports of all earlier examinations of the same condition. After delivery the party causing the examination shall be entitled upon request to receive from the party against whom the order is made a like report of any examination, previously or thereafter made, of the same condition, unless, in the case of a report of examination of a person not a party, the party shows that such party is unable to obtain it. The court on motion may make an order against a party requiring delivery of a report on such terms as are just, and if an examiner fails or refuses to make a report the court may exclude the examiner's testimony if offered at trial.

(2) By requesting and obtaining a report of the examination so ordered or by taking the deposition of the examiner, the party examined waives any privilege the party may have in that action or any other involving the same controversy, regarding the testimony of every other person who has examined or may thereafter examine the party in respect of the same mental or physical condition.

(3) This subdivision applies to examinations made by agreement of the parties, unless the agreement expressly provides otherwise. This subdivision does not preclude discovery of a report of an examiner or the taking of a deposition of the examiner in accordance with the provisions of any other rule.

As amended 1970, 1987, 1988, 1991.

Rule 36.
REQUESTS FOR ADMISSION

(a) Request for Admission. A party may serve upon any other party a written request for the admission, for purposes of the pending action only, of the truth of any matters within the scope of Rule 26(b)(1) set forth in the request that relate to statements or opinions of fact or of the application of law to fact, including the genuineness of any documents described in the request. Copies of documents shall be served with the request unless they have been or are otherwise furnished or made available for inspection and copying. Without leave of court or written stipulation, requests for admission may not be served before the time specified in Rule 26(d).

Each matter of which an admission is requested shall be separately set forth. The matter is admitted unless, within 30 days after service of the request, or within such shorter or longer time as the court may allow or as the parties may agree to in writing, subject to Rule 29, the party to whom the request is directed serves upon the party requesting the admission a written answer or objection addressed to the matter, signed by the party or by the party's attorney. If objection is made, the reasons therefor shall be stated. The answer shall specifically deny the matter or set forth in detail the reasons why the answering party cannot truthfully admit or deny the matter. A denial shall fairly meet the substance of the requested admission, and when good faith requires that a party qualify an answer or deny only a part of the matter of which an admission is requested, the party shall specify so much of it as is true and qualify or deny the remainder. An answering party may not give lack of information or knowledge as a reason for failure to admit or deny unless the party states that the party has made reasonable inquiry and that the information known or readily obtainable by the party is insufficient to enable the party to admit or deny. A party who considers that a matter of which an admission has been requested presents a genuine issue for trial may not, on that ground alone, object to the request; the party may, subject to the provisions of Rule 37(c), deny the matter or set forth reasons why the party cannot admit or deny it.

The party who has requested the admissions may move to determine the sufficiency of the answers or objections. Unless the court determines that an objection is justified, it shall order that an answer be served. If the court determines that an answer does not comply with the requirements of this rule, it may order either that the matter is admitted or that an amended answer be served. The court may, in lieu of these orders, determine that final disposition of the request be made at a pre-trial conference or at a designated time prior to trial. The provisions of Rule 37(a)(4) apply to the award of expenses incurred in relation to the motion.

(b) Effect of Admission. Any matter admitted under this rule is conclusively established unless the court on motion permits withdrawal or amendment of the admission. Subject to the provisions of Rule 16 governing amendment of a pre-trial order, the court may permit withdrawal or amendment when the presentation of the merits of the action will be subserved thereby and the party who obtained the admission fails to satisfy the court that withdrawal or amendment will prejudice that party in maintaining the action or defense on the merits. Any admission made by a party under this rule is for the purpose of the pending action only and is not an admission for any other purpose nor may it be used against the party in any other proceeding.

As amended 1948, 1970, 1987, 1993.

Rule 37.
FAILURE TO MAKE DISCLOSURE OR COOPERATE IN DISCOVERY. SANCTIONS

(a) Motion for Order Compelling Disclosure or Discovery. A party, upon reasonable notice to other parties and all persons affected thereby, may apply for an order compelling disclosure or discovery as follows:

(1) *Appropriate Court.* An application for an order to a party shall be made to the court in which the action is pending. An application for an order to a person who is not a party shall be made to the court in the district where the discovery is being, or is to be, taken.

(2) *Motion.*

(A) If a party fails to make a disclosure required by Rule 26(a), any other party may move to compel disclosure and for appropriate sanctions. The motion must include a certification that the movant has in good faith conferred or attempted to confer with the party not making the disclosure in an effort to secure the disclosure without court action.

(B) If a deponent fails to answer a question propounded or submitted under Rules 30 or 31, or a corporation or other entity fails to make a designation under Rule 30(b)(6) or 31(a), or a party fails to answer an interrogatory submitted under Rule 33, or if a party, in response to a request for inspection submitted under Rule 34, fails to respond that inspection will be permitted as requested or fails to permit inspection as requested, the discovering party may move for an order compelling an answer, or a designation, or an order compelling inspection in accordance with the request. The motion must include a certification that the movant has in good faith conferred or attempted to confer with the person or party failing to make the discovery in an effort to secure the information or material without court action. When taking a deposition on oral examination, the proponent of the question may complete or adjourn the examination before applying for an order.

(3) *Evasive or Incomplete Disclosure, Answer, or Response.* For purposes of this subdivision an evasive or incomplete disclosure, answer, or response is to be treated as a failure to disclose, answer, or respond.

(4) *Expenses and Sanctions.*

(A) If the motion is granted or if the disclosure or requested discovery is provided after the motion was filed, the court shall, after affording an opportunity to be heard, require the party or deponent whose conduct necessitated the motion or the party or attorney advising such conduct or both of them to pay to the moving party the reasonable expenses incurred in making the motion, including attorney's fees, unless the court finds that the motion was filed without the movant's first making a good faith effort to obtain the disclosure or discovery without court action, or that the opposing party's nondisclosure, response, or objection was substantially justified, or that other circumstances make an award of expenses unjust.

(B) If the motion is denied, the court may enter any protective order authorized under Rule 26(c) and shall, after affording an opportunity to be heard, require the moving party or the attorney filing the motion or both of them to pay to the party or deponent who opposed the motion the reasonable expenses incurred in opposing the motion, including attorney's fees, unless the court finds that the making of the motion was substantially justified or that other circumstances make an award of expenses unjust.

(C) If the motion is granted in part and denied in part, the court may enter any protective order authorized under Rule 26(c) and may, after affording an opportunity to be heard, apportion the reasonable expenses incurred in relation to the motion among the parties and persons in a just manner.

(b) Failure to Comply with Order.

(1) *Sanctions by Court in District Where Deposition Is Taken.* If a deponent fails to be sworn or to answer a question after being directed to do so by the court in the district in which the deposition is being taken, the failure may be considered a contempt of that court.

(2) *Sanctions by Court in Which Action Is Pending.* If a party or an officer, director, or managing agent of a party or a person designated under Rule 30(b)(6) or 31(a) to testify on behalf of a party fails to obey an order to provide or permit discovery, including an order made under subdivision (a) of this rule or Rule 35, or if a party fails to obey an order entered under Rule 26(f), the court in which the action is pending may make such orders in regard to the failure as are just, and among others the following:

(A) An order that the matters regarding which the order was made or any other designated facts shall be taken to be established for the purposes of the action in accordance with the claim of the party obtaining the order;

(B) An order refusing to allow the disobedient party to support or oppose designated claims or defenses, or prohibiting that party from introducing designated matters in evidence;

(C) An order stilling out pleadings or parts thereof, or staying further proceedings until the order is obeyed, or dismissing the action or proceeding or any part thereof, or rendering a judgment by default against the disobedient party;

(D) In lieu of any of the foregoing orders or in addition thereto, an order treating as a contempt of court the failure to obey any orders except an order to submit to a physical or mental examination;

(E) Where a party has failed to comply with an order under Rule 35(a) requiring that party to produce another for examination, such orders as are listed in paragraphs (A), (B), and (C) of this subdivision, unless the party failing to comply shows that that party is unable to produce such person for examination.

In lieu of any of the foregoing orders or in addition thereto, the court shall require the party failing to obey the order or the attorney advising that party or both to pay the reasonable expenses, including attorney's fees, caused by the failure, unless the court finds that the failure was substantially justified or that other circumstances make an award of expenses unjust.

(c) Failure to Disclose; False or Misleading Disclosure; Refusal to Admit.

(1) A party that without substantial justification fails to disclose information required by Rule 26(a) or 26(e)(1) shall not, unless such failure is harmless, be permitted to use as evidence at a trial, at a hearing, or on a motion any witness or information not so disclosed. In addition to or in lieu of this sanction, the court, on motion and after affording an opportunity to be heard, may impose other appropriate sanctions. In addition to requiring payment of reasonable expenses, including attorney's fees, caused by the failure, these sanctions may include any of the actions authorized under subparagraphs (A), (B), and (C) of subdivision (b)(2) of this rule and may include informing the jury of the failure to make the disclosure.

(2) If a party fails to admit the genuineness of any document or the truth of any matter as requested under Rule 36, and if the party requesting the admissions thereafter proves the genuineness of the document or the truth of the matter, the requesting party may apply to the court for an order requiring the other party to pay the reasonable expenses incurred in making that proof, including reasonable attorney's fees. The court shall make the order unless it finds that (A) the request was held objectionable pursuant to Rule 36(a), or (B) the admission

sought was of no substantial importance, or (C) the party failing to admit had reasonable ground to believe that the party might prevail on the matter, or (D) there was other good reason for the failure to admit.

(d) Failure of Party to Attend at Own Deposition or Serve Answers to Interrogatories or Respond to Request for Inspection. If a party or an officer, director, or managing agent of a party or a person designated under Rule 30(b)(6) or 31(a) to testify on behalf of a party fails (1) to appear before the officer who is to take the deposition, after being served with a proper notice, or (2) to serve answers or objections to interrogatories submitted under Rule 33, after proper service of the interrogatories, or (3) to serve a written response to a request for inspection submitted under Rule 34, after proper service of the request, the court in which the action is pending on motion may make such orders in regard to the failure as are just, and among others it may take any action authorized under subparagraphs (A), (B), and (C) of subdivision (b)(2) of this rule. Any motion specifying a failure under clause (2) or (3) of this subdivision shall include a certification that the movant has in good faith conferred or attempted to confer with the party failing to answer or respond in an effort to obtain such answer or response without court action. In lieu of any order or in addition thereto, the court shall require the party failing to act or the attorney advising that party or both to pay the reasonable expenses, including attorney's fees, caused by the failure, unless the court finds that the failure was substantially justified or that other circumstances make an award of expenses unjust.

The failure to act described in this subdivision may not be excused on the ground that the discovery sought is objectionable unless the party failing to act has a pending motion for a protective order as provided by Rule 26(c).

(e) Subpoena of Person in Foreign Country. Abrogated Apr. 29, 1980, eff. Aug. 1, 1980.

(f) Expenses Against United States. Repealed by P.L. 96–481, eff. Oct. 1, 1981.

(g) Failure to Participate in the Framing of a Discovery Plan. If a party or a party's attorney fails to participate in good faith in the development and submission of a proposed discovery plan as required by Rule 26(f), the court may, after opportunity for hearing, require such party or attorney to pay to any other party the reasonable expenses, including attorney's fees, caused by the failure.

As amended 1949, 1970, 1980, 1981, 1987, 1993.

VI. TRIALS

Rule 38.
JURY TRIAL OF RIGHT

(a) Right Preserved. The right of trial by jury as declared by the Seventh Amendment to the Constitution or as given by a statute of the United States shall be preserved to the parties inviolate.

(b) Demand. Any party may demand a trial by jury of any issue triable of right by a jury by (1) serving upon the other parties a demand therefor in writing at any time after the commencement of the action and not later than 10 days after the service of the last pleading directed to such issue, and (2) filing the demand as required by Rule 5(d). Such demand may be indorsed upon a pleading of the party.

(c) Same: Specification of Issues. In the demand a party may specify the issues which the party wishes so tried; otherwise the party shall be deemed to have demanded trial by jury for all the issues so triable. If the party has demanded trial by jury for only some of the issues, any other party within 10 days after service of the demand or such lesser time as the court may order, may serve a demand for trial by jury of any other or all of the issues of fact in the action.

(d) Waiver. The failure of a party to serve and file a demand as required by this rule constitutes a waiver by the party of trial by jury. A demand for trial by jury made as herein provided may not be withdrawn without the consent of the parties.

(e) Admiralty and Maritime Claims. These rules shall not be construed to create a right to trial by jury of the issues in an admiralty or maritime claim within the meaning of Rule 9(h).

As amended 1966, 1987, 1993.

MIG 1 JURISDICTION

PERSONAL JURISDICTION

- Types
  - In personam.
  - In-Rem.
  - Quasi-In-Rem does ***not*** bind Δ personally.

In Personam: Jurisdiction over Δ personally and/or his property

In Rem: Jurisdiction over a ***particular item*** of Δ's property. Ct has power to adjudicate rights of ***all persons*** in world over the property.

Quasi-in-Rem: Ct has jurisdiction over ***particular individuals*** with respect to specificproperty.

- Jurisdiction based upon
  - Personal service inside forum state.
  - Domiciliary.
  - Consent.
  - Minimum contacts.
  - Long-Arm statutes within 100 miles of Federal Ct.

SUBJECT MATTER JURISDICTION (Federal question jurisdiction)

Extends → To all civil actions arising under U.S. Constitution, treaties and federal laws.

Amount in controversy → No minimum amount required.

Diversity → No diversity of parties required.

Joinder of claims → If subject matter jurisdiction exists, federal court may add (append) related state law actions to federal claim.

DIVERSITY JURISDICTION

- Requirements
  - Diversity Δ & π = different states
  - $75,000 + amount in controversy
  - Aggregation of amount allowed
- Erie doctrine (Fed. Ct.)
  - Must apply substantive law of forum st.
  - Procedural rules apply fed. rules of civil procedure.
- Pendent or Supplemental Jurisdiction
  - π has both a fed & state claim against Δ.
  - Fed. Ct. may join both claims

MIG 2 VENUE

VENUE (Judicial district where action may be brought)

- Diversity cases
  - District where any Δ resides.
  - Where claim occurred.
  - Or substantial part of claim occurred.
- Federal claim cases
  - (i) Where any Δ resides.
  - (ii) Where property that is subject of action is located.
  - If (i) & (ii) cannot be satisfied then wherever Δ can be found.
- Corporate Residency
  - Corporate Δ resides where it has sufficient contacts.
  - Corporate π resides in state of its incorporation.

TRANSFER OF VENUE (Fed. Ct. may transfer venue to another district)

- Factors
  - Convenience of parties.
  - Convenienceof witnesses.
  - Forum non conveniens
  - Where material event occurred.
- Law applicable upon transfer
  - Law of transferor Ct. generally applies
  - Transferee Ct. law applies if original venue was improper.

REMOVAL JURISDICTION

- Permitted
  - Δ may remove a fed. question action from state to fed. ct.
- Limitation
  - Diversity removal ***not*** permitted if one of Δs is a citizen of the same state as the π.

Dismissal of nondiverse party. — Removal Allowable → If diversity does not exist because a party is a co-citizen of an opposing party their removal is permitted if non-diverse parties are thereafter dismissed.

MIG 3 PRETRIAL MOTION PRACTICE

MOTION TO DISMISS (Fed. Rule 12b)

- Grounds for dismissal
  - Lack of sub. matter jurisdiction.
  - Lack of personal jurisdiction.
  - Improper venue.
  - Insufficient process.
  - Failure to state a claim.
  - Failure to join necessary party.
- Judgment on pleadings (Fed. Rule 12c)
  - After all pleadings completed.
  - Motion denied unless there are no facts to support cause of action.
- Summary Judgment
  - Motion may be made at any time usually after pleadings.
  - Motion granted if no genuine issue of material fact exists.

COLLATERAL ATTACK

- Personal Jurisdiction — Δ never makes an appearance & default judgment is entered. → Can Δ collaterally attack for lack of personal jurisdiction? Yes, but if Δ loses on personal jurisdiction issue, default judgment stands.
- Summary Judgment
  - Can Δ collaterally attack judg. bec. of lack of subj. matter jurisdiction?
  - Yes, if judgment was by default. No, if it was a contested action.

CONSOLIDATION

- Fed. Rule 12(g)
  - Requires consolidation of defenses into motion.
  - Failure to consolidate leads to waiver.
- WAIVER — Defenses waived if not pleaded.
  - Lack of personal jurisdiction.
  - Improper venue.
  - Insufficient of process.
- NO WAIVER — Defenses preserved if not originally pleaded.
  - Failure to state a claim.
  - Failure to join necessary party.

MIG 4 JOINDER

JOINDER OF CLAIMS

- Permitted (Permissive) → Party allowed to join as many claims as she has against opposing party.

JOINDER OF CLAIMS

- Compelled (Compulsory)
  - If failure to join could result in splitting of cause of action.
  - Example: π has suffered both property loss & personal injury resulting from auto accident.

JOINDER OF PARTIES

- Permissive
  - Multiple πs may join if each seeks relief on same claim from same transaction.
  - One π may join several Δs in one claim that arises from same transaction.

NECESSARY (INDISPENSABLE PARTIES)

- Motion to Dismiss
  - May be granted for failure to join indispensible party.
  - Exception: If joinder is impossible (e.g. joinder would destroy diversity) action may proceed w/outsider viewed as a necessary ***not*** indispensable party.

IMPLEADER

- 3rd party practice to add persons to the suit
  - If person "is or may be liable" to Δ.
  - Δ seeks indemnity or contribution.

INTERPLEADER

- Person has interest in property that is subject of litigation.
  - "Stakeholder" may bring in other claimants to decide matter in a single law suit.
  - In personam action and court must have personal jurisdiction over all parties.

MIG 5 BINDING EFFECT OF JUDGMENT

RES JUDICATA (Applies in civil actions *NOT* criminal cases.)

- Claim Preclusion
  - Precludes re-litigation of claim if final judgment is rendered.
  - Example: π sues Δ for negligence. Judgment rendered for Δ. π
- Parties Bound
  - Same parties are bound.
  - Non-parties not bound.
- SPLITTING A CLAIM
  - Merger → π wins an earlier lawsuit, his cause of action ***merges*** w/the judgment and he cannot sue again.
  - Bar → If Δ wins, the π is "barred" by the adverse judgment and cannot sue again.

COLLATERAL ESTOPPEL (Applies in both civil and criminal cases.)

- Issue Preclusion (Civil case) → A judgment for π or Δ precludes relitigation of same issues by same parties.

  Example: π sues Δ for negligence. π is found to be contributorily negligent. The issue of contributory negligence cannot be relitigated.
- Criminal Case → Δ asserts intoxication as defense in a larceny prosecution. Jury finds Δ was not intoxicated when he stole prop. Δ now prosecuted for battery (arising out of same incident) because he struck victim when he took her prop.

NON-MUTUAL COLLATERAL ESTOPPEL

- Cannot be used against a non-party to the previous action.
- Can a non-party use collateral estoppel against someone who was a party?

Yes, as a "defensive shield" (e.g., A is involved in an auto accident w/B, a driver for C Corp. A sues B for negligence and losses. A cannot sue C).

Yes, as an "offensive sword" (e.g. SEC sued Δ for stock fraud and won. A, private π, sued Δ for same violation established in SEC action, π can establish violation on Δ's part based on SEC action.

MIG 6 DISCOVERY

DISCOVERY DEVICES
- Oral deposition
- Written deposition
- Interrogatories
- Document production
- Physical/mental exam

INFORMATION REQUESTED
- Must be relevant.
- Privileged matter not discoverable.
- Insurance agreements discoverable.
- Qualified immunity: Attorney's work product.
- Limited discovery: Expert trial witnesses.

PROCEDURAL ASPECTS OF DISCOVERY
- Motion to compel where there has been a failure to comply w/discovery request.
- Protective order: Ct. may grant a protective order over confidential documents.

DISCOVERY SANCTIONS
- Discovery conference (failure to participate may result in sanctions).
- Discovery request (failure to supply info may result in sanctions).
- Discovery motions and discovery requests must be signed by attorney. If info is false, attorney may also be sanctioned.